MARVEL 1602
NEW WORLD

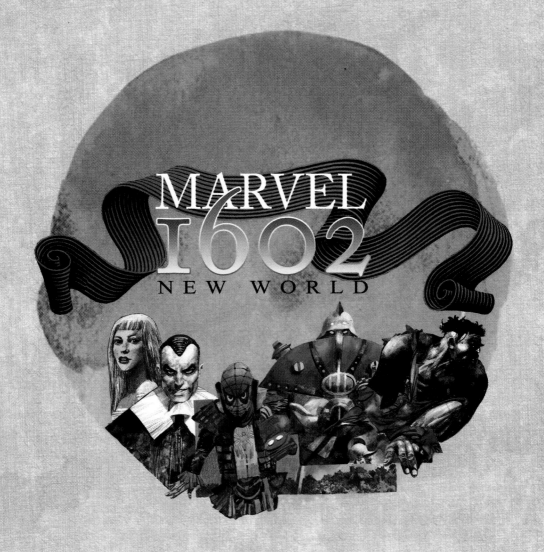

WRITER: Greg Pak
PENCILER: Greg Tocchini
INKERS: Greg Tocchini, Oclair Albert,
Mark Morales & Edde Wagner
COLORS: Laura Villari with Morry Hollowell,
Wil Quintana, Laura Martin & Chris Chuckry
LETTERS: Todd Klein
COVER ART: Sergio Toppi
ASSISTANT EDITOR: Sean Ryan
EDITOR: Nick Lowe
CONSULTING EDITOR: Mike Marts
CREATIVE CONSULTANT: Neil Gaiman

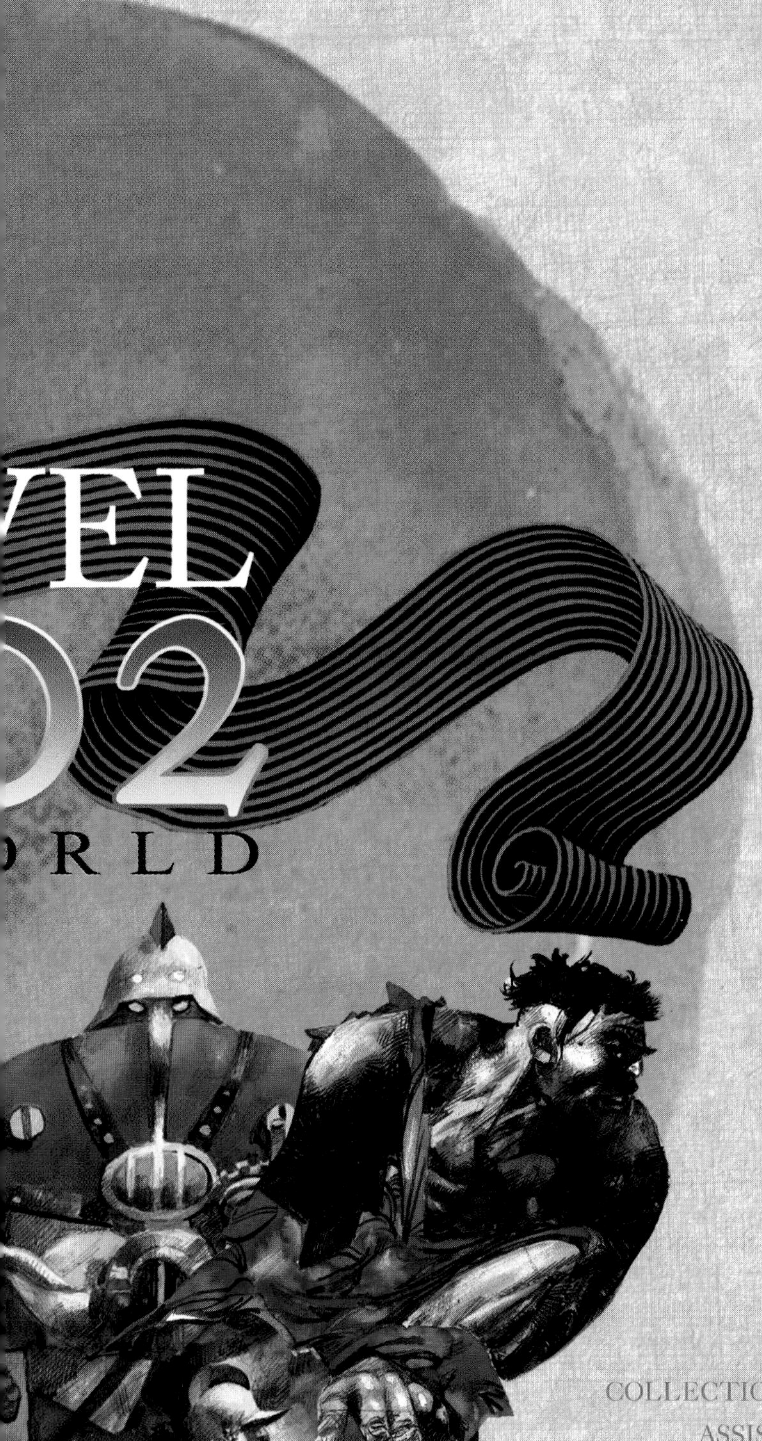
VEL
02
ORLD

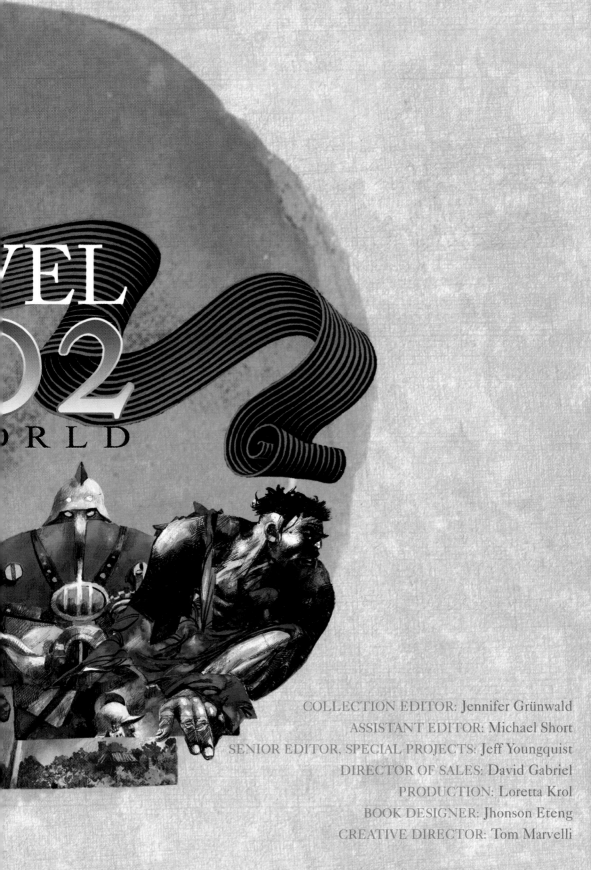

COLLECTION EDITOR: Jennifer Grünwald
ASSISTANT EDITOR: Michael Short
SENIOR EDITOR, SPECIAL PROJECTS: Jeff Youngquist
DIRECTOR OF SALES: David Gabriel
PRODUCTION: Loretta Krol
BOOK DESIGNER: Jhonson Eteng
CREATIVE DIRECTOR: Tom Marvelli

EDITOR IN CHIEF: Joe Quesada
PUBLISHER: Dan Buckley

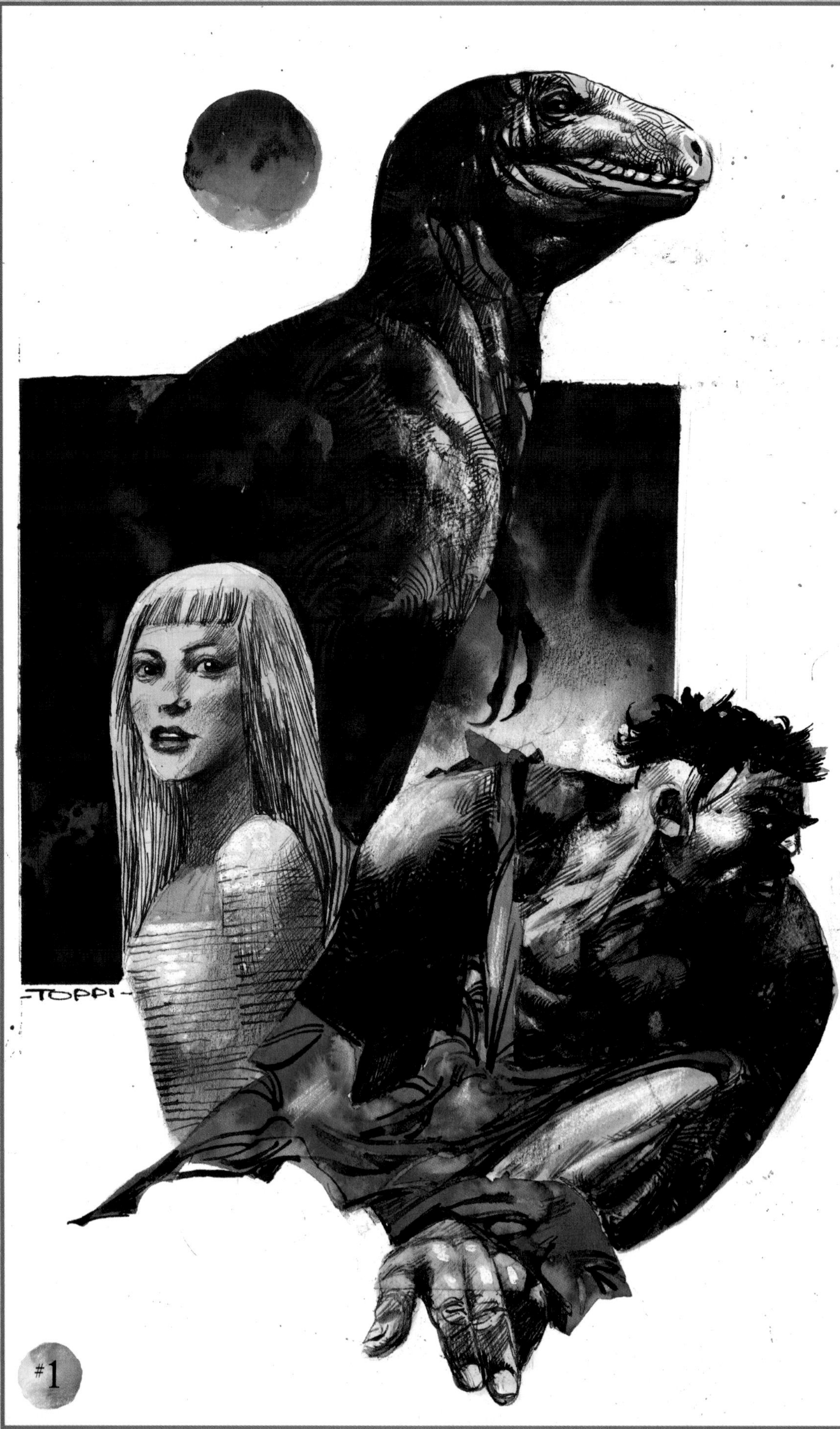
TOPPI

#1

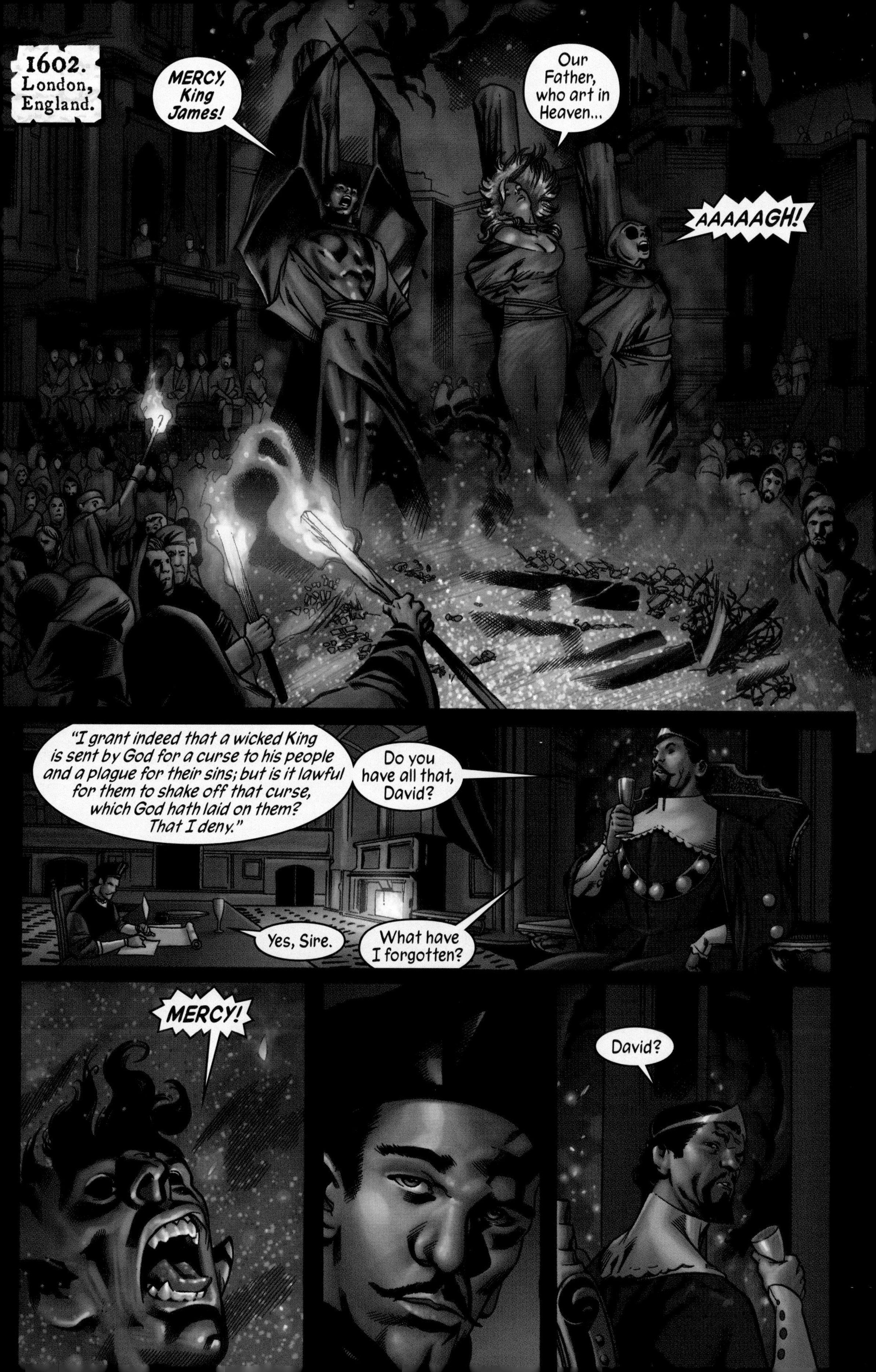
1602. London, England.
MERCY, King James!
Our Father, who art in Heaven...
AAAAAGH!
"I grant indeed that a wicked King is sent by God for a curse to his people and a plague for their sins; but is it lawful for them to shake off that curse, which God hath laid on them? That I deny."
Do you have all that, David?
Yes, Sire.
What have I forgotten?
MERCY!
David?

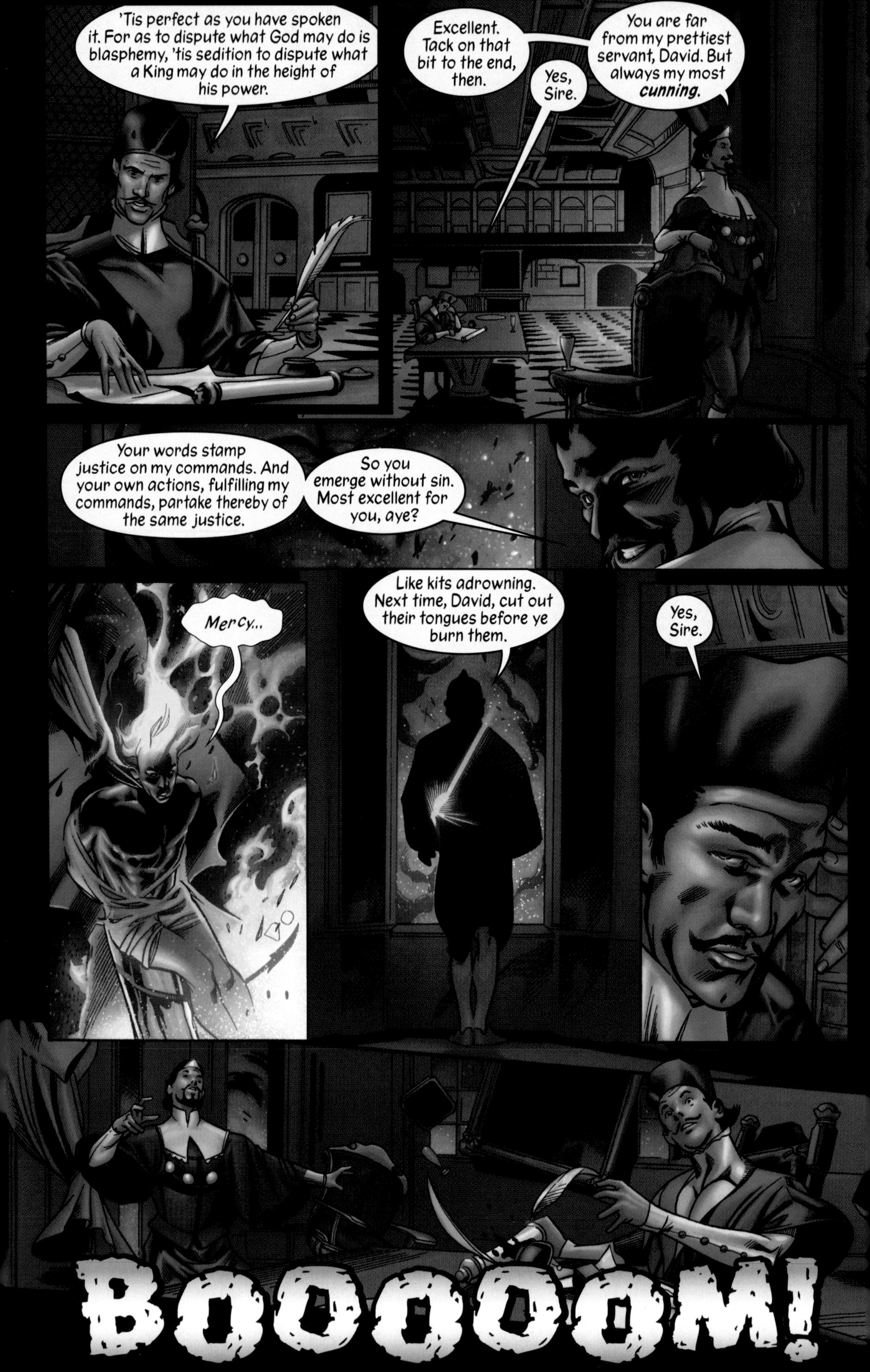
'Tis perfect as you have spoken it. For as to dispute what God may do is blasphemy, 'tis sedition to dispute what a King may do in the height of his power.
Excellent. Tack on that bit to the end, then.
Yes, Sire.
You are far from my prettiest servant, David. But always my most cunning.
Your words stamp justice on my commands. And your own actions, fulfilling my commands, partake thereby of the same justice.
So you emerge without sin. Most excellent for you, aye?
Mercy...
Like kits adrowning. Next time, David, cut out their tongues before ye burn them.
Yes, Sire.
BOOOOOM!

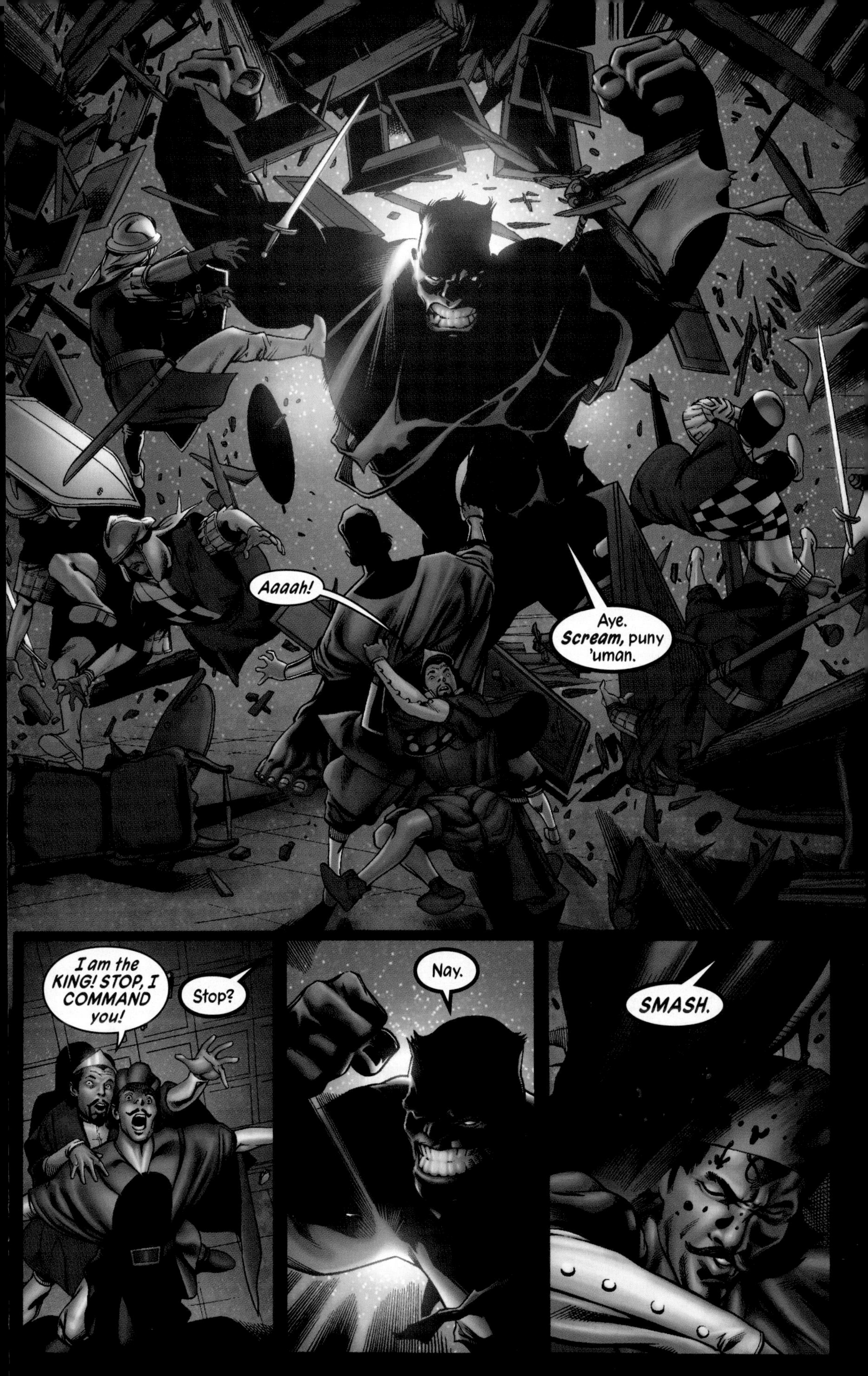
Aaaah!
Aye. Scream, puny 'uman.
I am the KING! STOP, I COMMAND you!
Stop?
Nay.
SMASH.

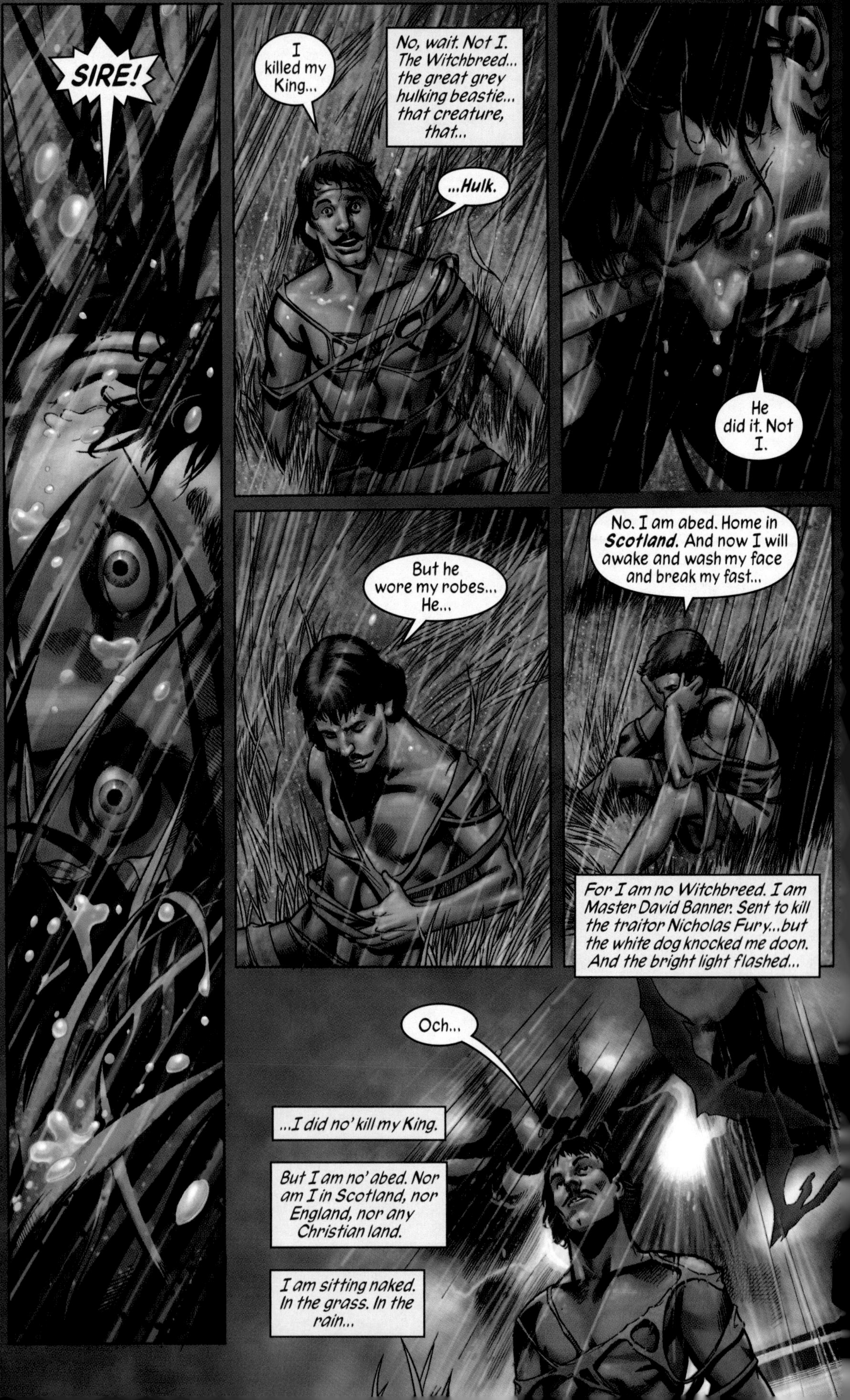
SIRE!
I killed my King...
No, wait. Not I. The Witchbreed... the great grey hulking beastie... that creature, that...
...Hulk.
He did it. Not I.
But he wore my robes... He...
No. I am abed. Home in Scotland. And now I will awake and wash my face and break my fast...
For I am no Witchbreed. I am Master David Banner. Sent to kill the traitor Nicholas Fury...but the white dog knocked me doon. And the bright light flashed...
Och...
...I did no' kill my King.
But I am no' abed. Nor am I in Scotland, nor England, nor any Christian land.
I am sitting naked. In the grass. In the rain...

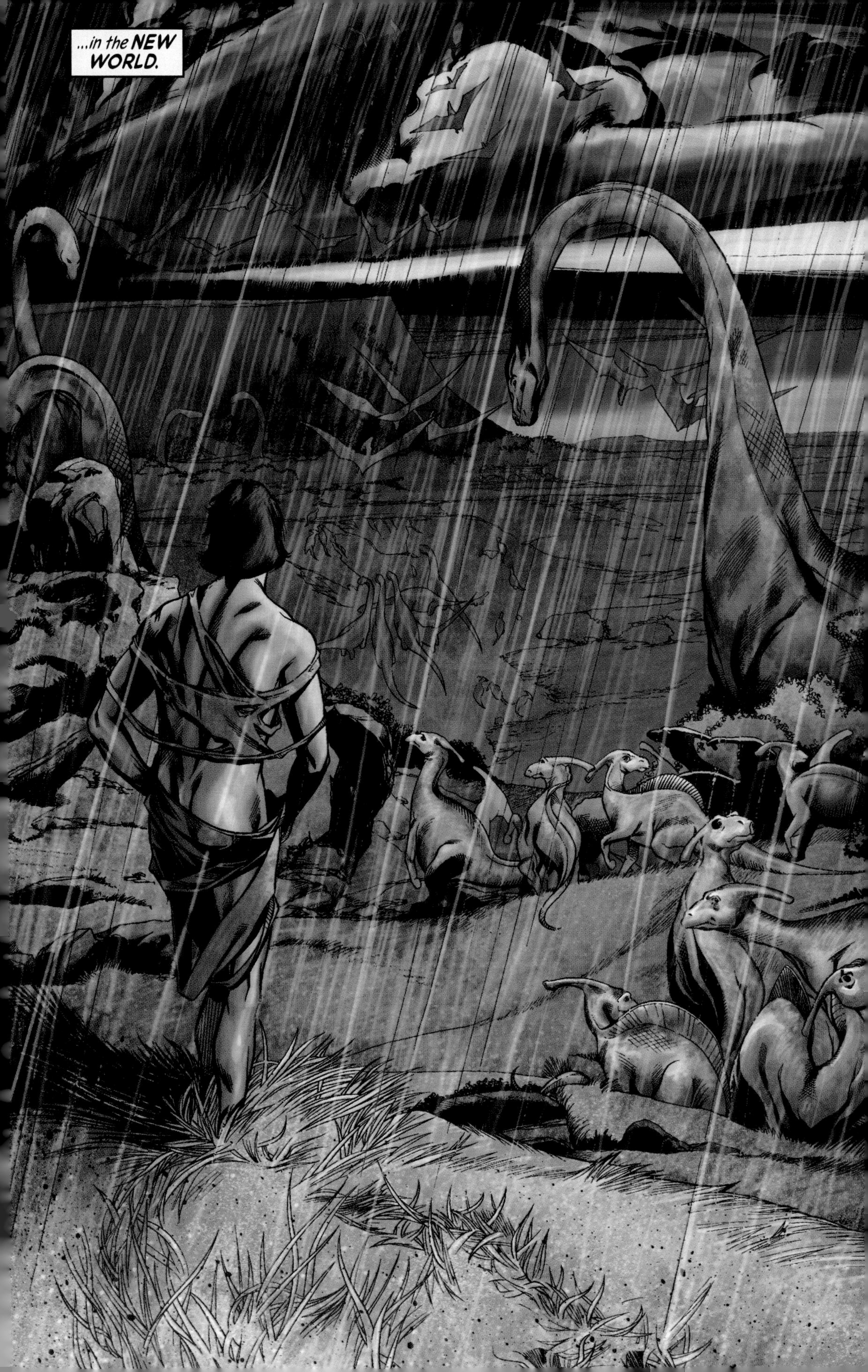
...in the NEW WORLD.

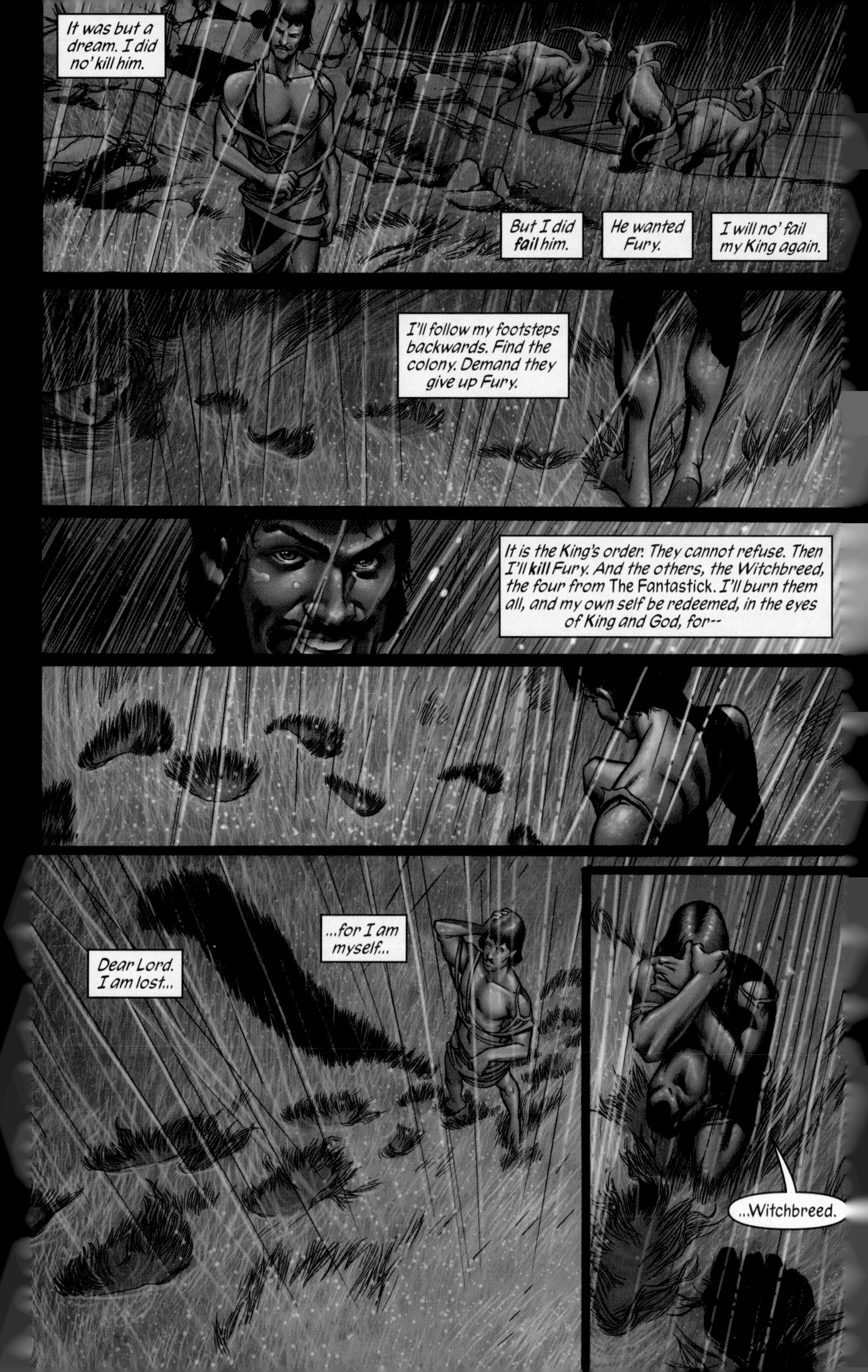
It was but a dream. I did no' kill him.
But I did **fail** him.
He wanted Fury.
I will no' fail my King again.
I'll follow my footsteps backwards. Find the colony. Demand they give up Fury.
It is the King's order. They cannot refuse. Then I'll **kill** Fury. And the others, the Witchbreed, the four from The Fantastick. I'll burn them all, and my own self be redeemed, in the eyes of King and God, for--
Dear Lord. I am lost...
...for I am myself...
...Witchbreed.

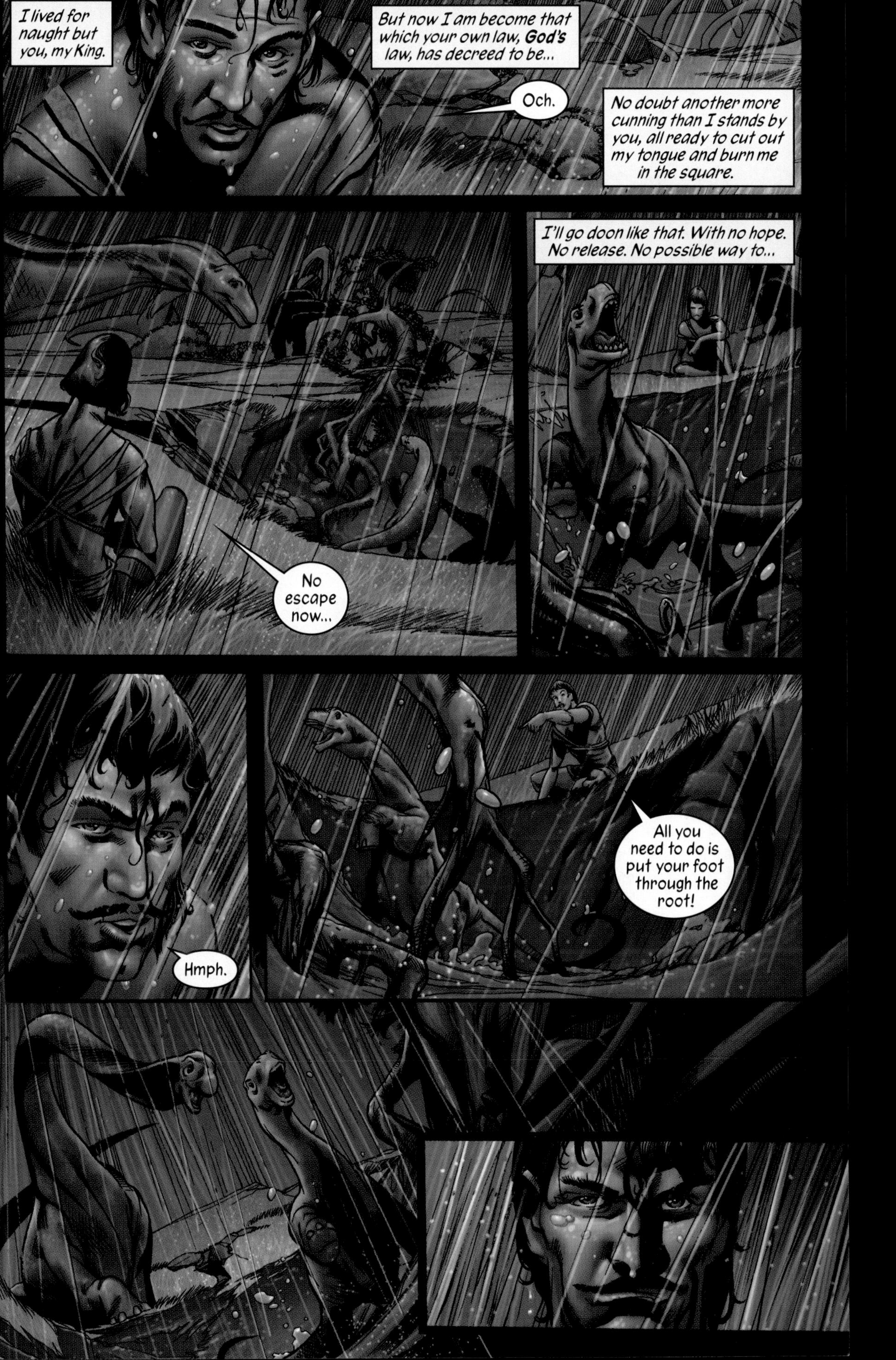

I lived for naught but you, my King.
But now I am become that which your own law, **God's** law, has decreed to be...
Och.
No doubt another more cunning than I stands by you, all ready to cut out my tongue and burn me in the square.
No escape now...
I'll go doon like that. With no hope. No release. No possible way to...
Hmph.
All you need to do is put your foot through the root!

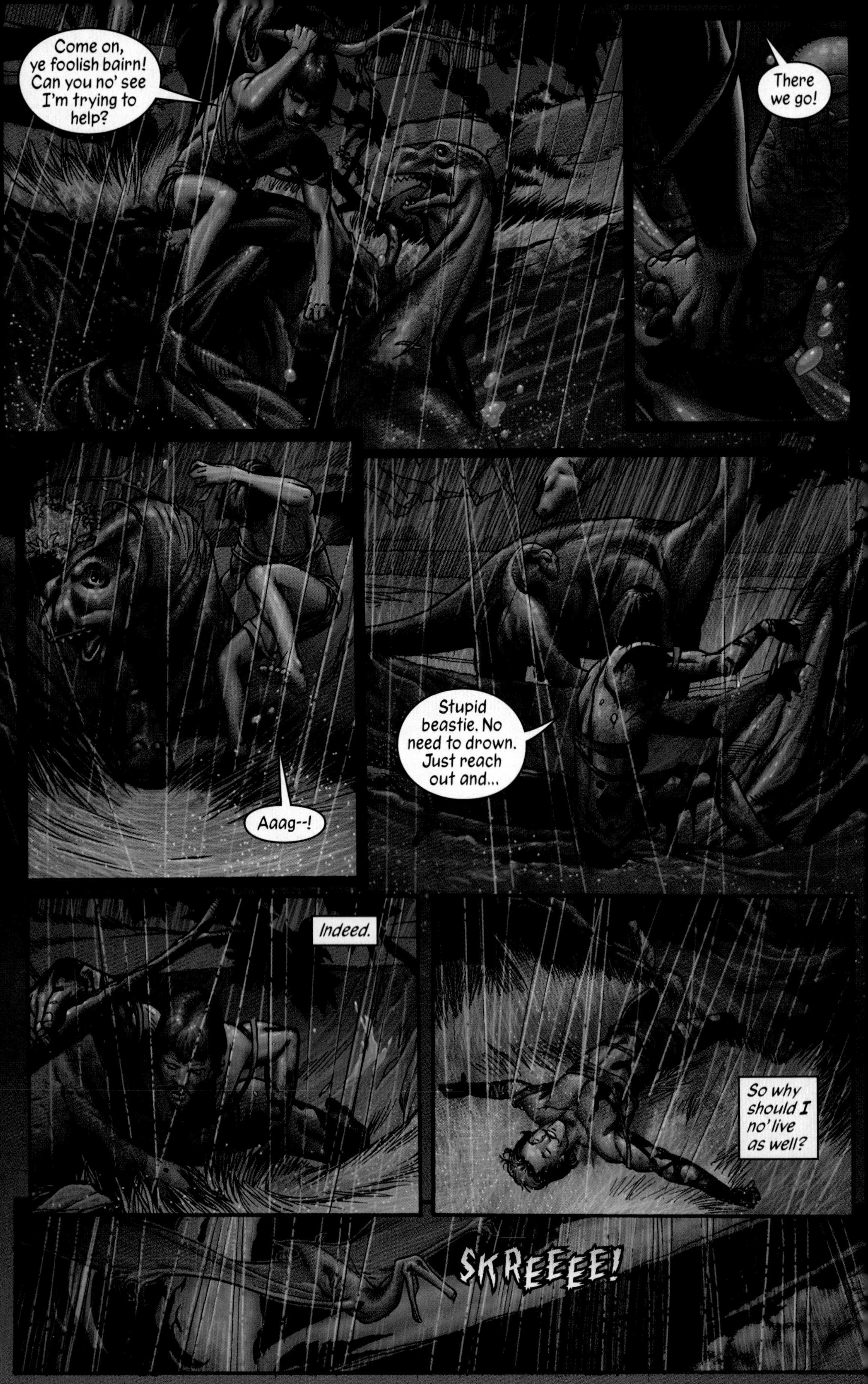
Come on, ye foolish bairn! Can you no' see I'm trying to help?
There we go!
Aaag--!
Stupid beastie. No need to drown. Just reach out and...
Indeed.
So why should I no' live as well?
SKREEEEE!

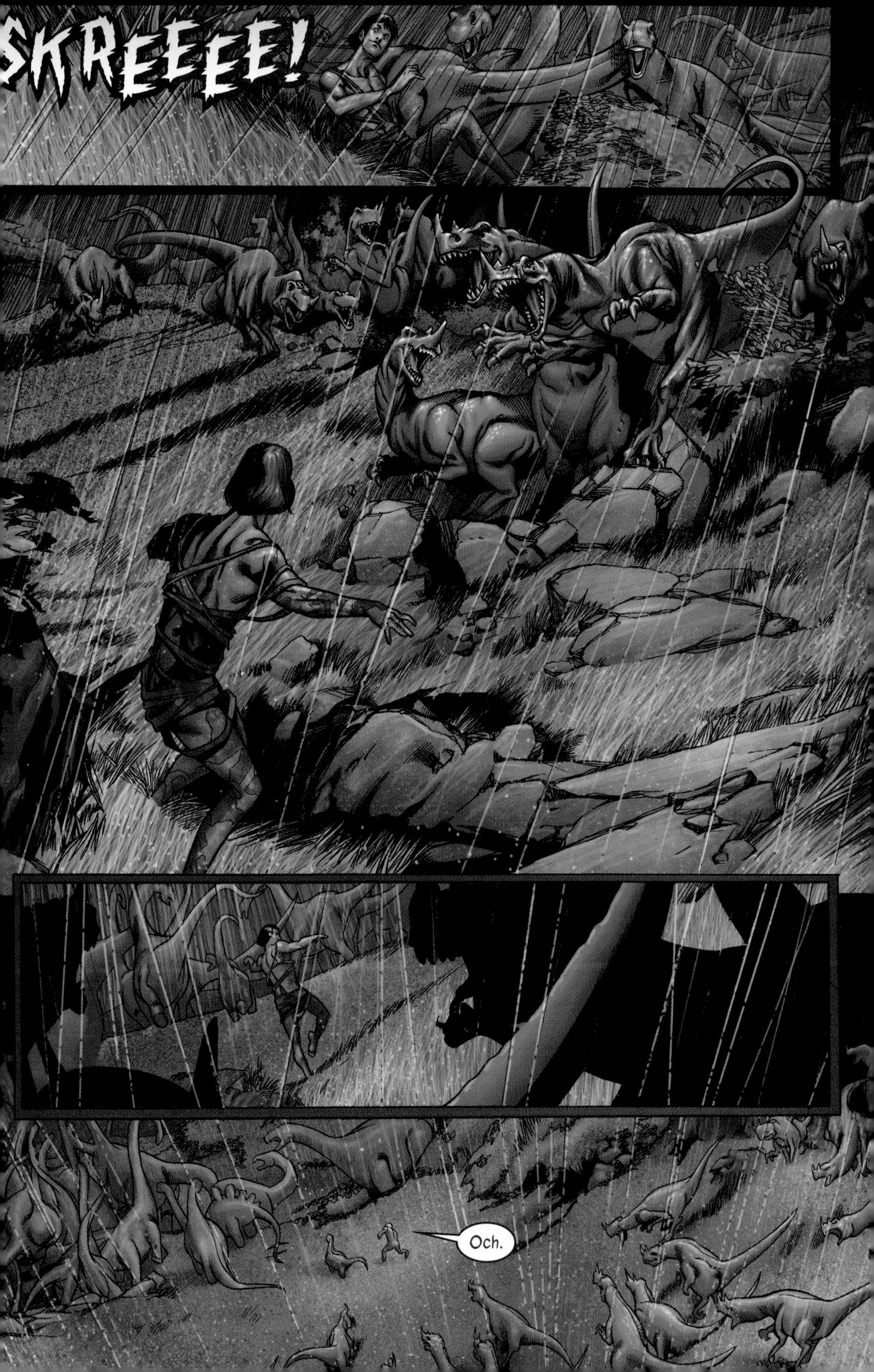
SKREEEE!
Och.

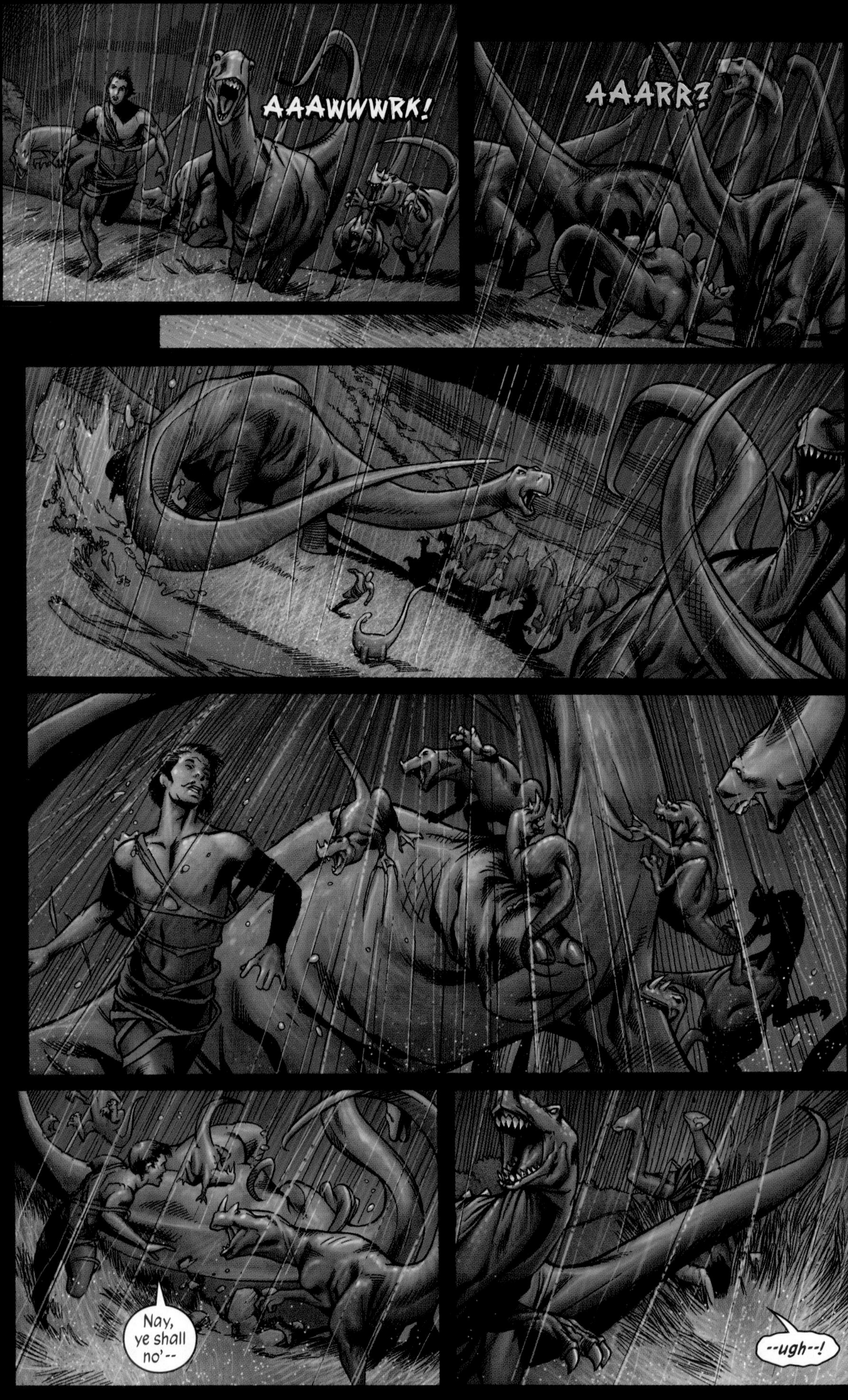
AAAWWWRK!
AAARR?
Nay, ye shall no'--
--ugh--!

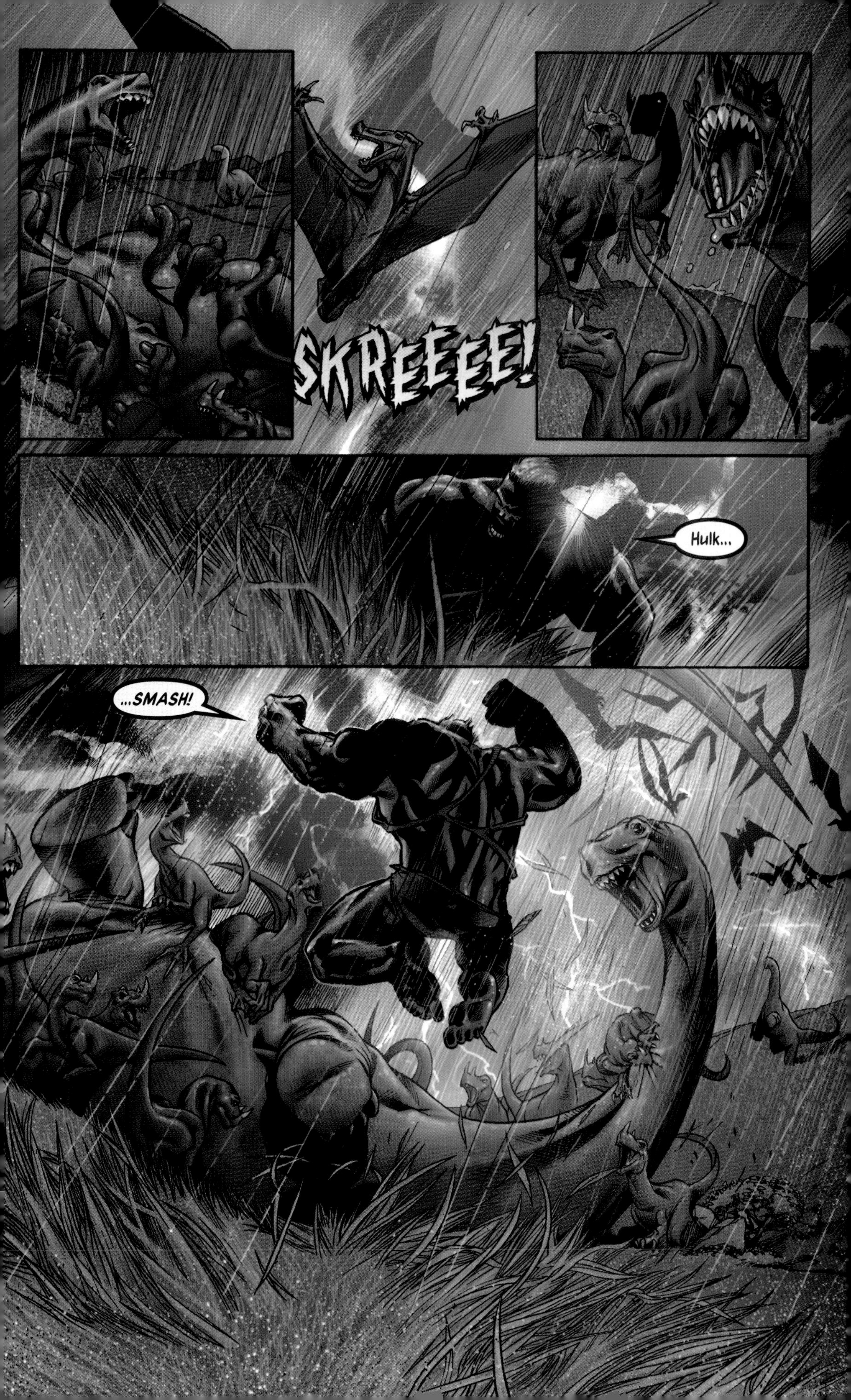
SKREEEEE!
Hulk...
...SMASH!

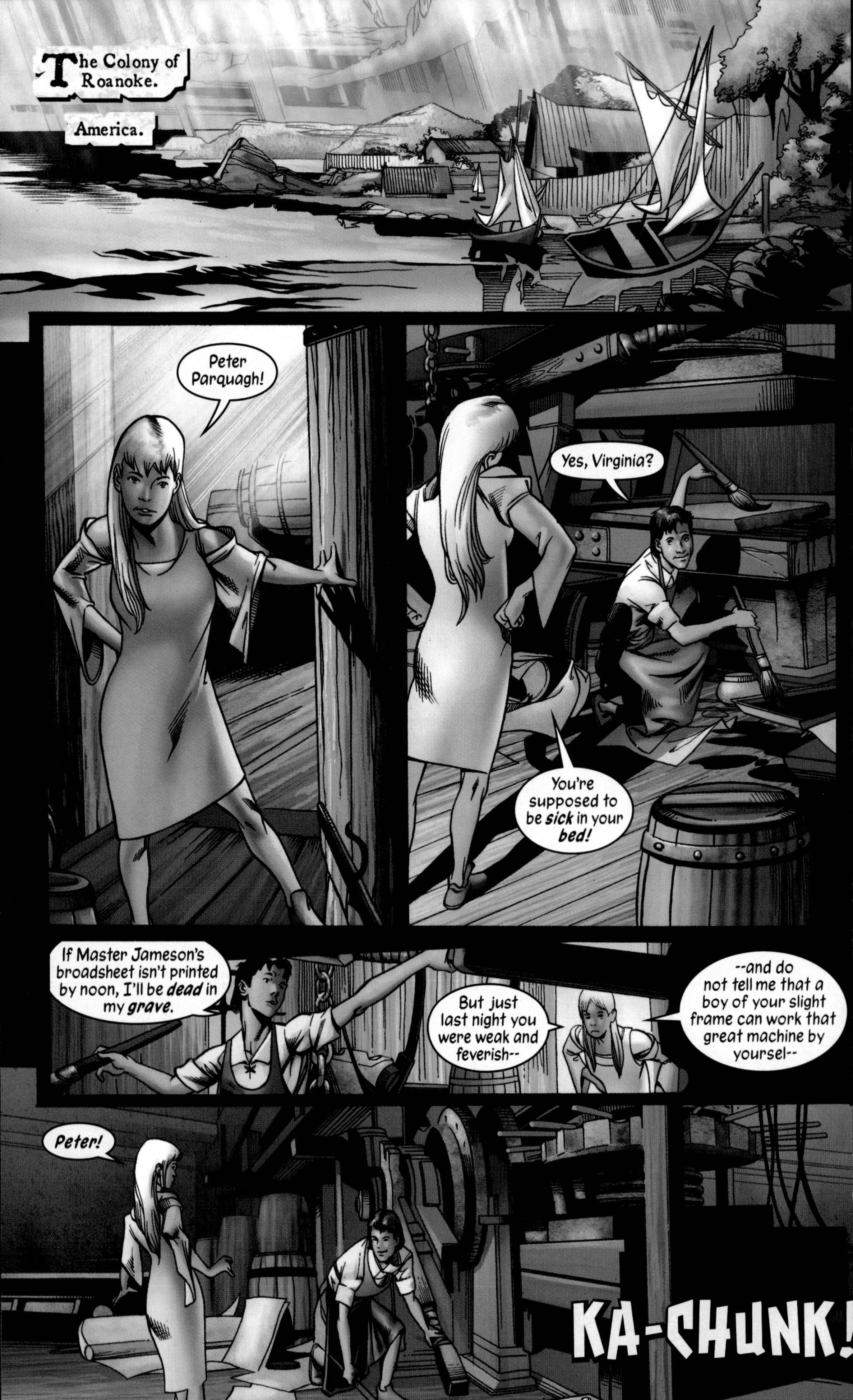
The Colony of Roanoke.
America.
Peter Parquagh!
Yes, Virginia?
You're supposed to be sick in your bed!
If Master Jameson's broadsheet isn't printed by noon, I'll be dead in my grave.
But just last night you were weak and feverish--
--and do not tell me that a boy of your slight frame can work that great machine by yoursel--
Peter!
KA-CHUNK!

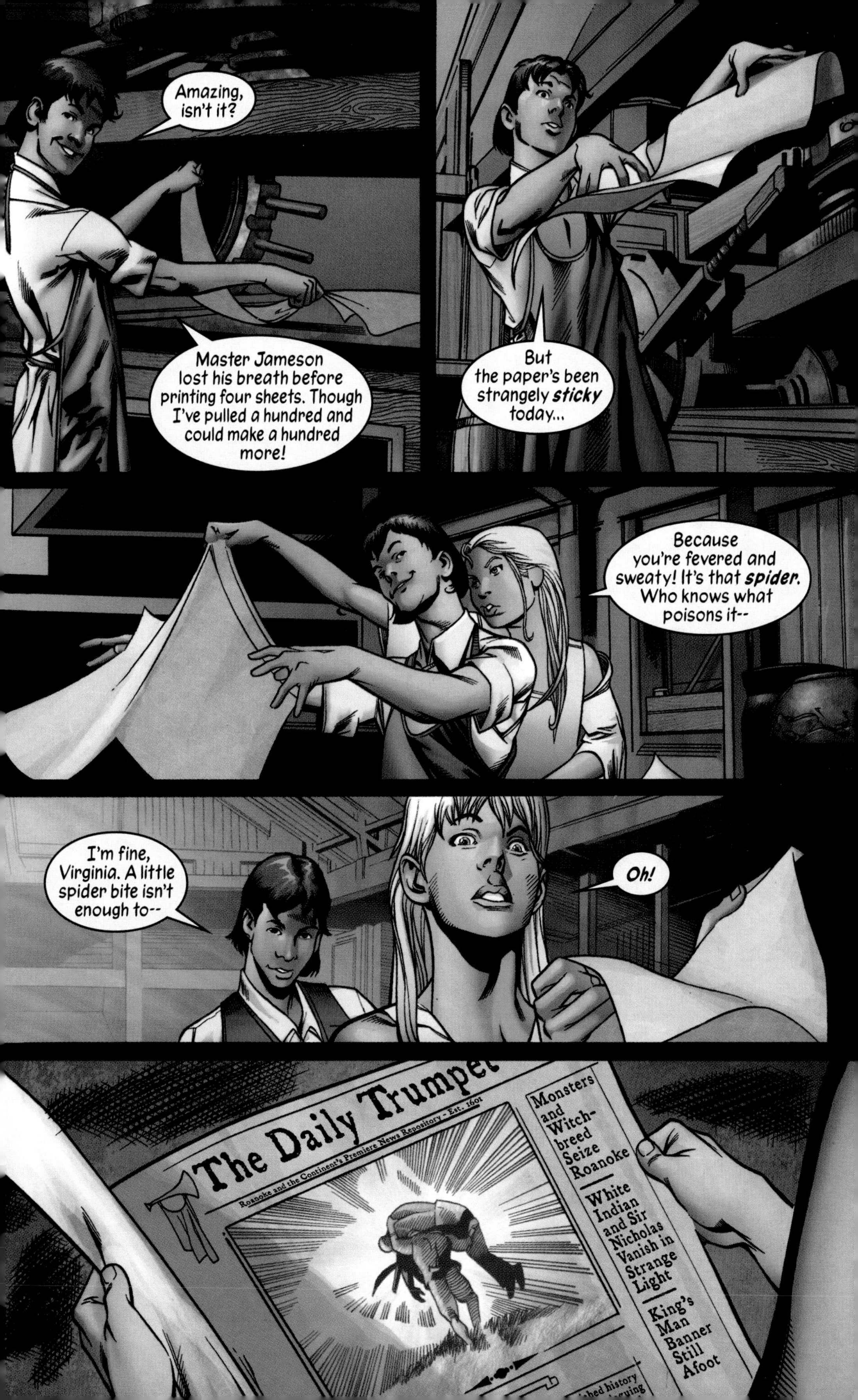
Amazing, isn't it?
Master Jameson lost his breath before printing four sheets. Though I've pulled a hundred and could make a hundred more!
But the paper's been strangely *sticky* today...
Because you're fevered and sweaty! It's that *spider*. Who knows what poisons it--
I'm fine, Virginia. A little spider bite isn't enough to--
Oh!
The Daily Trumpet
Roanoke and the Continent's Premiere News Repository - Est. 1601
Monsters and Witch-breed Seize Roanoke
White Indian and Sir Nicholas Vanish in Strange Light
King's Man Banner Still Afoot

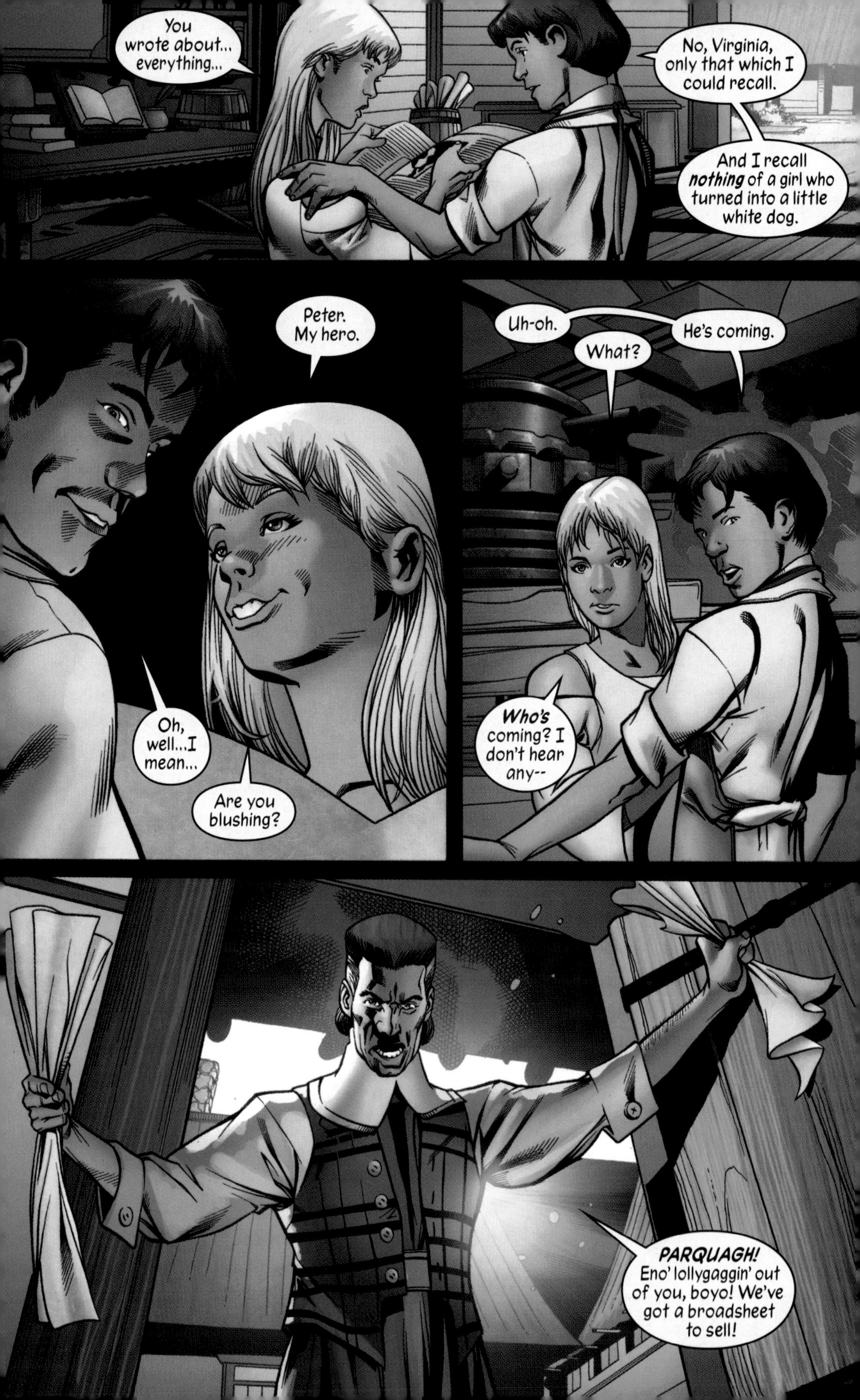
You wrote about... everything...
No, Virginia, only that which I could recall.
And I recall *nothing* of a girl who turned into a little white dog.
Peter. My hero.
Oh, well...I mean...
Are you blushing?
Uh-oh.
What?
He's coming.
Who's coming? I don't hear any--
PARQUAGH! Eno' lollygaggin' out of you, boyo! We've got a broadsheet to sell!

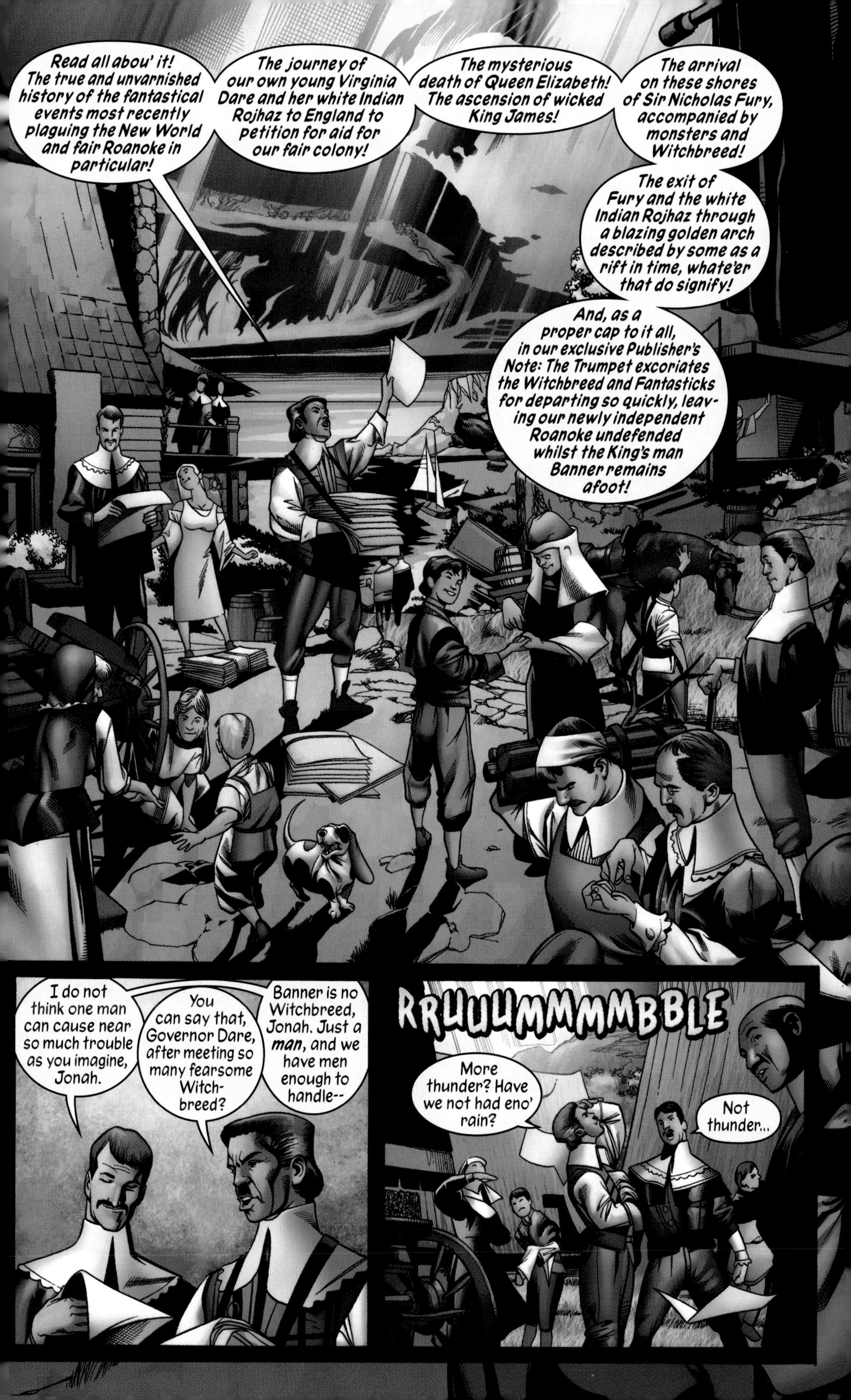
Read all abou' it! The true and unvarnished history of the fantastical events most recently plaguing the New World and fair Roanoke in particular!
The journey of our own young Virginia Dare and her white Indian Rojhaz to England to petition for aid for our fair colony!
The mysterious death of Queen Elizabeth! The ascension of wicked King James!
The arrival on these shores of Sir Nicholas Fury, accompanied by monsters and Witchbreed!
The exit of Fury and the white Indian Rojhaz through a blazing golden arch described by some as a rift in time, whate'er that do signify!
And, as a proper cap to it all, in our exclusive Publisher's Note: The Trumpet excoriates the Witchbreed and Fantasticks for departing so quickly, leaving our newly independent Roanoke undefended whilst the King's man Banner remains afoot!
I do not think one man can cause near so much trouble as you imagine, Jonah.
You can say that, Governor Dare, after meeting so many fearsome Witchbreed?
Banner is no Witchbreed, Jonah. Just a *man*, and we have men enough to handle--
RRUUUMMMMMBBLE
More thunder? Have we not had eno' rain?
Not thunder...

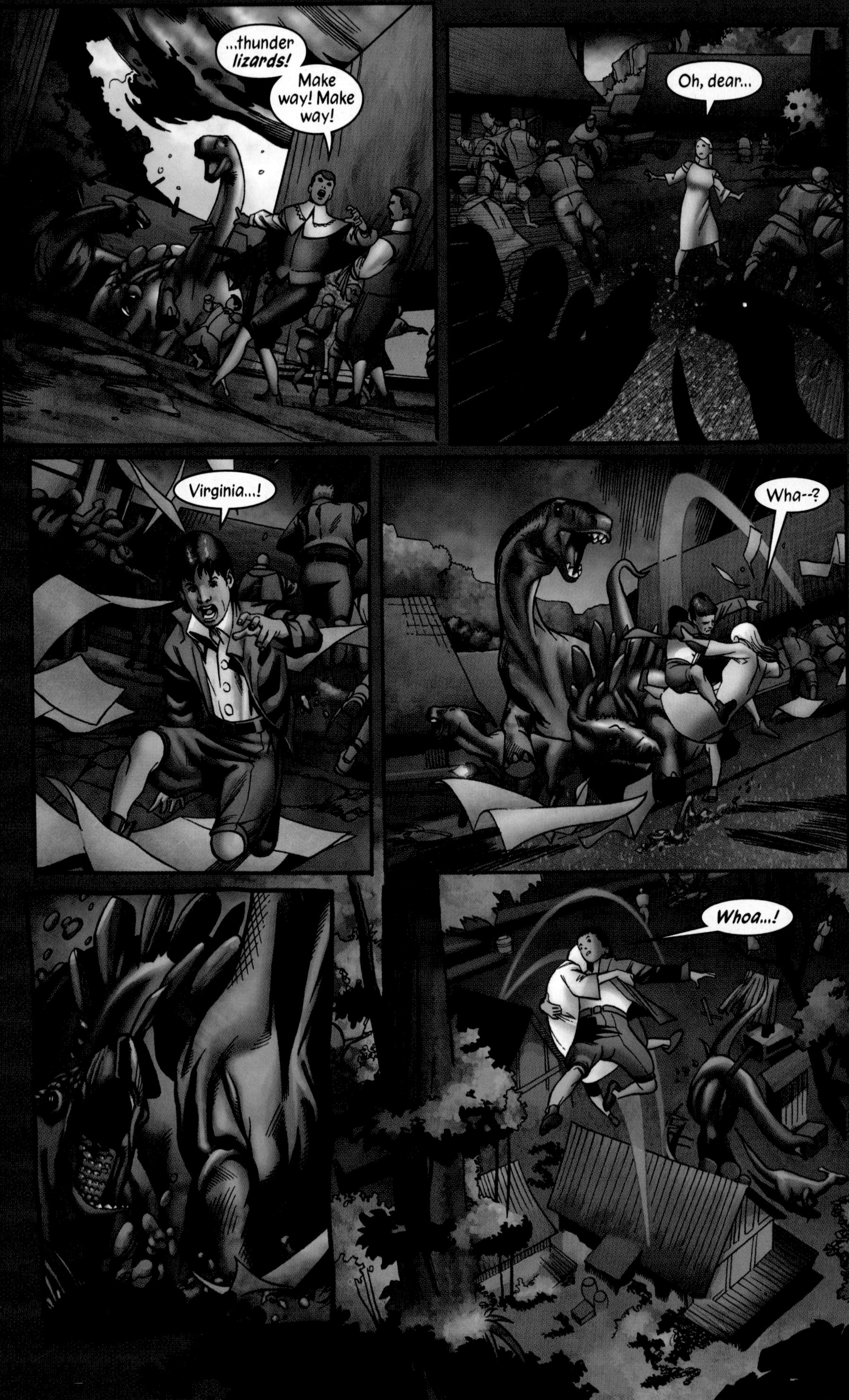
...thunder *lizards!*
Make way! Make way!
Oh, dear...
Virginia...!
Wha--?
Whoa...!

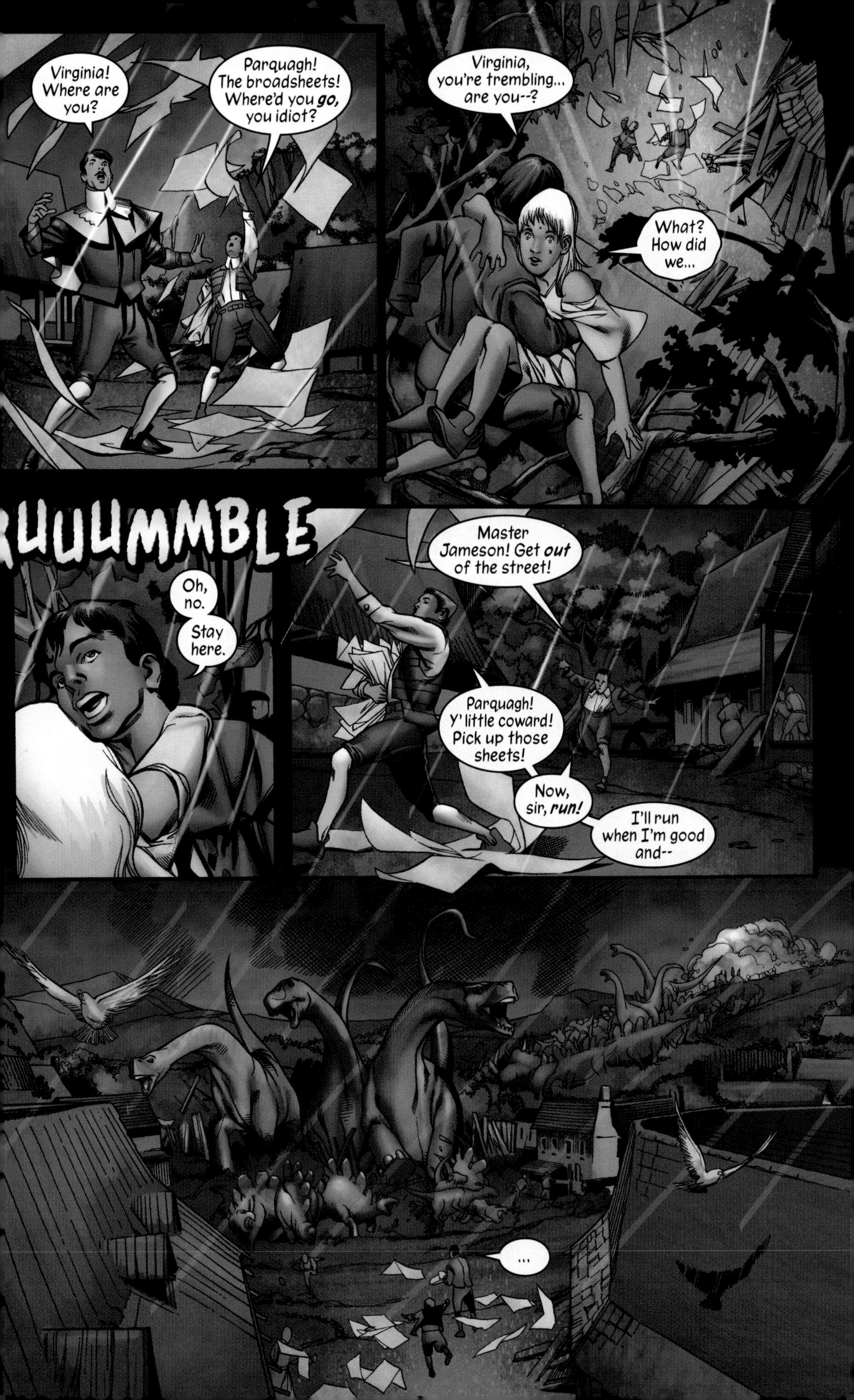

Virginia! Where are you?
Parquagh! The broadsheets! Where'd you *go,* you idiot?
Virginia, you're trembling... are you--?
What? How did we...
RUUUMMBLE
Oh, no.
Stay here.
Master Jameson! Get *out* of the street!
Parquagh! Y' little coward! Pick up those sheets!
Now, sir, *run!*
I'll run when I'm good and--
...

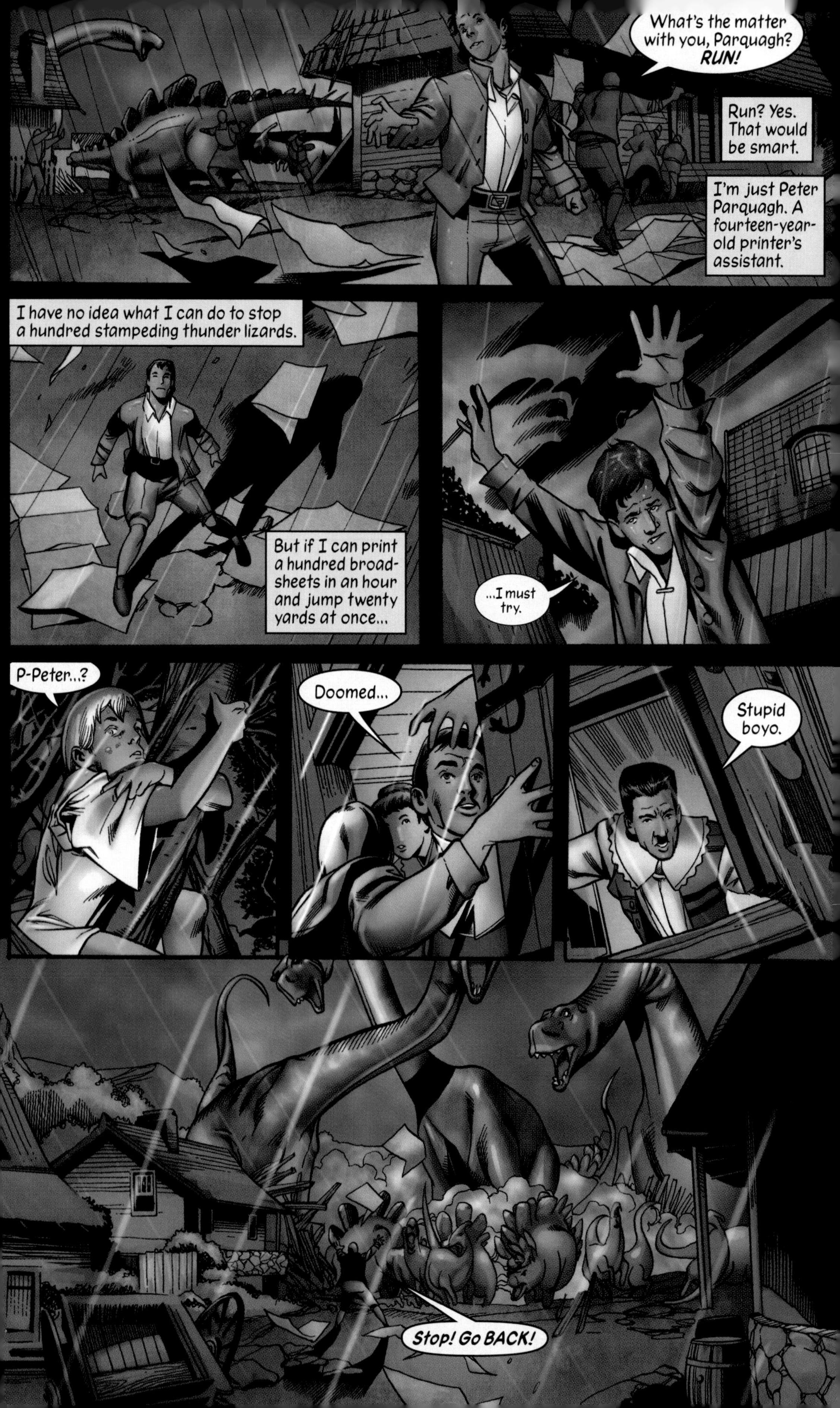
What's the matter with you, Parquagh? RUN!
Run? Yes. That would be smart.
I'm just Peter Parquagh. A fourteen-year-old printer's assistant.
I have no idea what I can do to stop a hundred stampeding thunder lizards.
But if I can print a hundred broad-sheets in an hour and jump twenty yards at once...
...I must try.
P-Peter...?
Doomed...
Stupid boyo.
Stop! Go BACK!

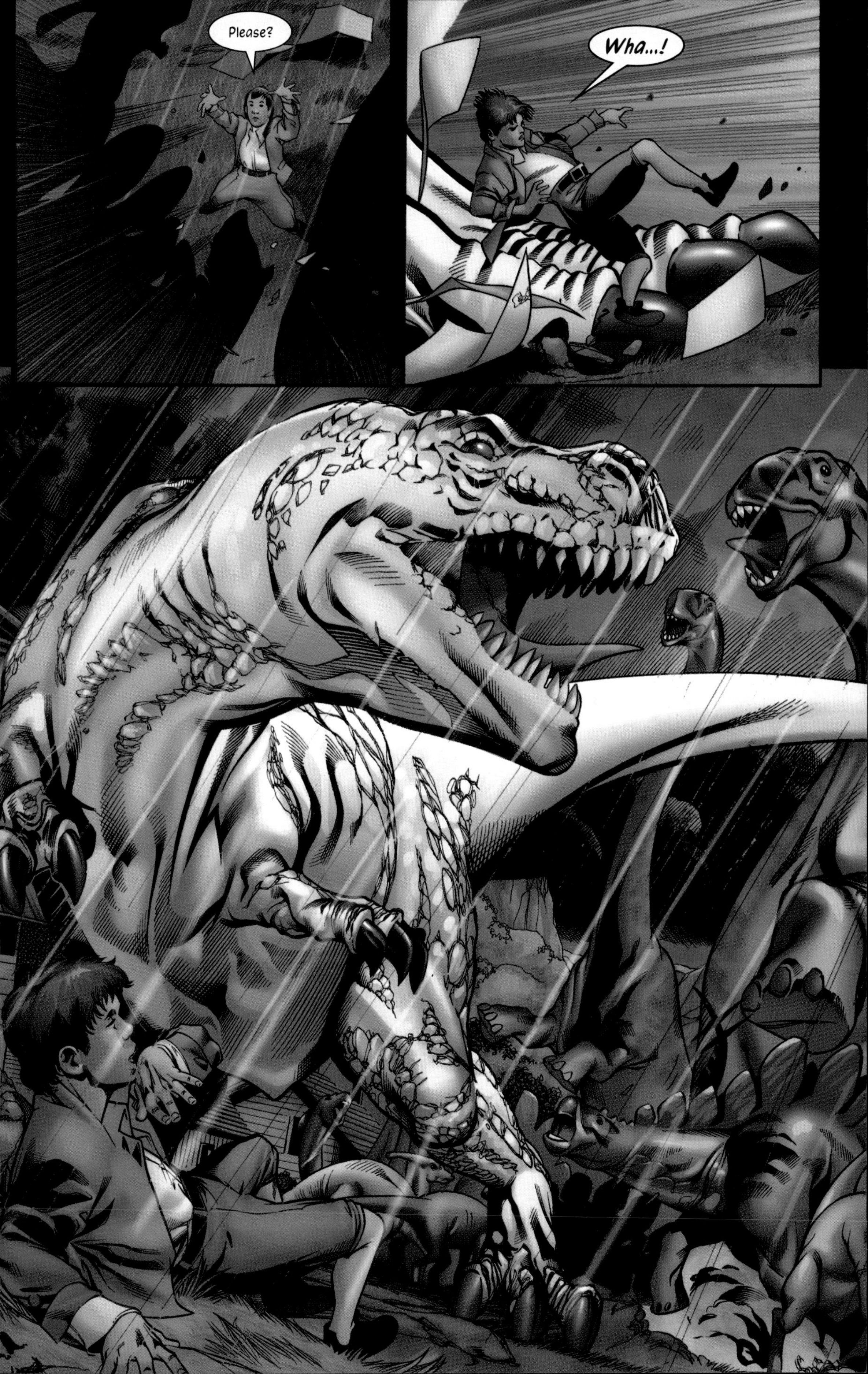
Please?
Wha...!

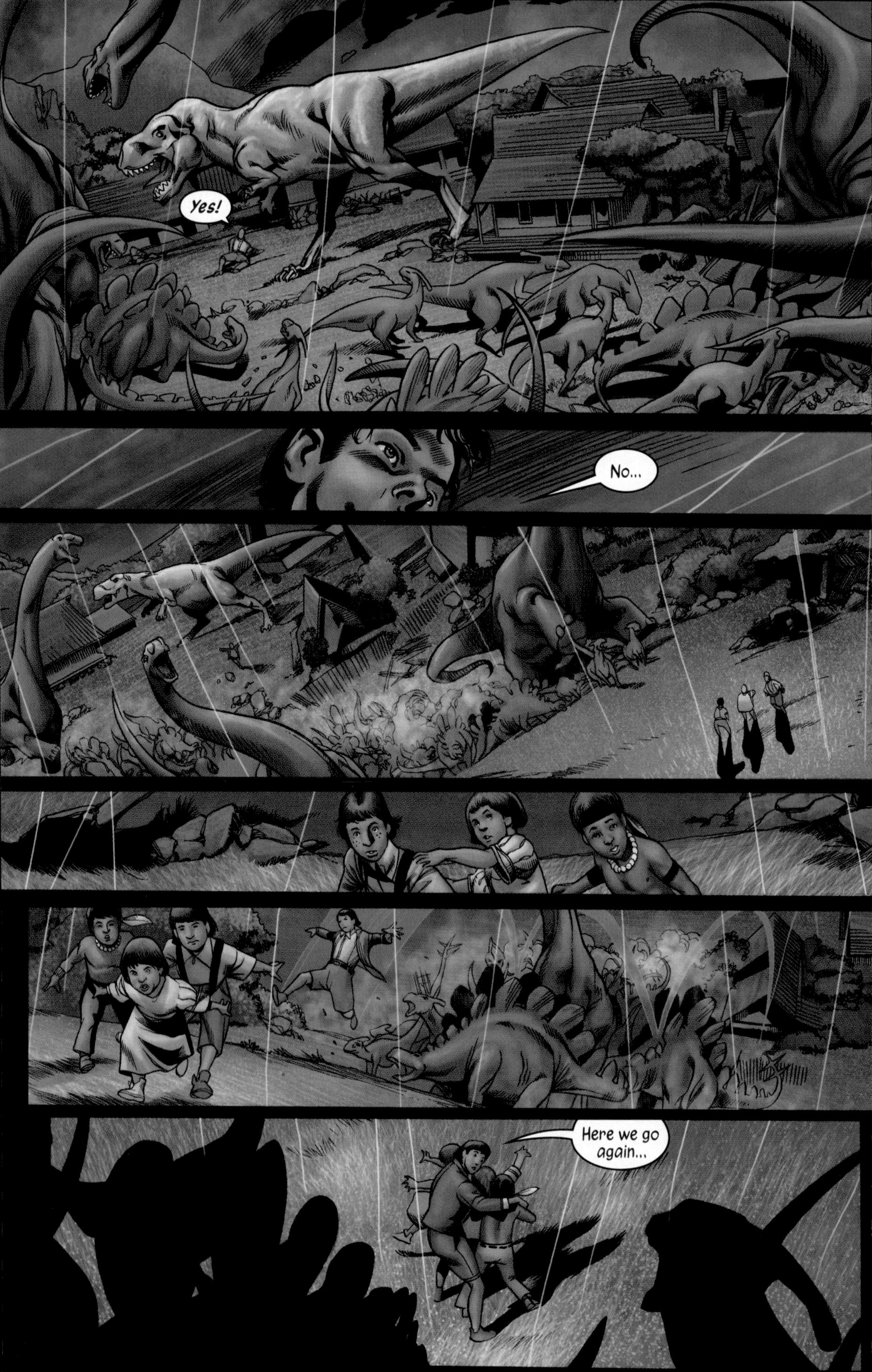
Yes!
No...
Here we go again...

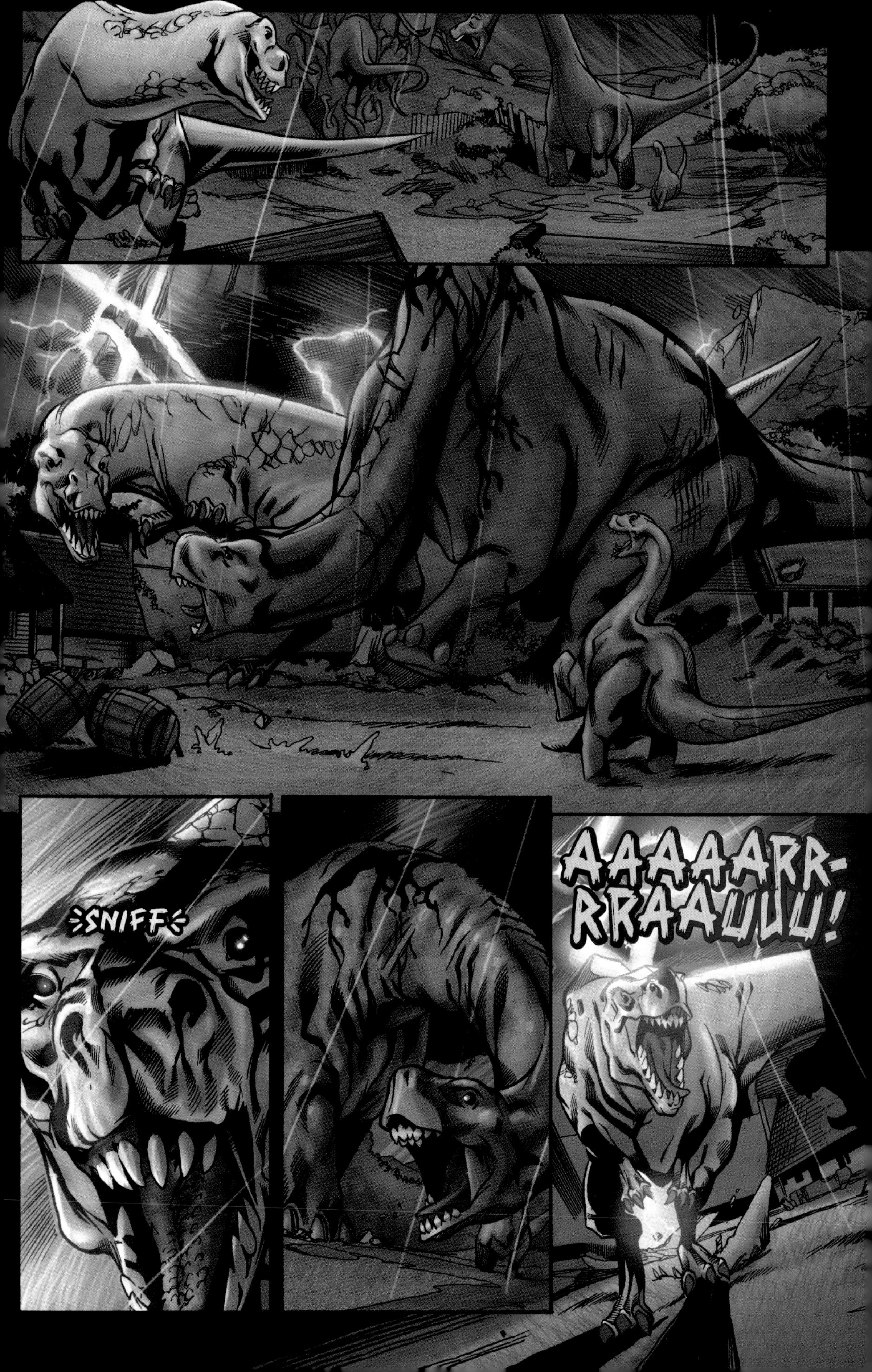
SNIFF
AAAAARR-
RRAAUUU!

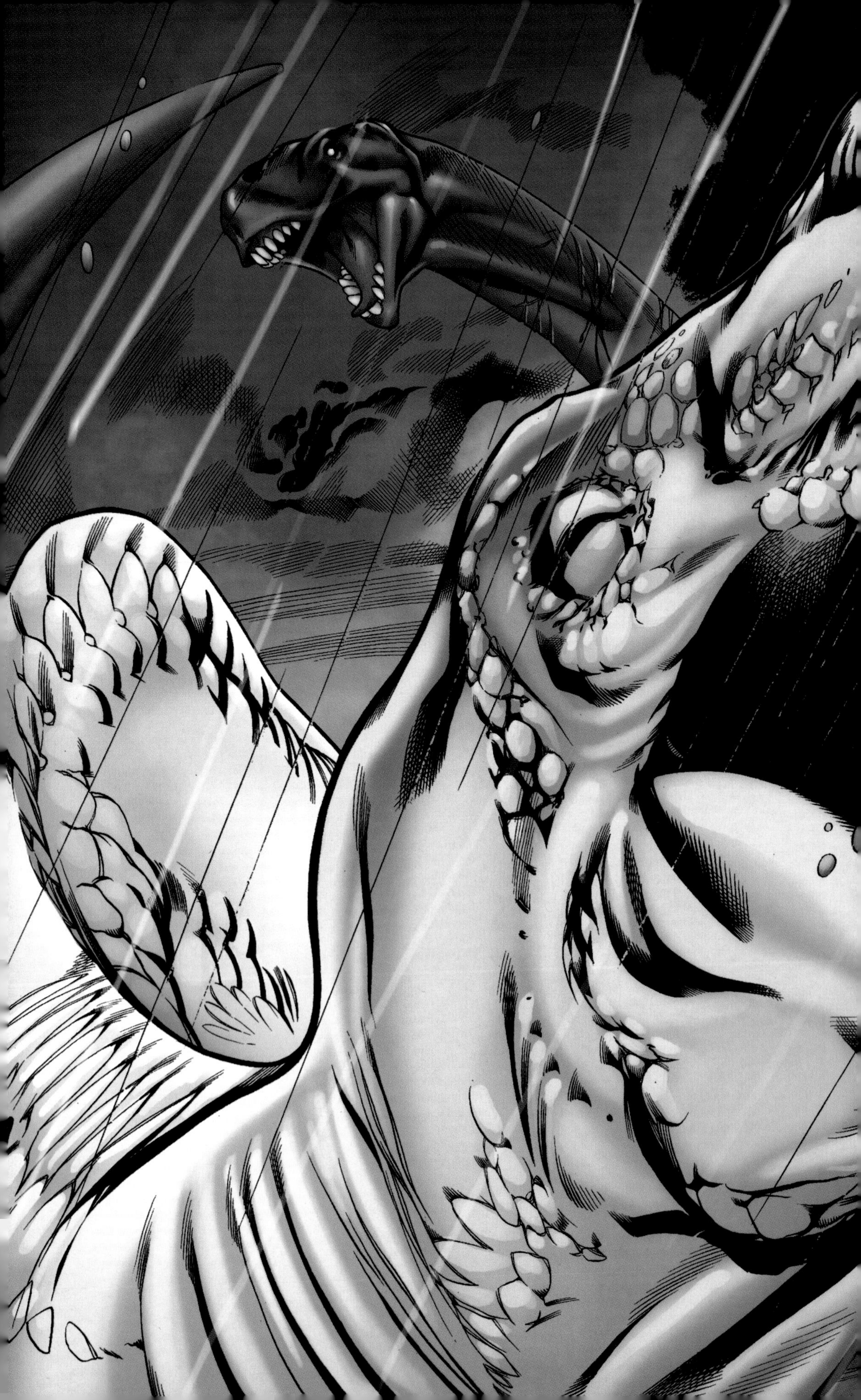

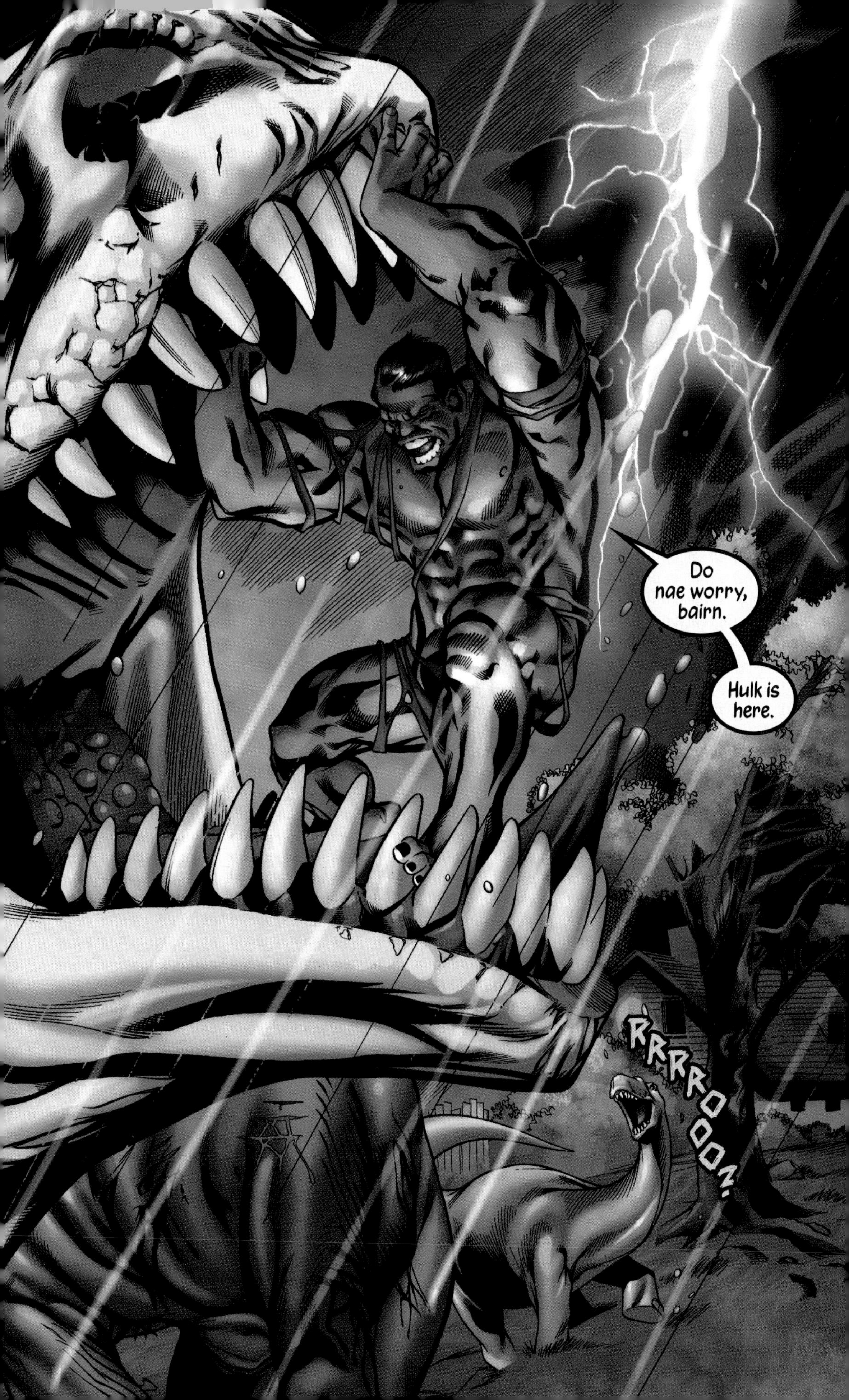
Do nae worry, bairn.
Hulk is here.
RRRROOON!

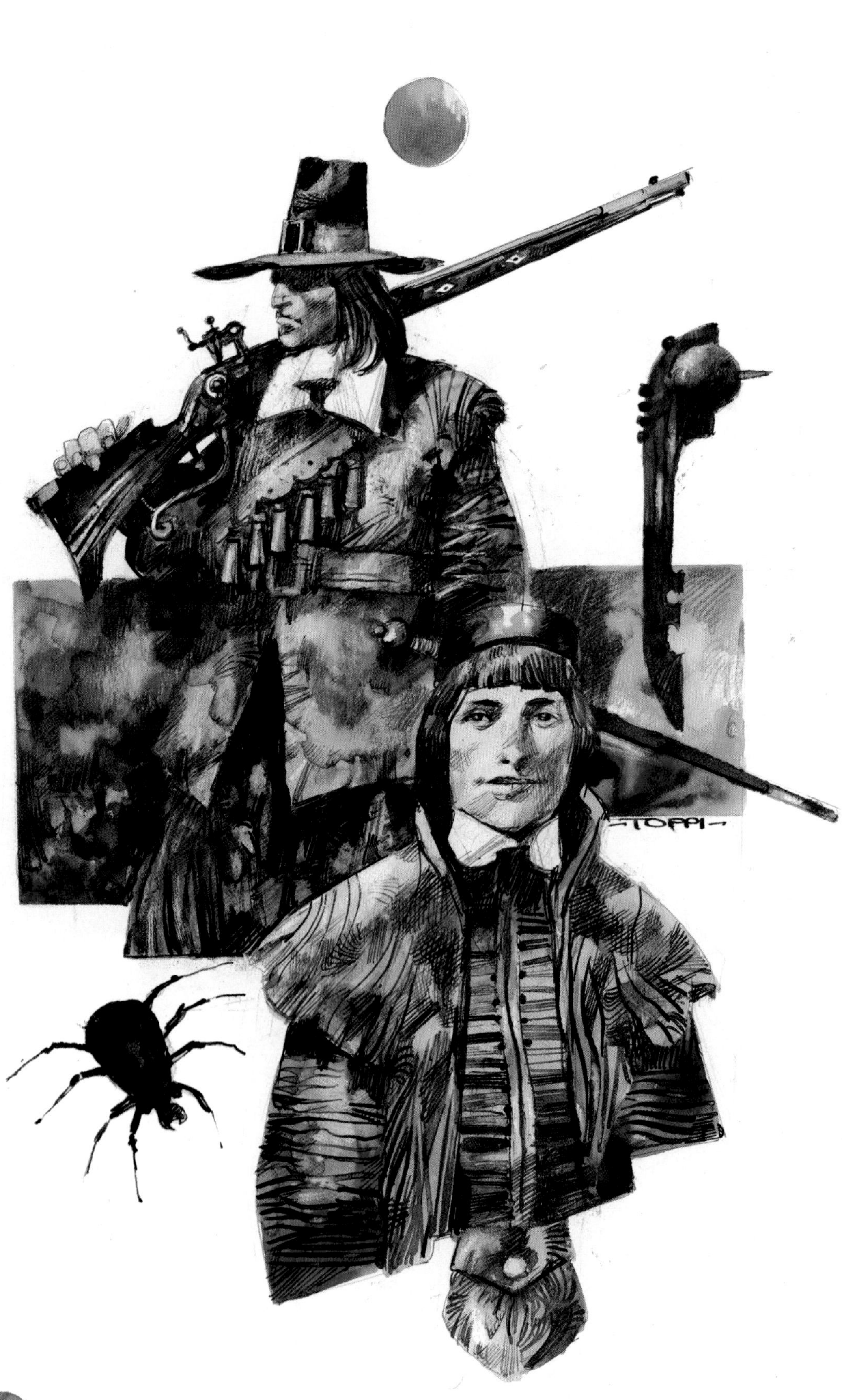
TOPPI

#2

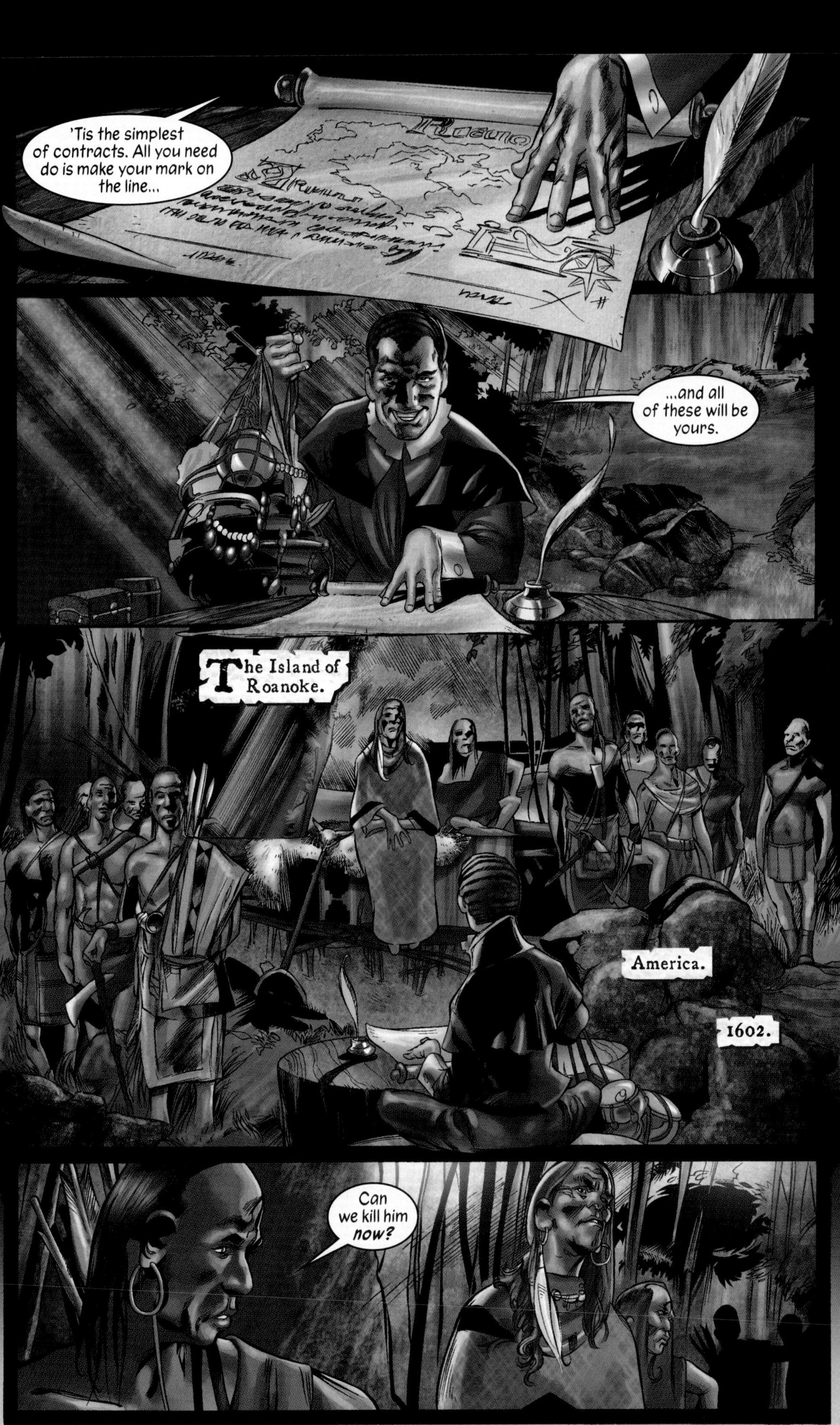

'Tis the simplest of contracts. All you need do is make your mark on the line...
...and all of these will be yours.
The Island of Roanoke.
America.
1602.
Can we kill him *now?*

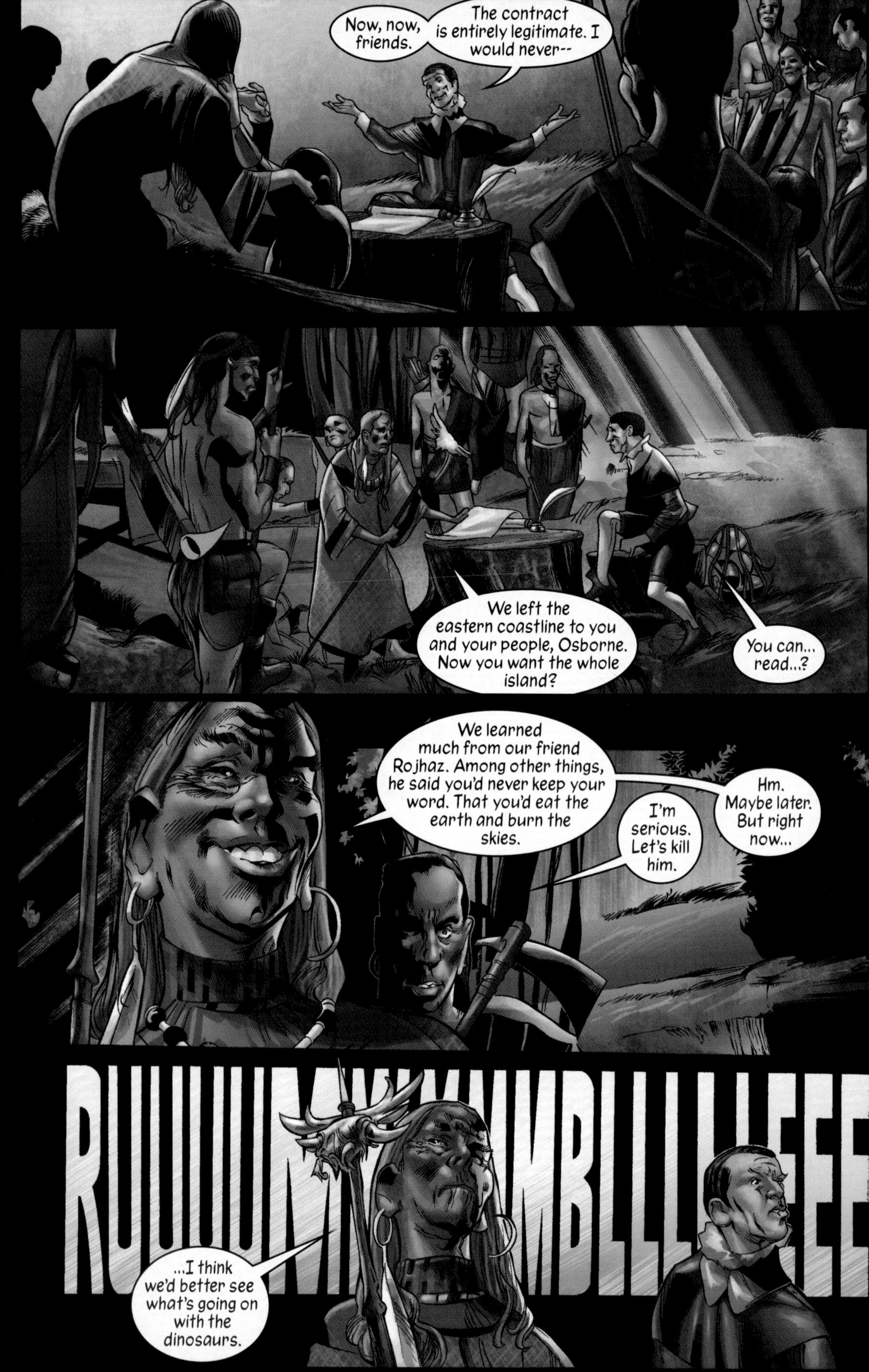
Now, now, friends.
The contract is entirely legitimate. I would never--
We left the eastern coastline to you and your people, Osborne. Now you want the whole island?
You can... read...?
We learned much from our friend Rojhaz. Among other things, he said you'd never keep your word. That you'd eat the earth and burn the skies.
I'm serious. Let's kill him.
Hm. Maybe later. But right now...
RUUUUMMMMMBLLLLEEE
...I think we'd better see what's going on with the dinosaurs.

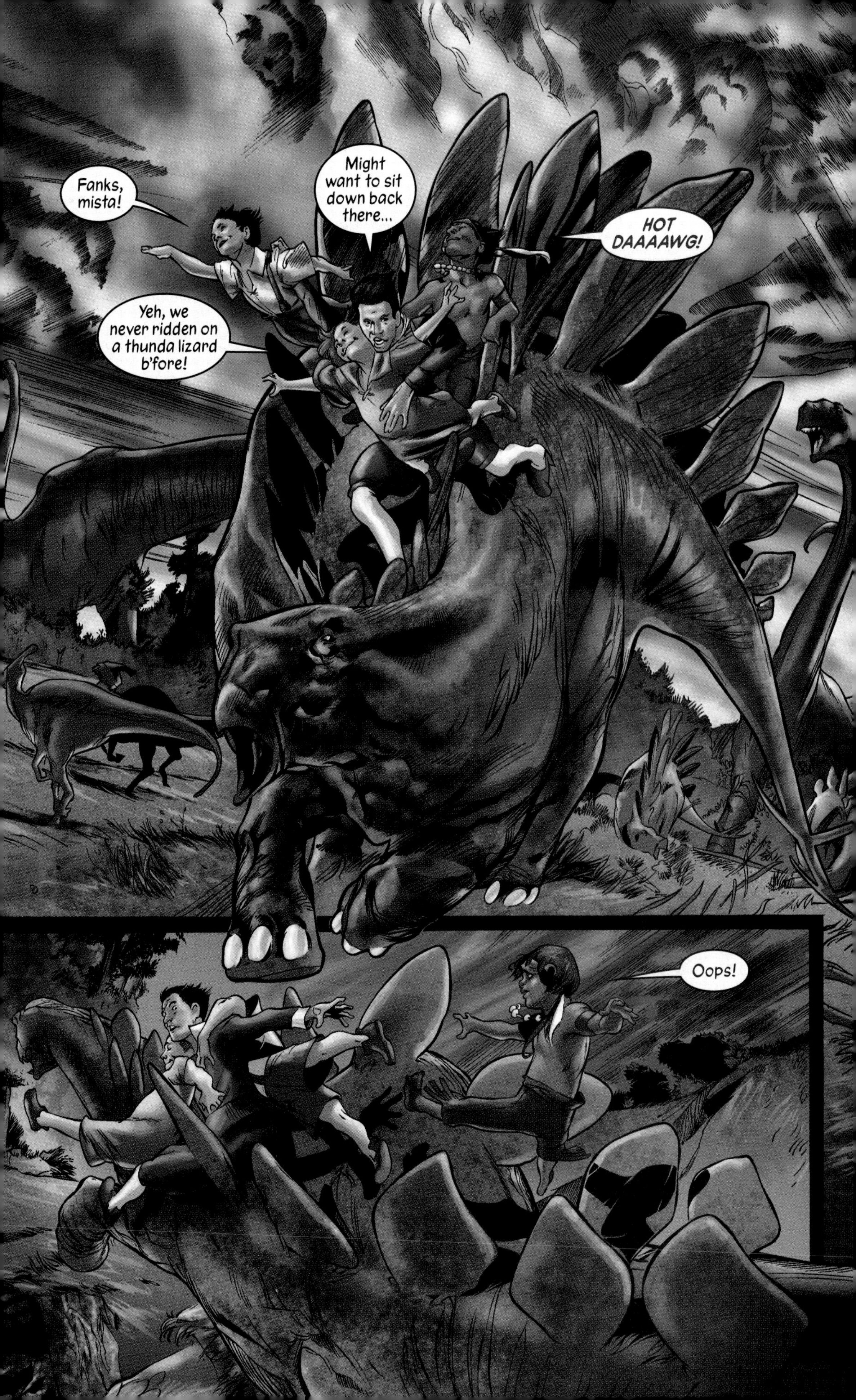

Fanks, mista!
Might want to sit down back there...
HOT DAAAAWG!
Yeh, we never ridden on a thunda lizard b'fore!
Oops!

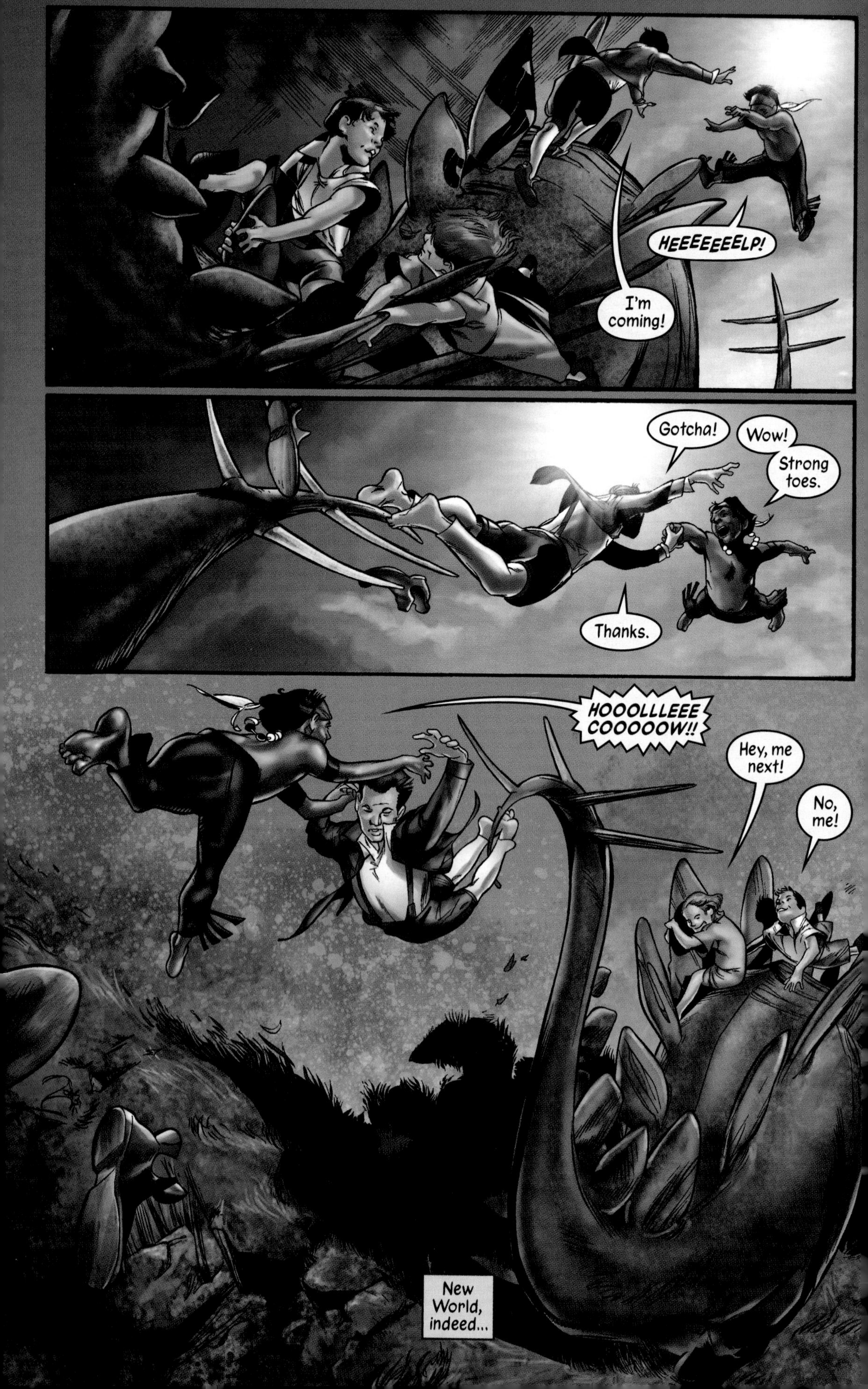
HEEEEEEELP!
I'm coming!
Gotcha!
Wow!
Strong toes.
Thanks.
HOOOLLLEEE COOOOOW!!
Hey, me next!
No, me!
New World, indeed...

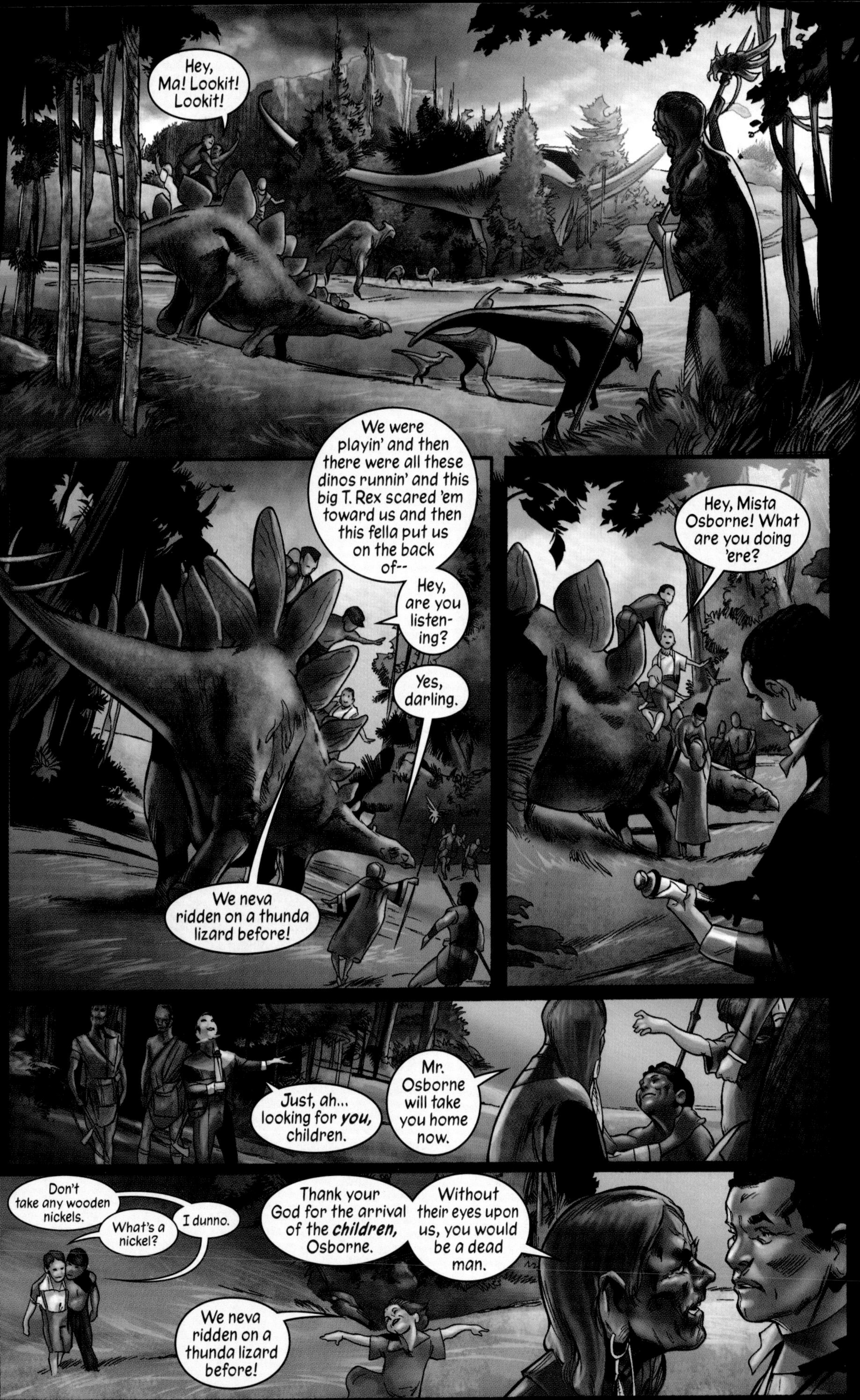
Hey, Ma! Lookit! Lookit!
We were playin' and then there were all these dinos runnin' and this big T. Rex scared 'em toward us and then this fella put us on the back of--
Hey, are you listen-ing?
Yes, darling.
We neva ridden on a thunda lizard before!
Hey, Mista Osborne! What are you doing 'ere?
Just, ah... looking for *you,* children.
Mr. Osborne will take you home now.
Don't take any wooden nickels.
What's a nickel?
I dunno.
Thank your God for the arrival of the ***children,*** Osborne.
Without their eyes upon us, you would be a dead man.
We neva ridden on a thunda lizard before!

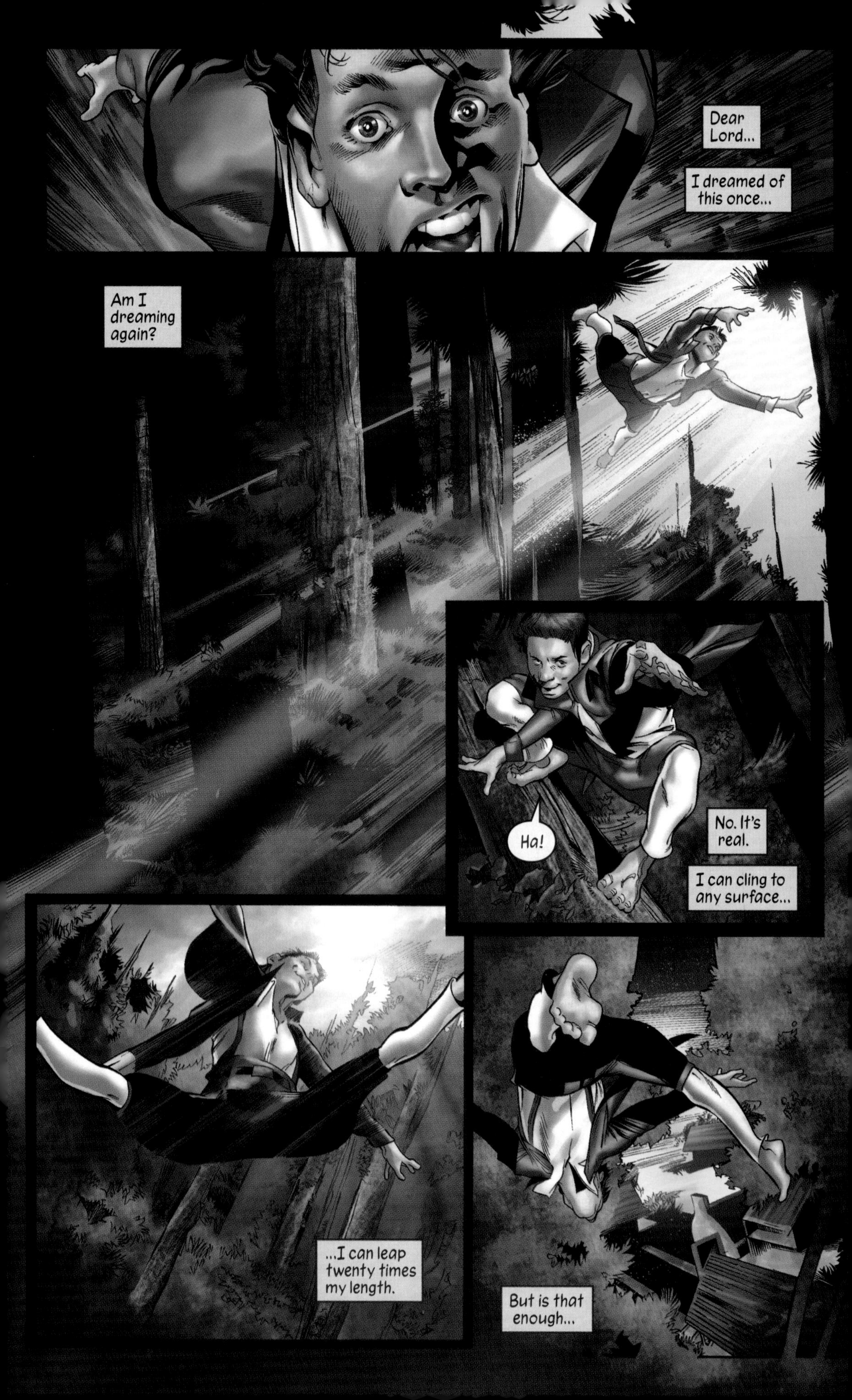
Dear Lord...
I dreamed of this once...
Am I dreaming again?
Ha!
No. It's real.
I can cling to any surface...
...I can leap twenty times my length.
But is that enough...

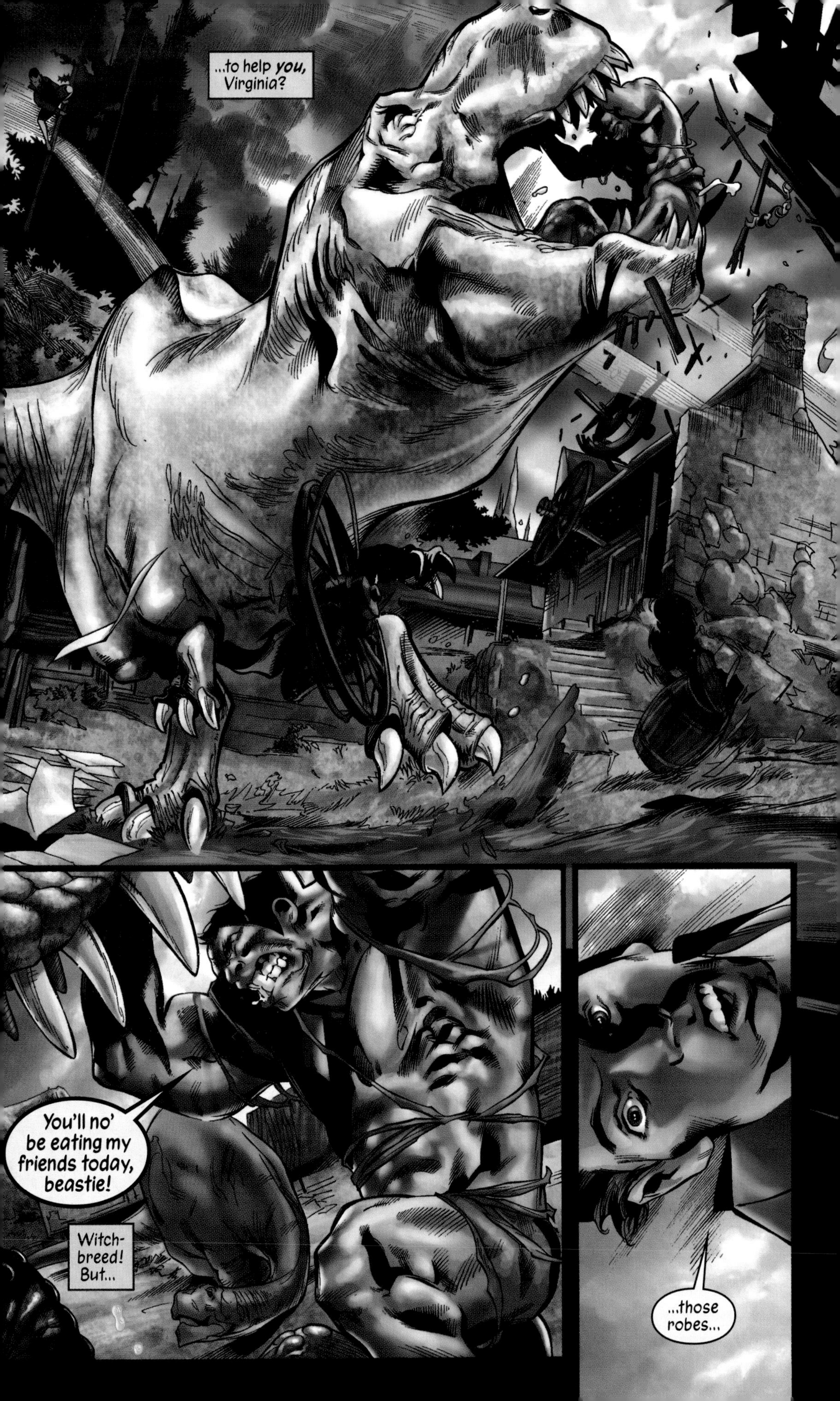
...to help *you*, Virginia?
You'll no' be eating my friends today, beastie!
Witch-breed! But...
...those robes...

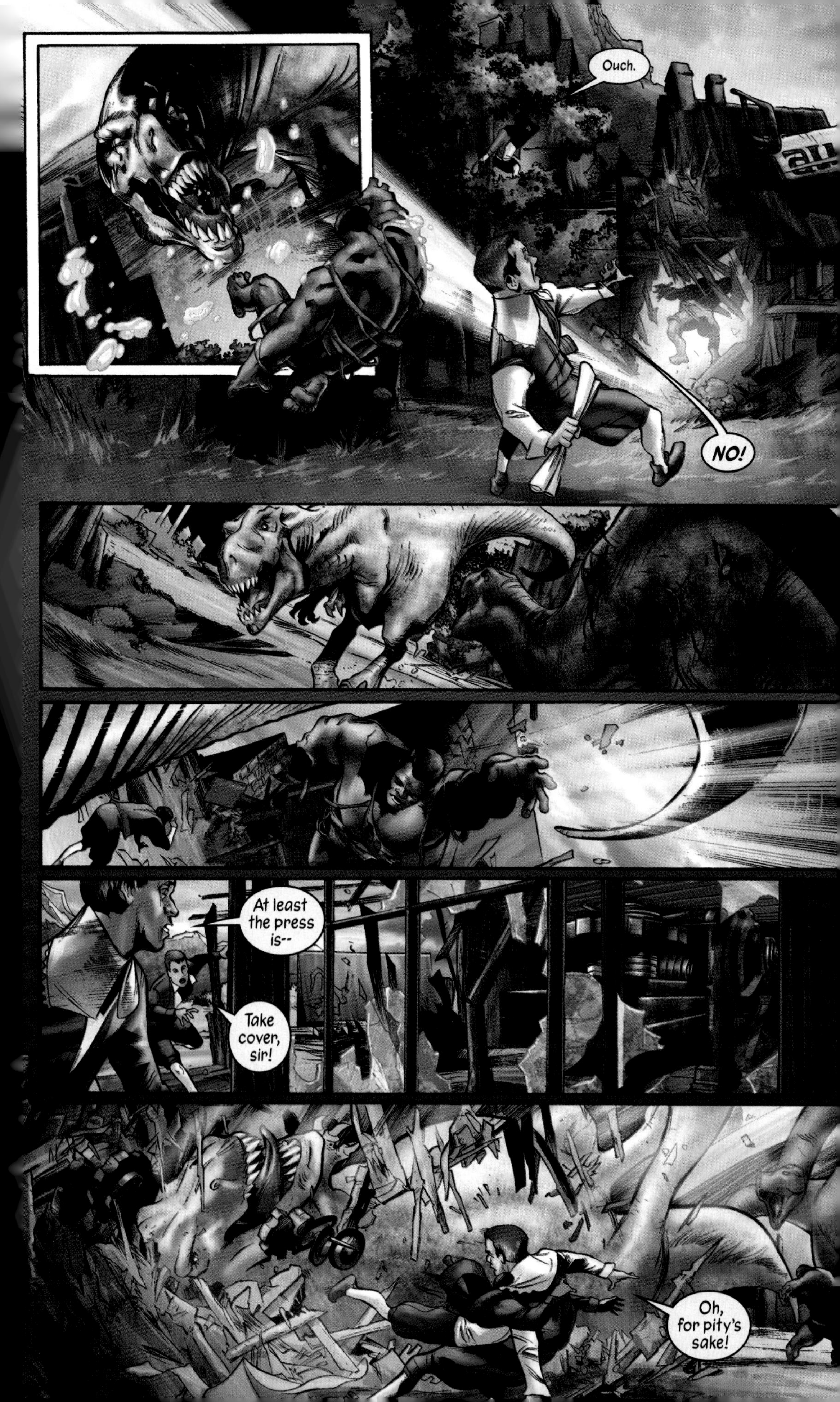

Ouch.
NO!
At least the press is--
Take cover, sir!
Oh, for pity's sake!

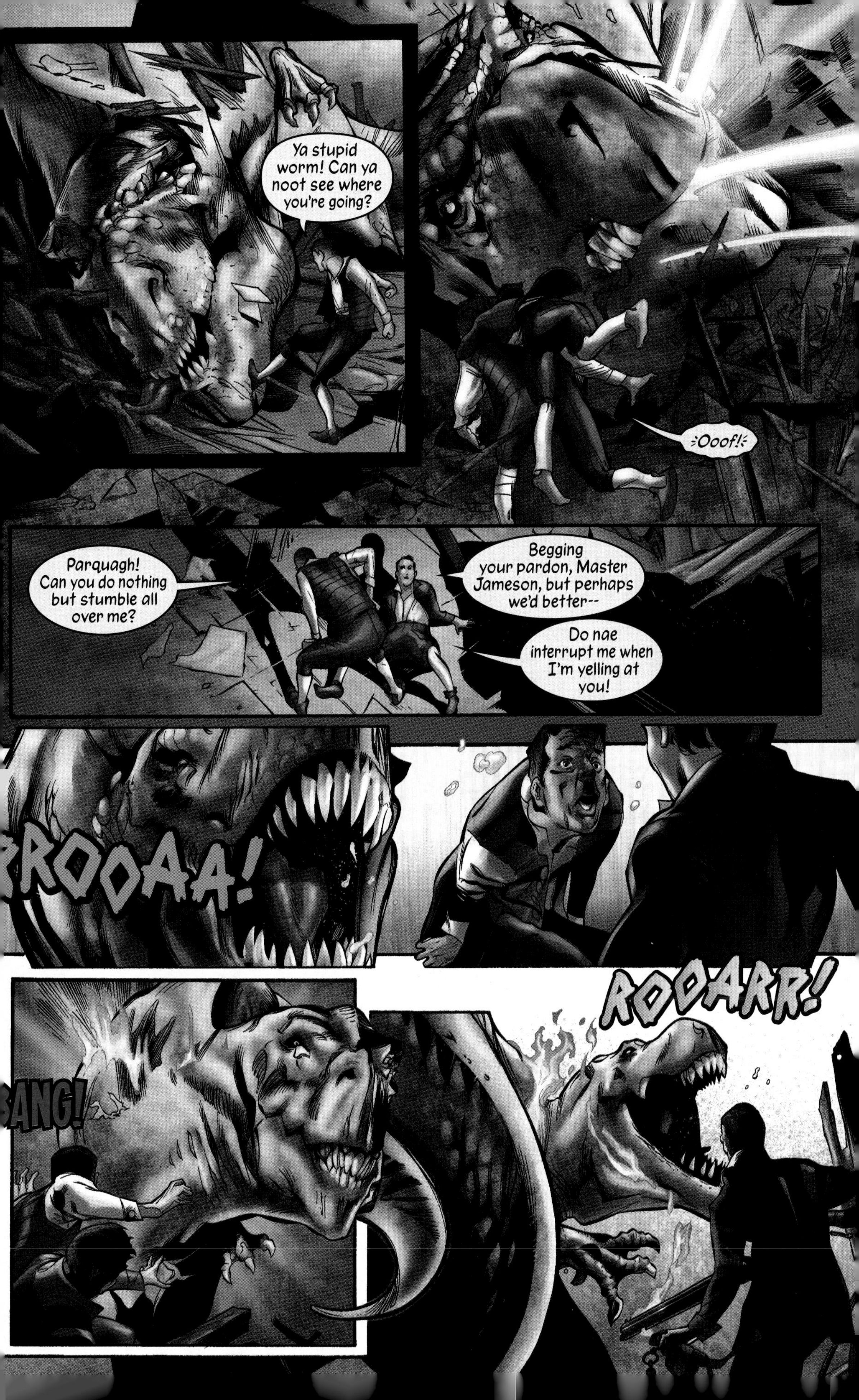
Ya stupid worm! Can ya noot see where you're going?
Ooof!
Parquagh! Can you do nothing but stumble all over me?
Begging your pardon, Master Jameson, but perhaps we'd better--
Do nae interrupt me when I'm yelling at you!
ROOAA!
BANG!
ROOARR!

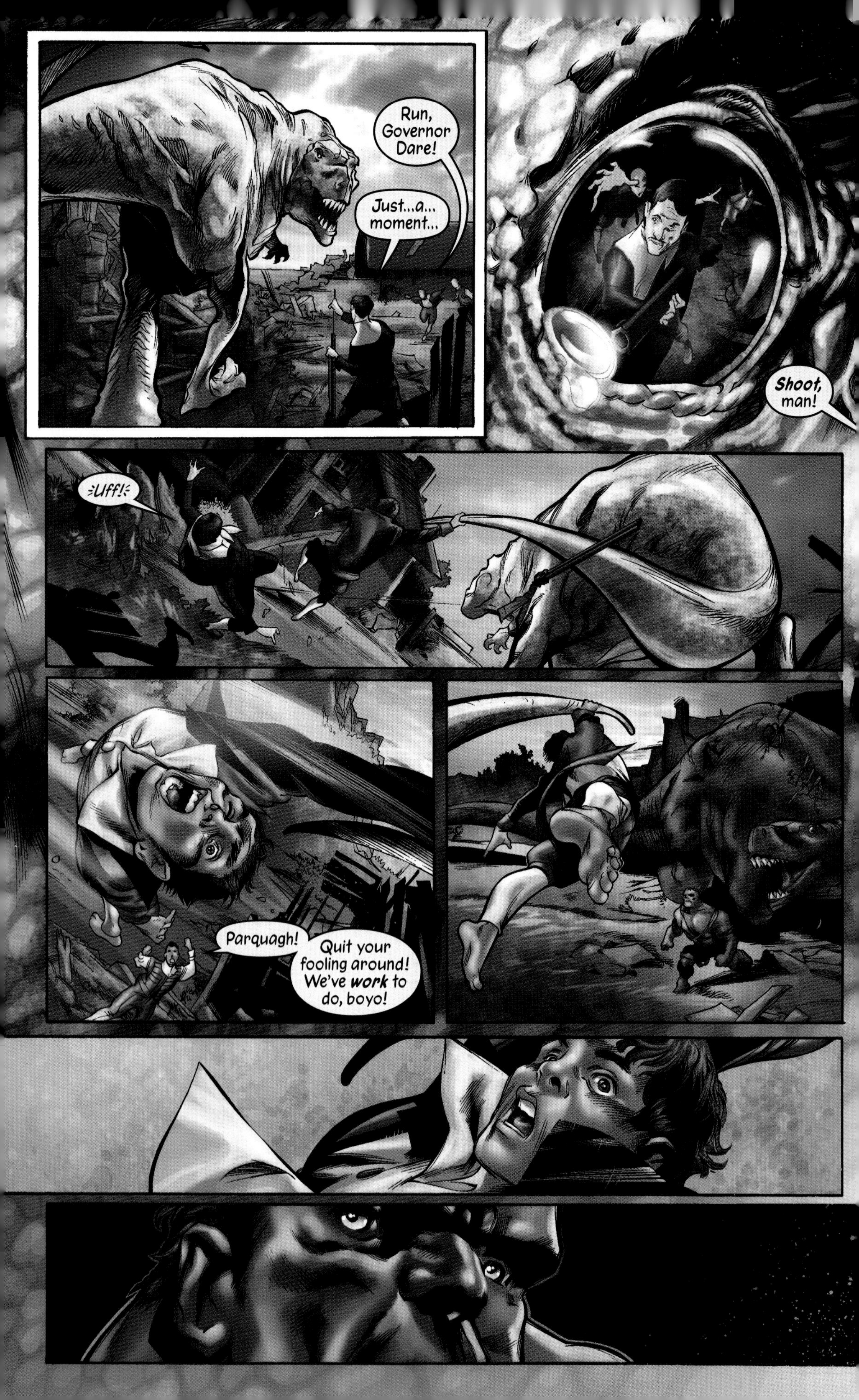

Run, Governor Dare!
Just...a... moment...
Shoot, man!
Uff!
Parquagh!
Quit your fooling around! We've work to do, boyo!

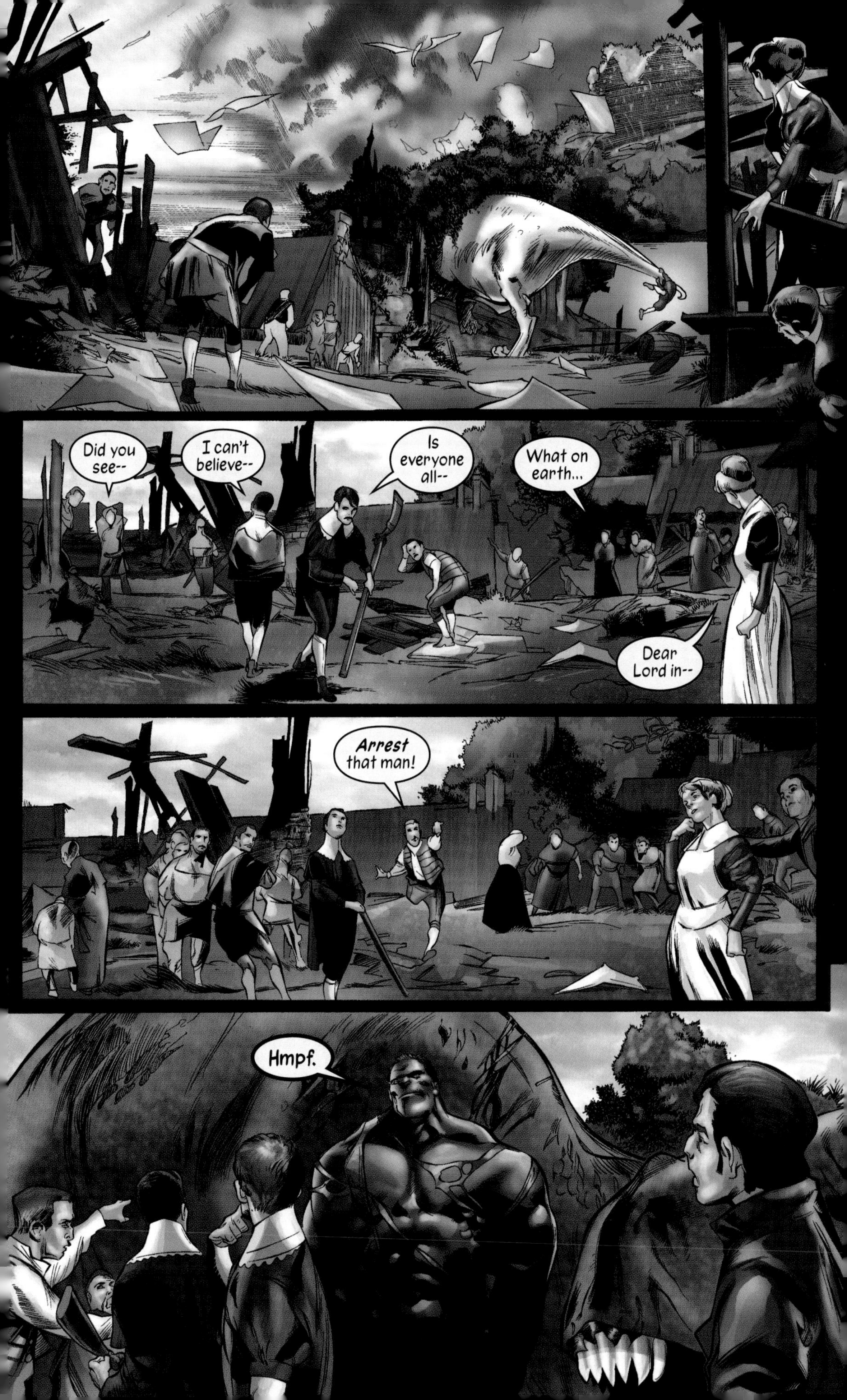
Did you see--
I can't believe--
Is everyone all--
What on earth...
Dear Lord in--
Arrest that man!
Hmpf.

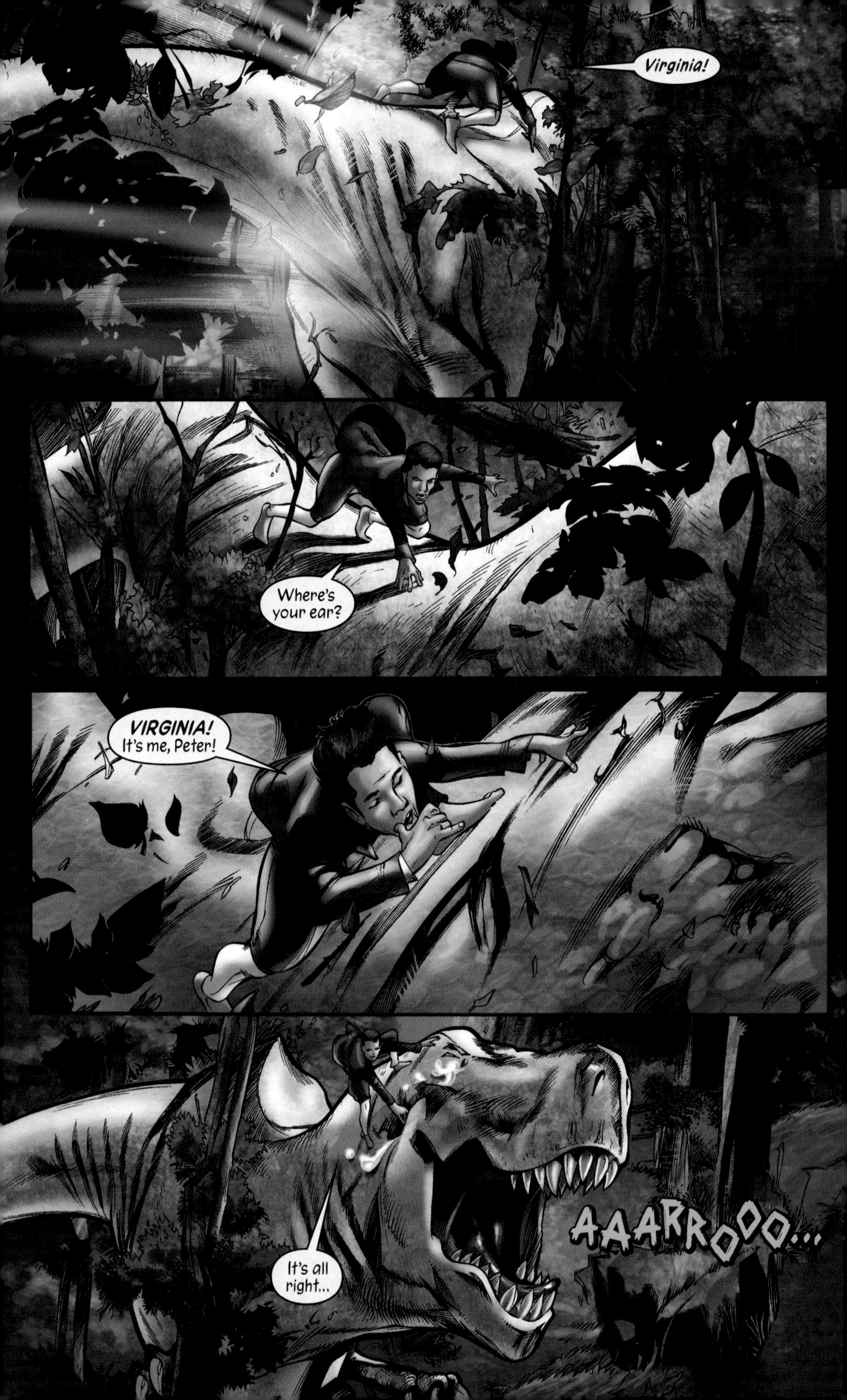
Virginia!
Where's your ear?
VIRGINIA! It's me, Peter!
It's all right...
AAARROOO...

...hush, now.

Do nae turn your back to me, you great gray lump!

Hulk.

Lump or Hulk, you've smashed my press! And ye shall *pay,* you menace! Governor Dare! Will you nae do your *duty?*

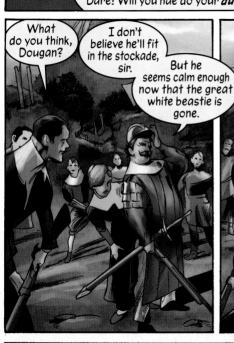

What do you think, Dougan?

I don't believe he'll fit in the stockade, sir.

But he seems calm enough now that the great white beastie is gone.

Master...Hulk. We thank you for your assistance in confronting the thunder lizard.

Get *away* from those newspapers, you stinking worm!

EEEE!

Puny, puling 'uman. Always screamin', lyin' hatin'.

Can you leave no thing *BE?*

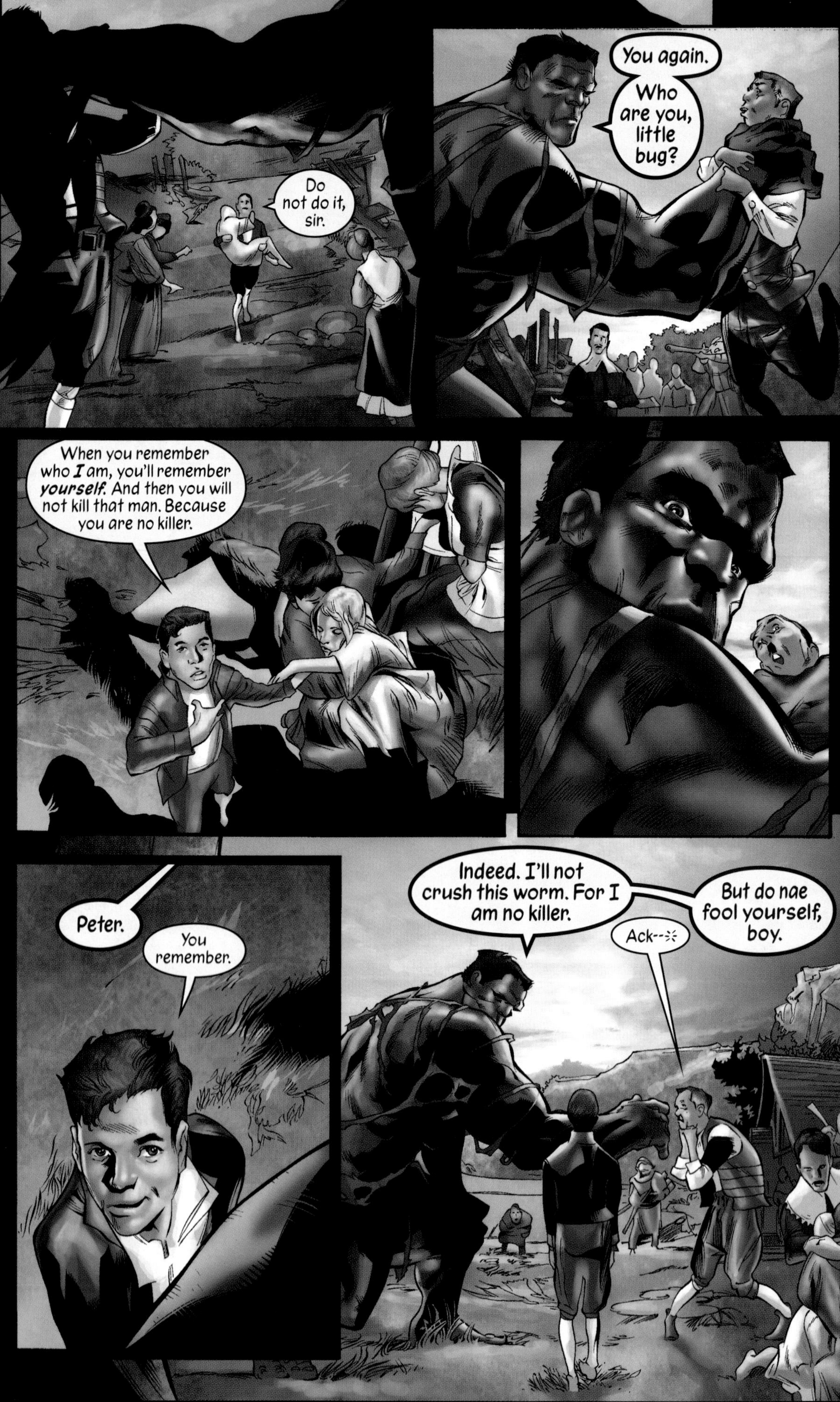
Do not do it, sir.
You again.
Who are you, little bug?
When you remember who *I* am, you'll remember *yourself.* And then you will not kill that man. Because you are no killer.
Peter.
You remember.
Indeed. I'll not crush this worm. For I am no killer.
Ack--
But do nae fool yourself, boy.

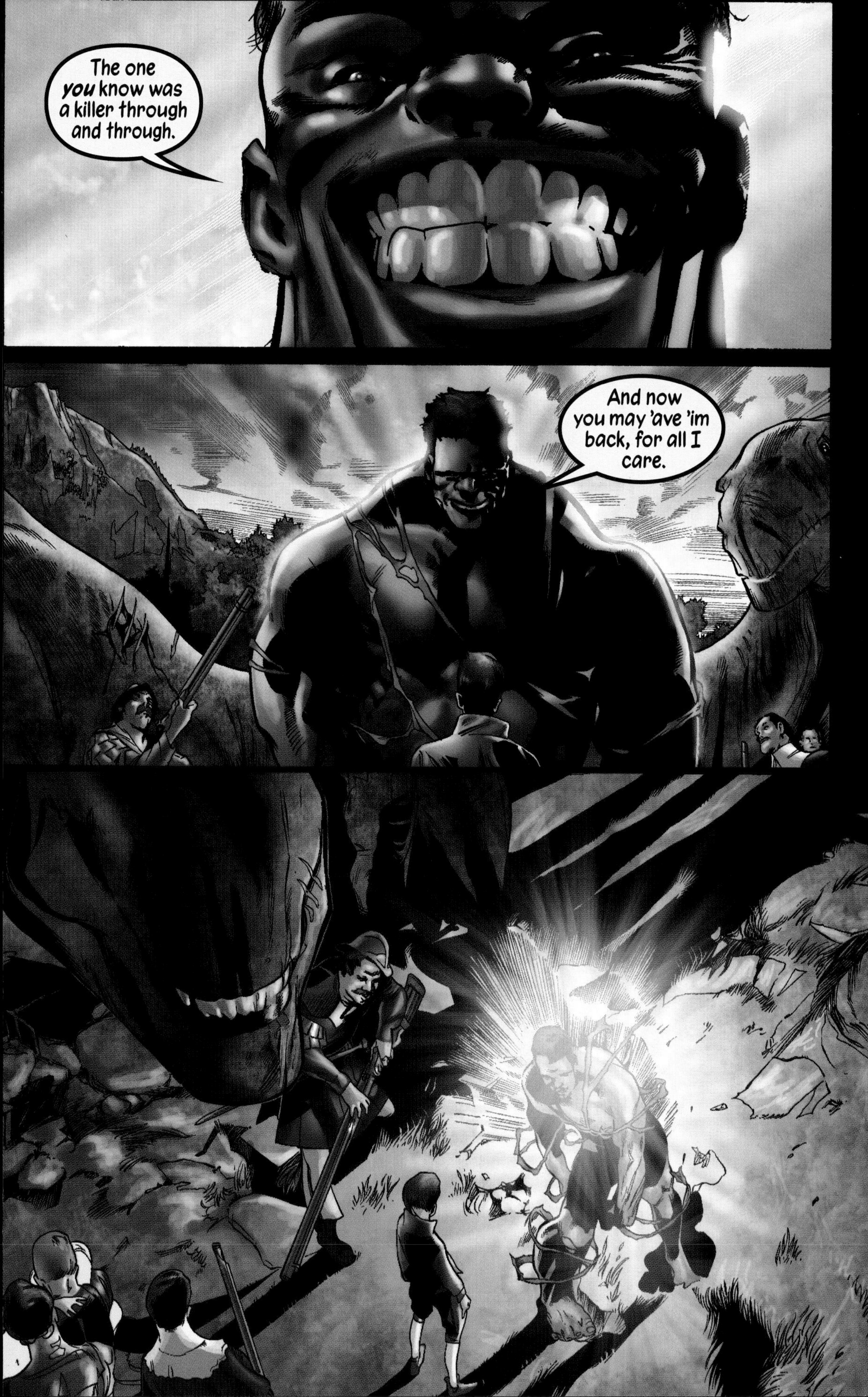
The one *you* know was a killer through and through.
And now you may 'ave 'im back, for all I care.

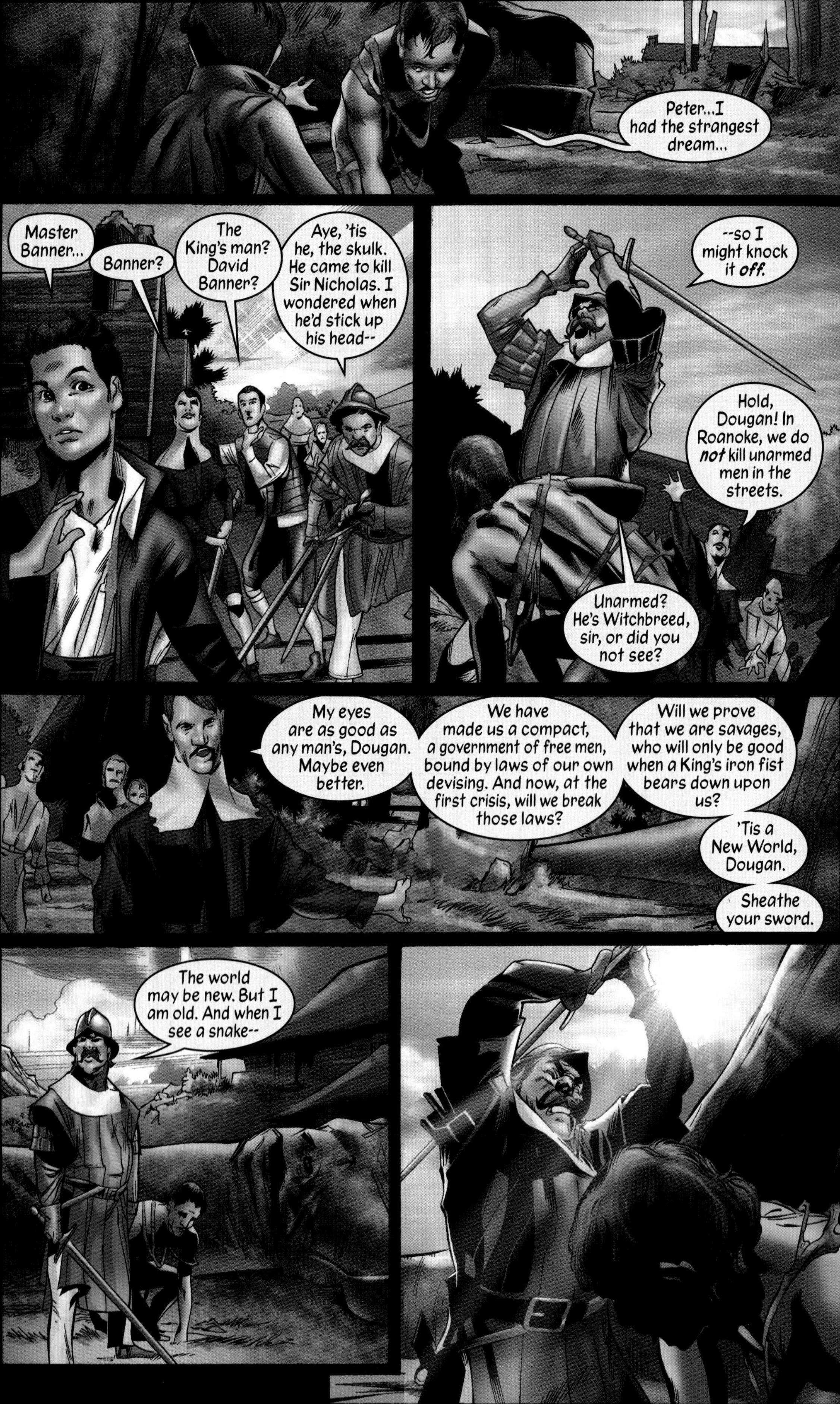
Peter...I had the strangest dream...
Master Banner...
Banner?
The King's man? David Banner?
Aye, 'tis he, the skulk. He came to kill Sir Nicholas. I wondered when he'd stick up his head--
--so I might knock it *off.*
Hold, Dougan! In Roanoke, we do *not* kill unarmed men in the streets.
Unarmed? He's Witchbreed, sir, or did you not see?
My eyes are as good as any man's, Dougan. Maybe even better.
We have made us a compact, a government of free men, bound by laws of our own devising. And now, at the first crisis, will we break those laws?
Will we prove that we are savages, who will only be good when a King's iron fist bears down upon us?
'Tis a New World, Dougan.
Sheathe your sword.
The world may be new. But I am old. And when I see a snake--

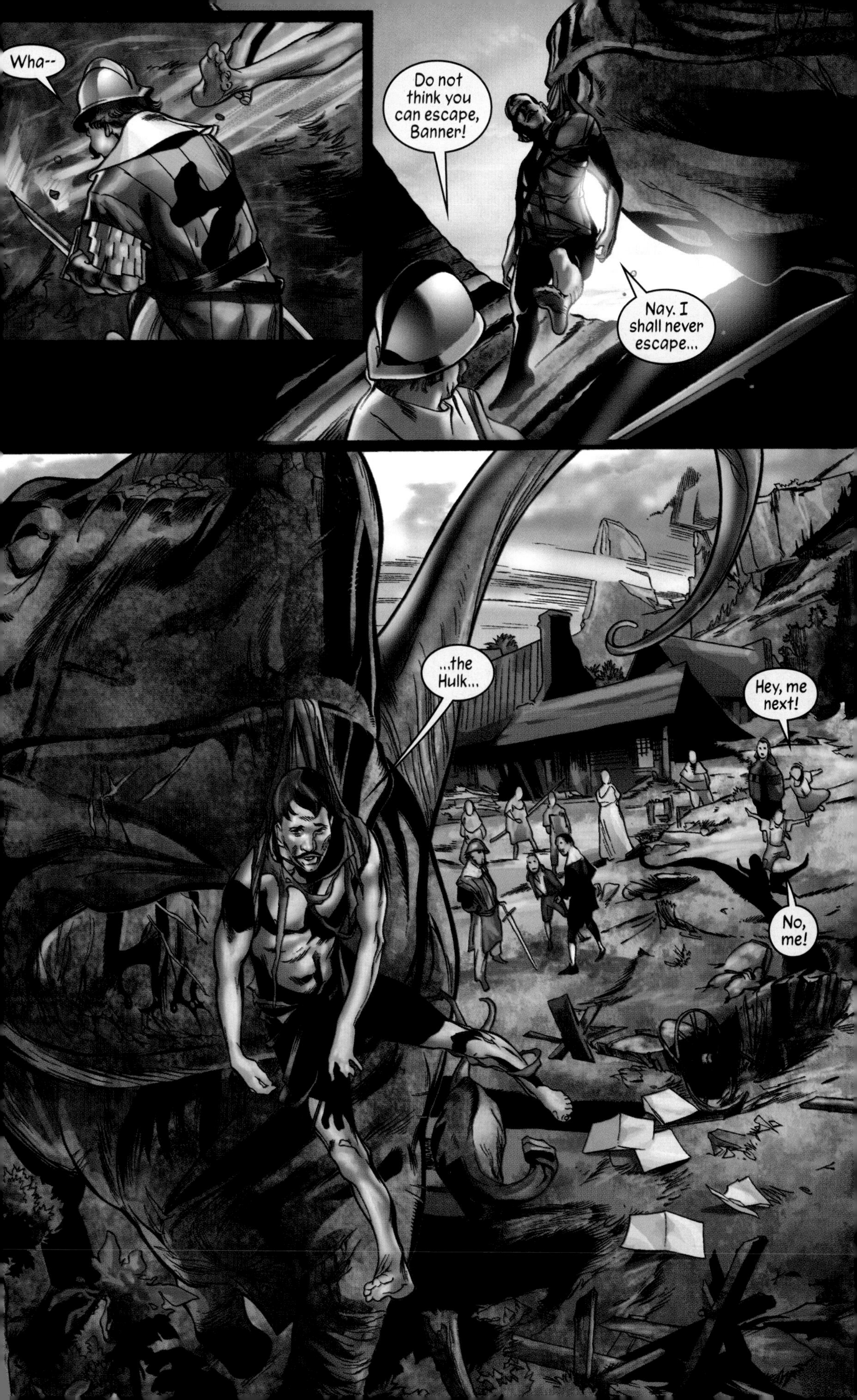
Wha--
Do not think you can escape, Banner!
Nay. I shall never escape...
...the Hulk...
Hey, me next!
No, me!

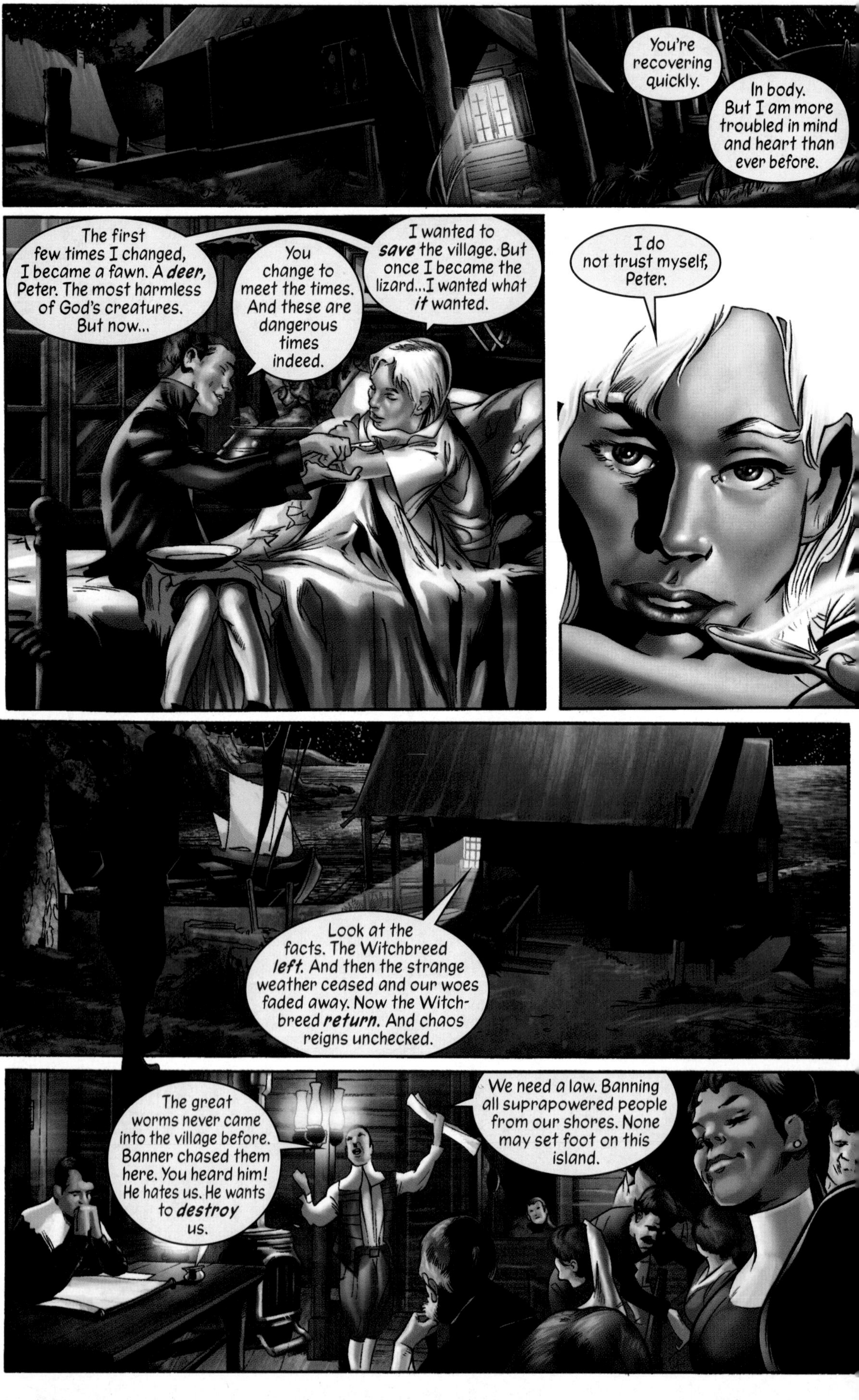
You're recovering quickly.
In body. But I am more troubled in mind and heart than ever before.
The first few times I changed, I became a fawn. A *deer,* Peter. The most harmless of God's creatures. But now...
I wanted to *save* the village. But once I became the lizard...I wanted what *it* wanted.
You change to meet the times. And these are dangerous times indeed.
I do not trust myself, Peter.
Look at the facts. The Witchbreed *left.* And then the strange weather ceased and our woes faded away. Now the Witch-breed *return.* And chaos reigns unchecked.
The great worms never came into the village before. Banner chased them here. You heard him! He hates us. He wants to *destroy* us.
We need a law. Banning all suprapowered people from our shores. None may set foot on this island.

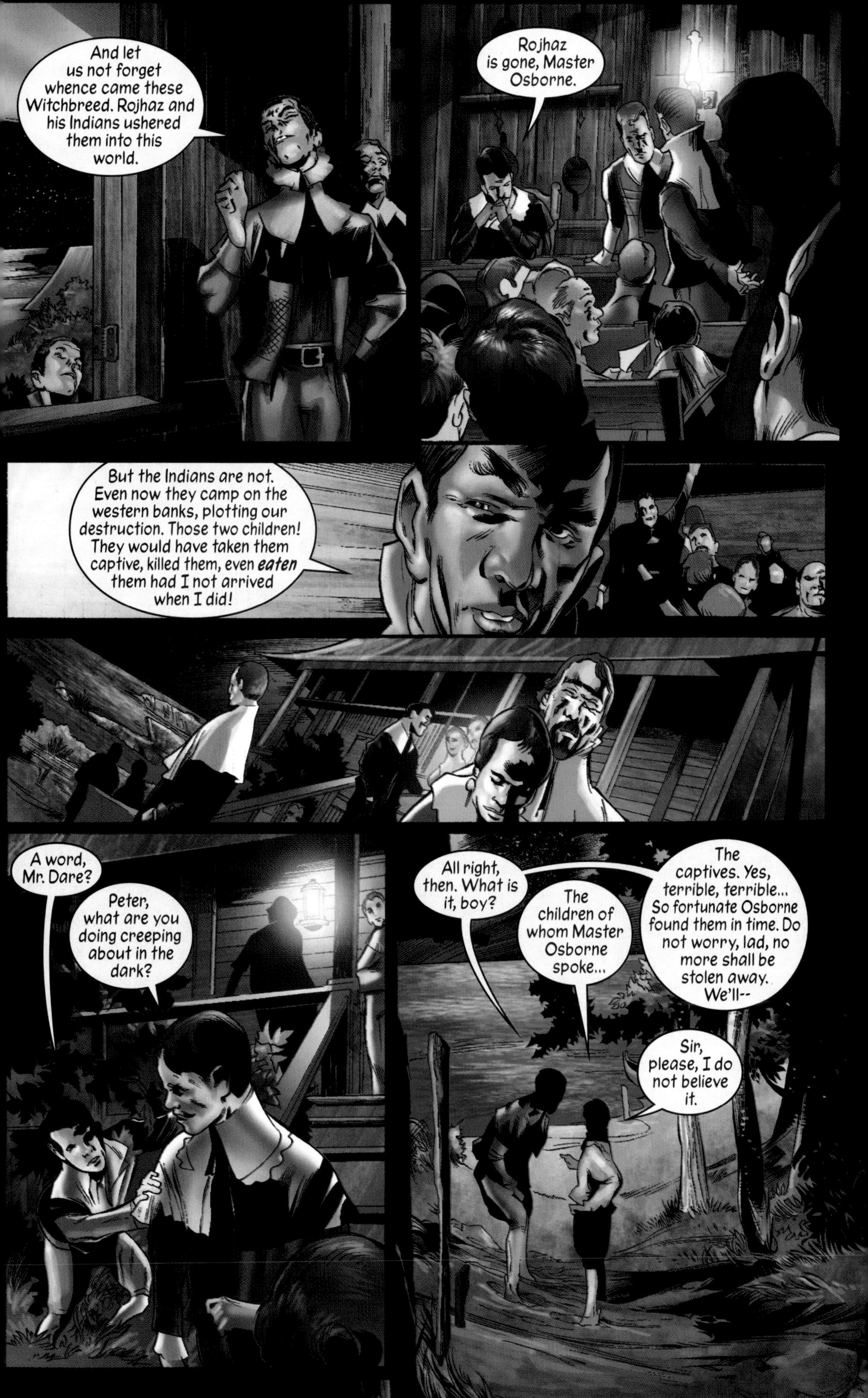
And let us not forget whence came these Witchbreed. Rojhaz and his Indians ushered them into this world.
Rojhaz is gone, Master Osborne.
But the Indians are not. Even now they camp on the western banks, plotting our destruction. Those two children! They would have taken them captive, killed them, even *eaten* them had I not arrived when I did!
A word, Mr. Dare?
Peter, what are you doing creeping about in the dark?
All right, then. What is it, boy?
The children of whom Master Osborne spoke...
The captives. Yes, terrible, terrible... So fortunate Osborne found them in time. Do not worry, lad, no more shall be stolen away. We'll--
Sir, please, I do not believe it.

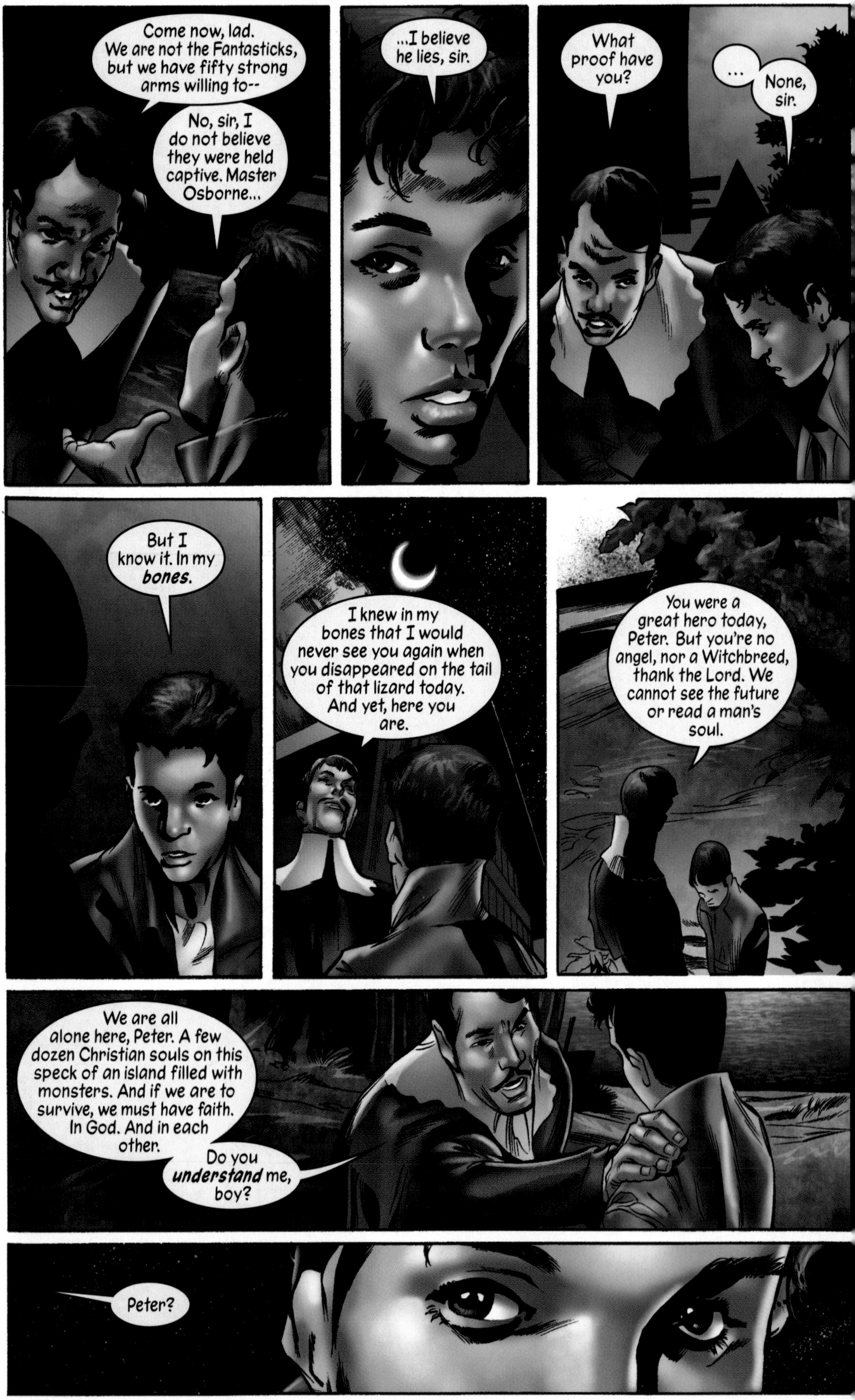
Come now, lad. We are not the Fantasticks, but we have fifty strong arms willing to--
No, sir, I do not believe they were held captive. Master Osborne...
...I believe he lies, sir.
What proof have you?
...
None, sir.
But I know it. In my *bones*.
I knew in my bones that I would never see you again when you disappeared on the tail of that lizard today. And yet, here you are.
You were a great hero today, Peter. But you're no angel, nor a Witchbreed, thank the Lord. We cannot see the future or read a man's soul.
We are all alone here, Peter. A few dozen Christian souls on this speck of an island filled with monsters. And if we are to survive, we must have faith. In God. And in each other.
Do you *understand* me, boy?
Peter?

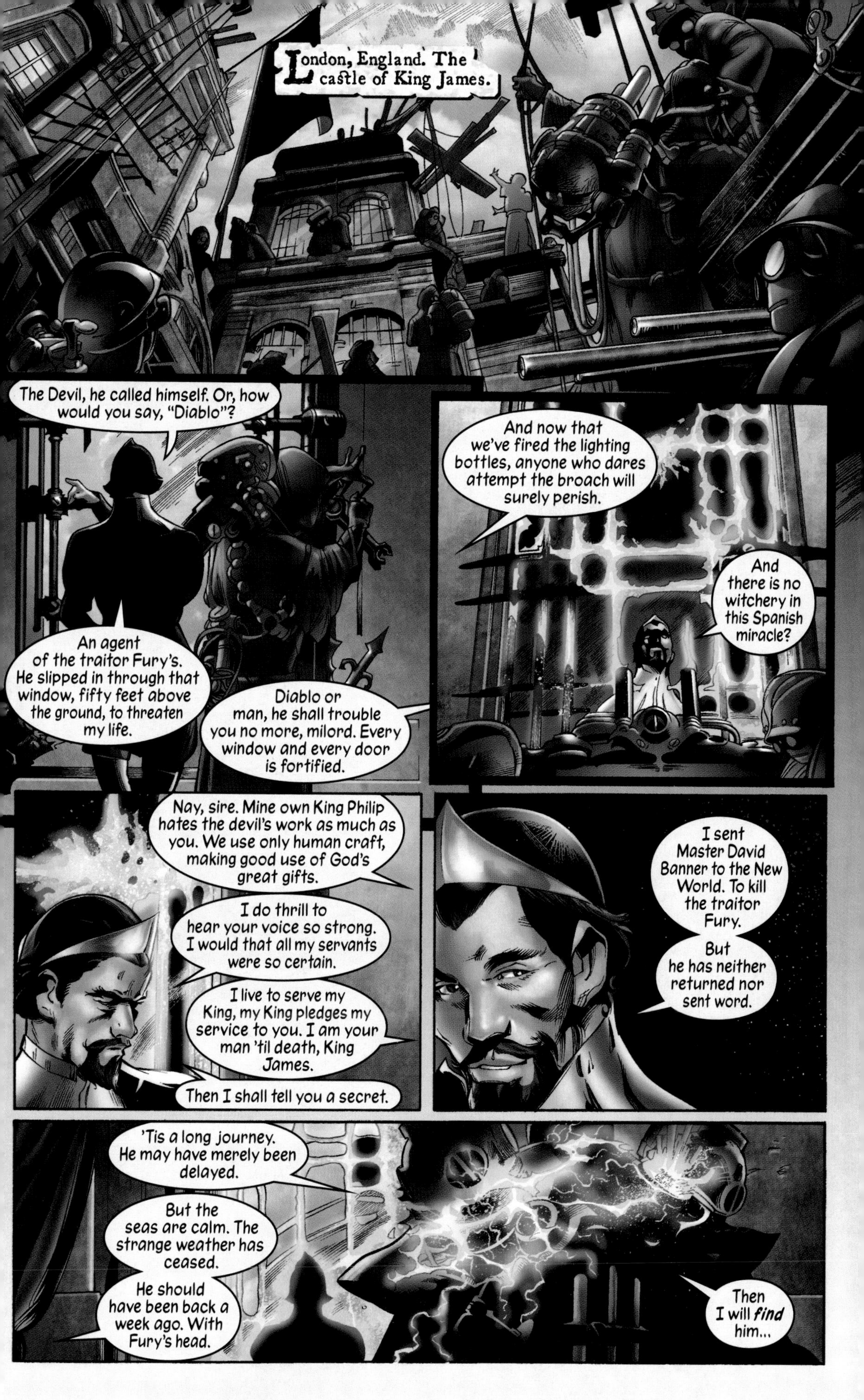
London, England. The castle of King James.
The Devil, he called himself. Or, how would you say, "Diablo"?
An agent of the traitor Fury's. He slipped in through that window, fifty feet above the ground, to threaten my life.
Diablo or man, he shall trouble you no more, milord. Every window and every door is fortified.
And now that we've fired the lighting bottles, anyone who dares attempt the broach will surely perish.
And there is no witchery in this Spanish miracle?
Nay, sire. Mine own King Philip hates the devil's work as much as you. We use only human craft, making good use of God's great gifts.
I do thrill to hear your voice so strong. I would that all my servants were so certain.
I live to serve my King, my King pledges my service to you. I am your man 'til death, King James.
Then I shall tell you a secret.
I sent Master David Banner to the New World. To kill the traitor Fury.
But he has neither returned nor sent word.
'Tis a long journey. He may have merely been delayed.
But the seas are calm. The strange weather has ceased.
He should have been back a week ago. With Fury's head.
Then I will *find* him...

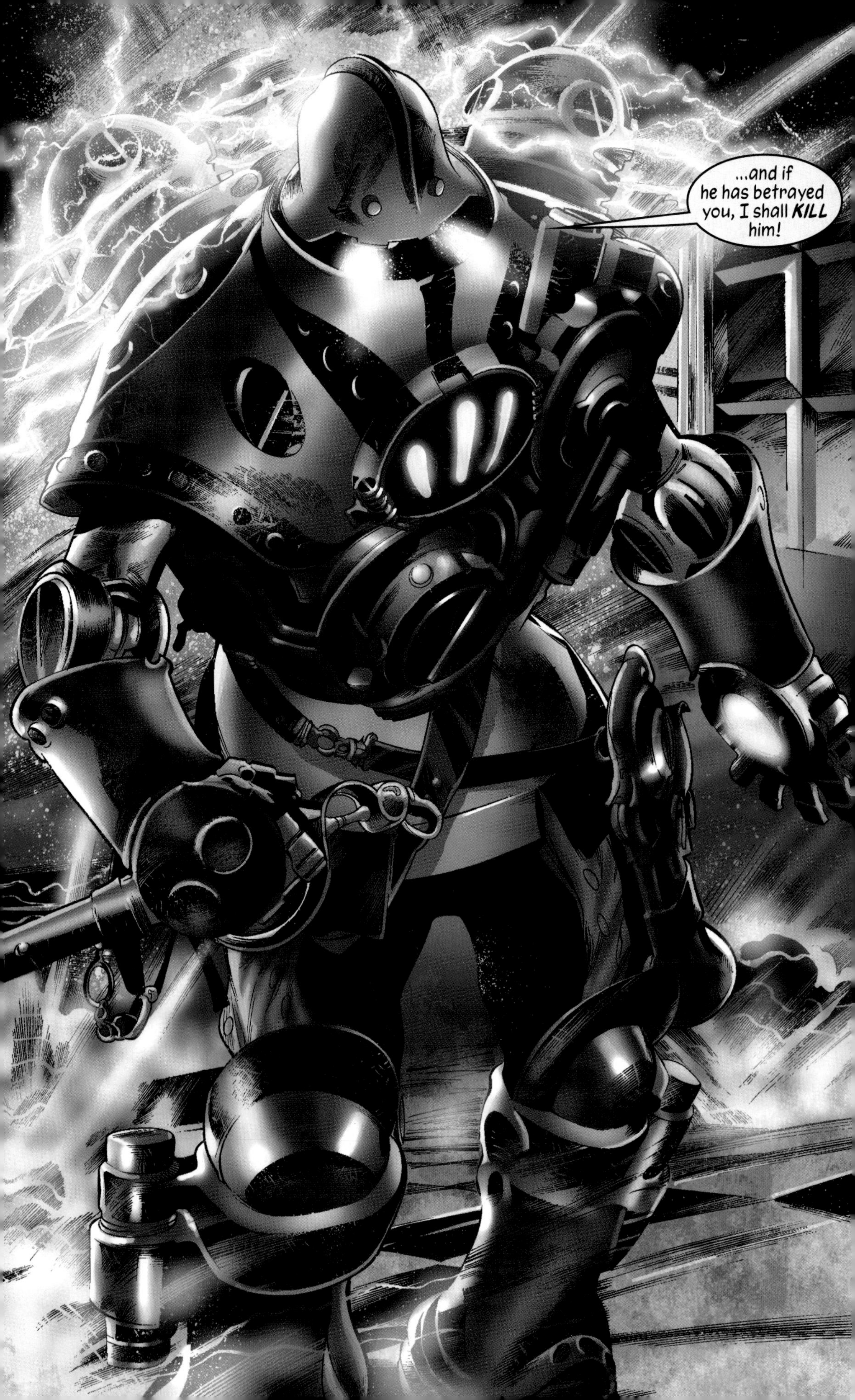
...and if he has betrayed you, I shall KILL him!

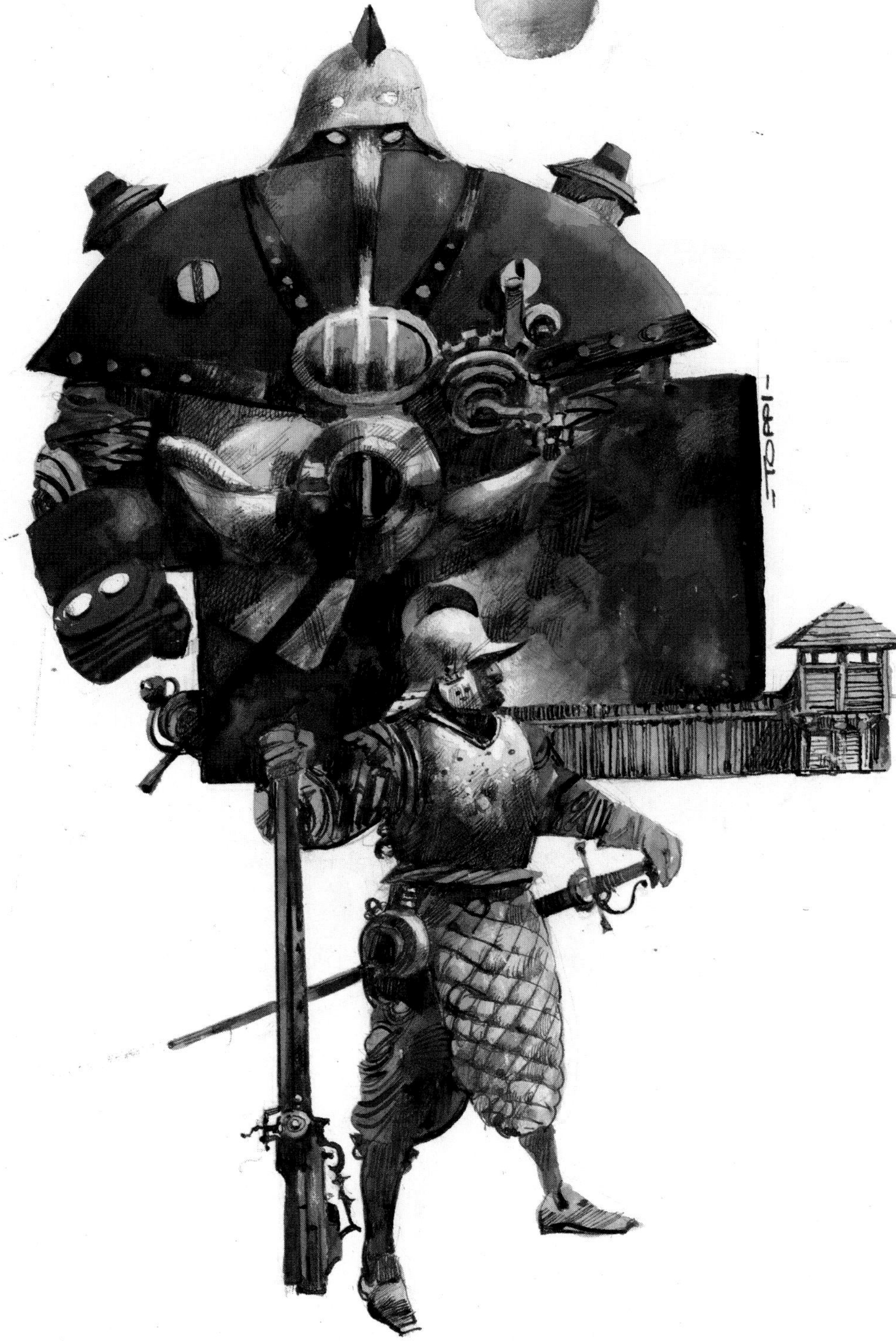

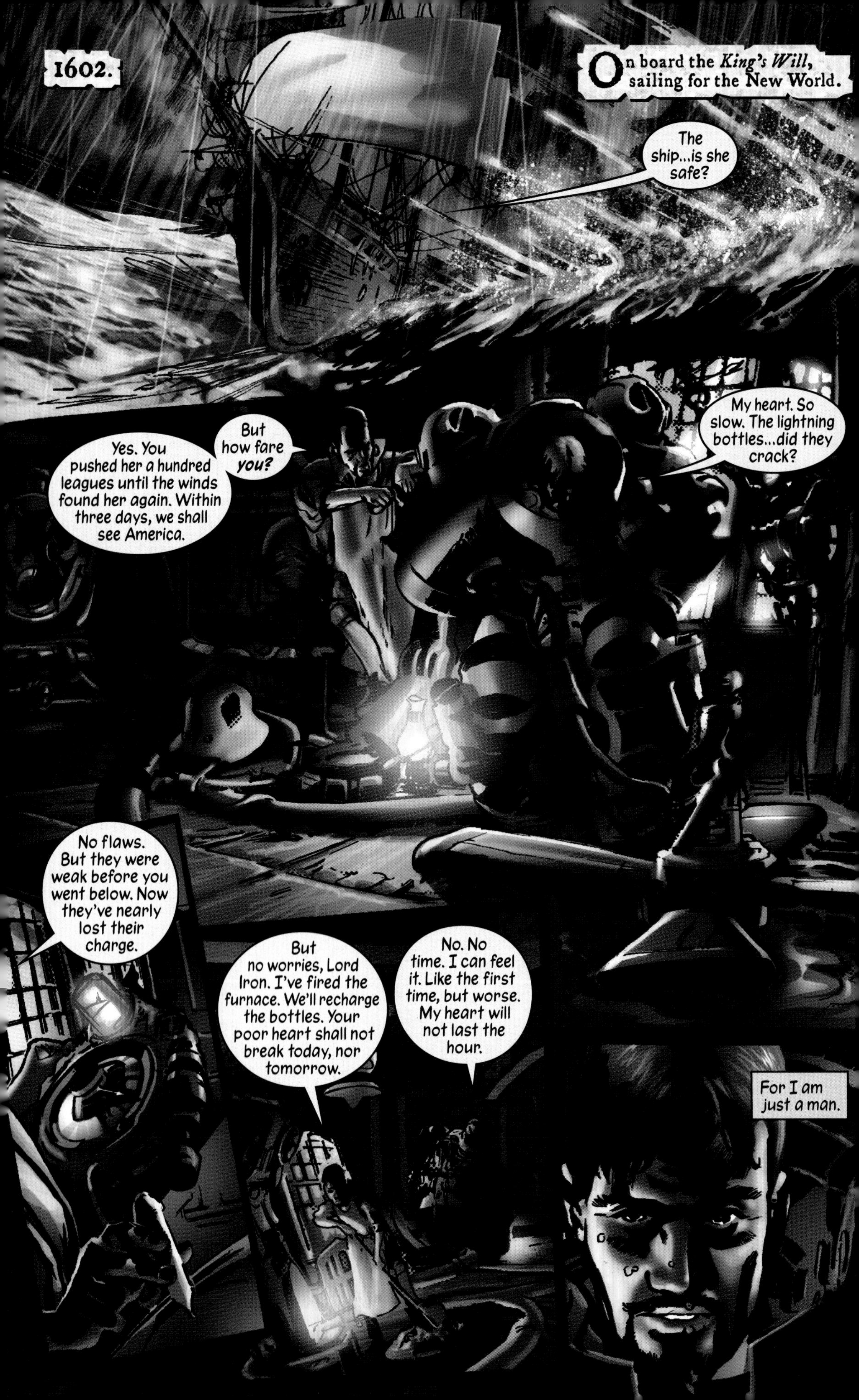
1602.
On board the *King's Will*, sailing for the New World.
The ship...is she safe?
Yes. You pushed her a hundred leagues until the winds found her again. Within three days, we shall see America.
But how fare *you?*
My heart. So slow. The lightning bottles...did they crack?
No flaws. But they were weak before you went below. Now they've nearly lost their charge.
But no worries, Lord Iron. I've fired the furnace. We'll recharge the bottles. Your poor heart shall not break today, nor tomorrow.
No. No time. I can feel it. Like the first time, but worse. My heart will not last the hour.
For I am just a man.

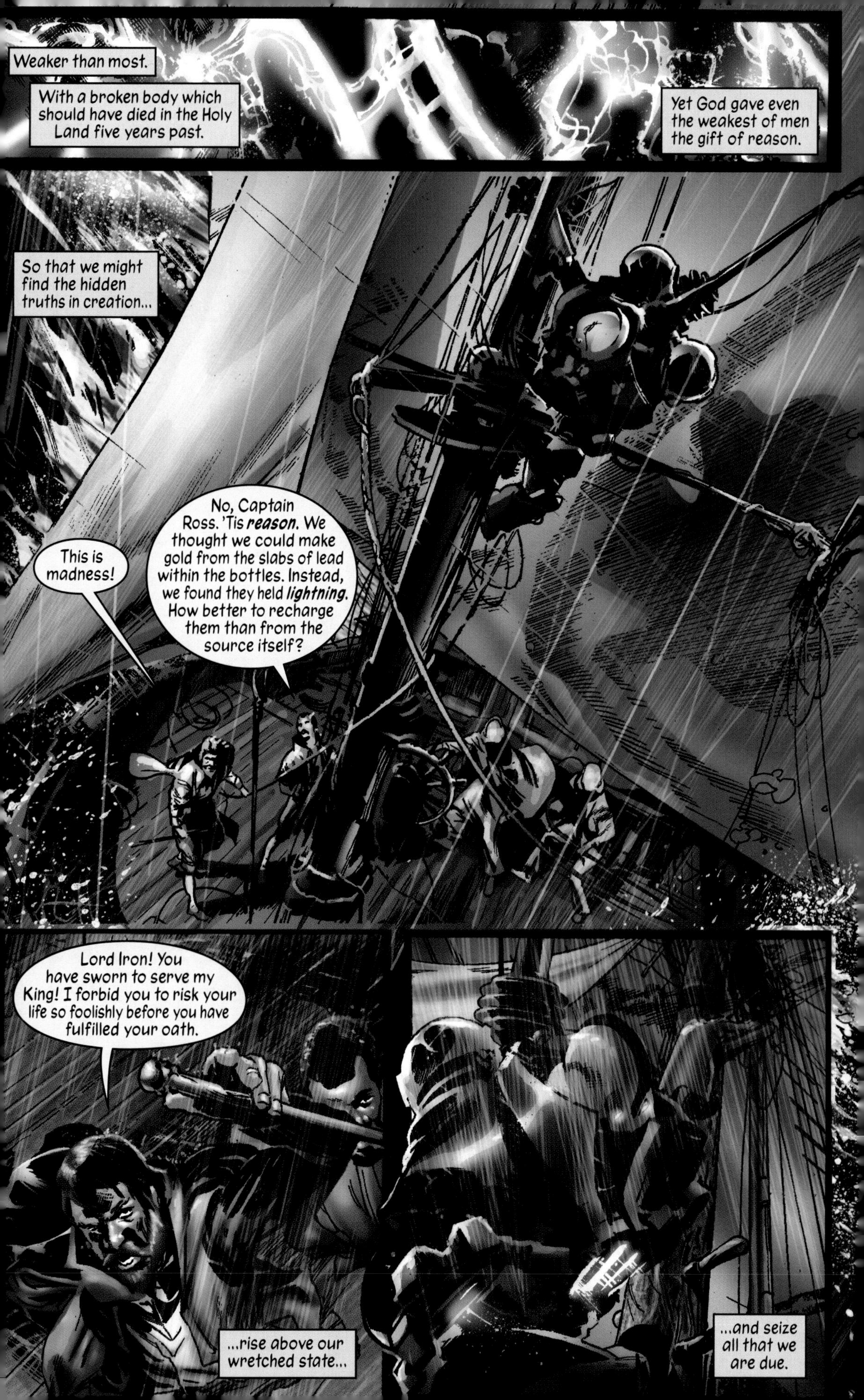
Weaker than most.
With a broken body which should have died in the Holy Land five years past.
Yet God gave even the weakest of men the gift of reason.
So that we might find the hidden truths in creation...
This is madness!
No, Captain Ross. 'Tis ***reason.*** We thought we could make gold from the slabs of lead within the bottles. Instead, we found they held ***lightning.*** How better to recharge them than from the source itself?
Lord Iron! You have sworn to serve my King! I forbid you to risk your life so foolishly before you have fulfilled your oath.
...rise above our wretched state...
...and seize all that we are due.

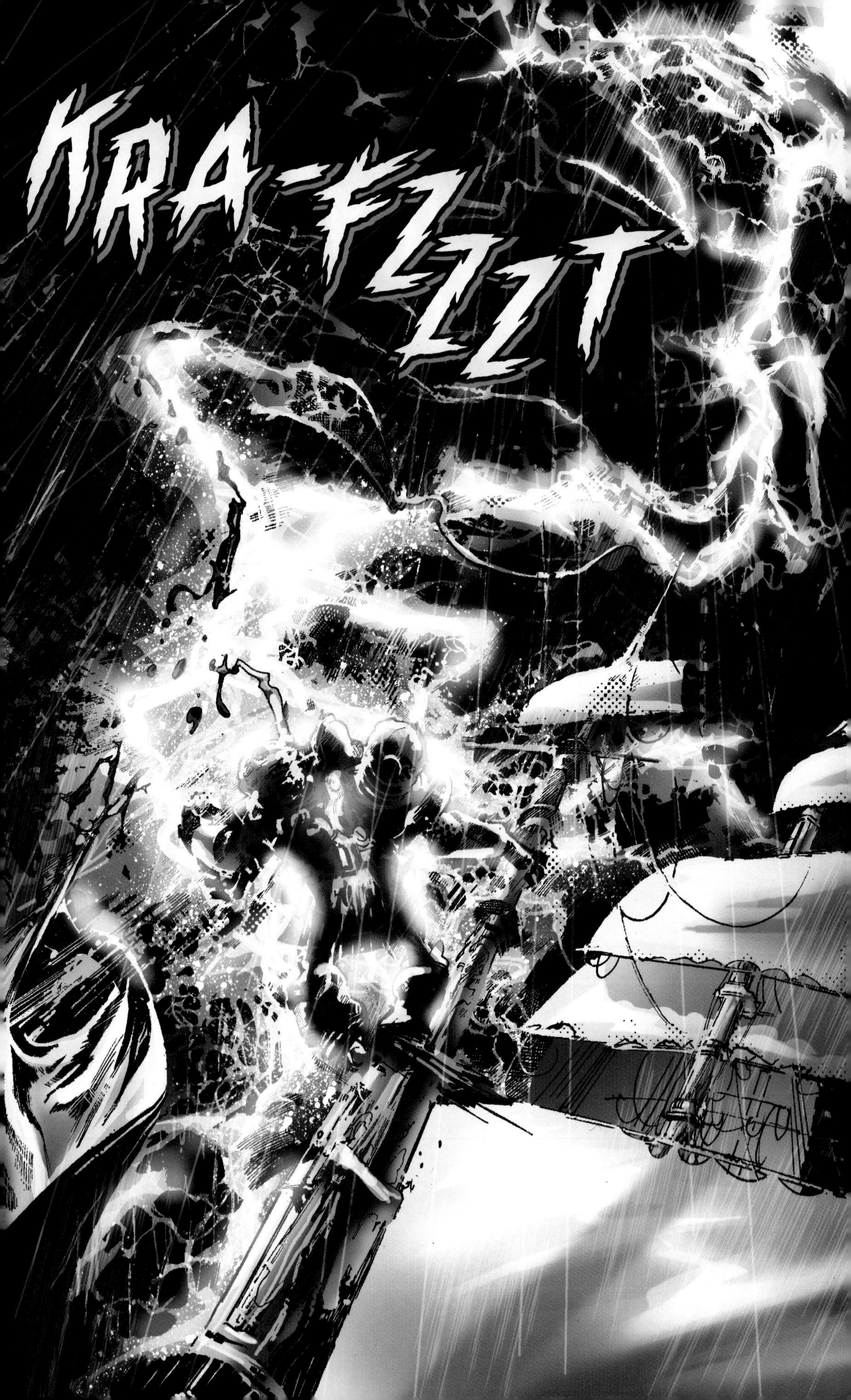
KRA-FZZZT

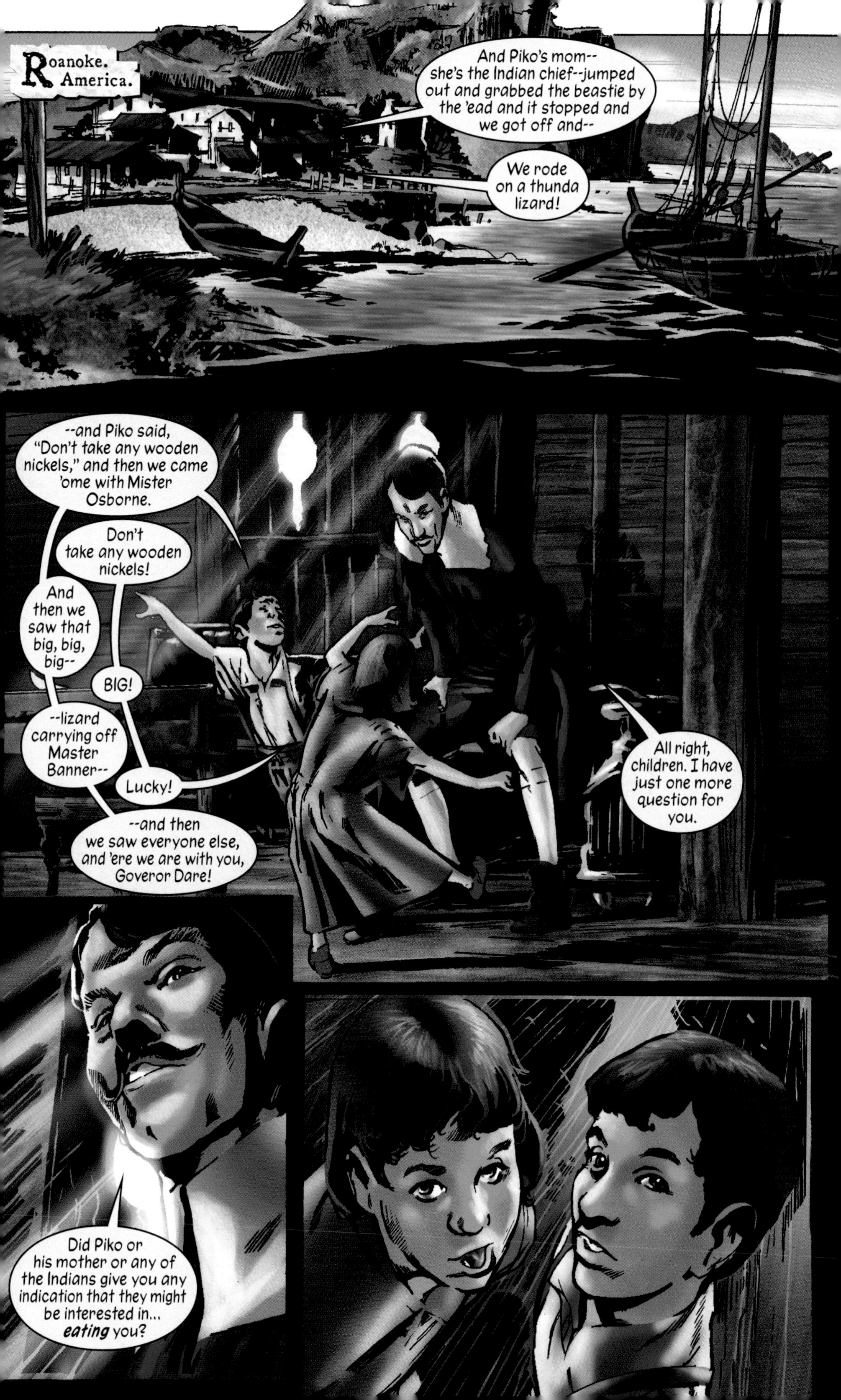
Roanoke. America.
And Piko's mom--she's the Indian chief--jumped out and grabbed the beastie by the 'ead and it stopped and we got off and--
We rode on a thunda lizard!
--and Piko said, "Don't take any wooden nickels," and then we came 'ome with Mister Osborne.
Don't take any wooden nickels!
And then we saw that big, big, big--
BIG!
--lizard carrying off Master Banner--
Lucky!
--and then we saw everyone else, and 'ere we are with you, Goveror Dare!
All right, children. I have just one more question for you.
Did Piko or his mother or any of the Indians give you any indication that they might be interested in... *eating* you?

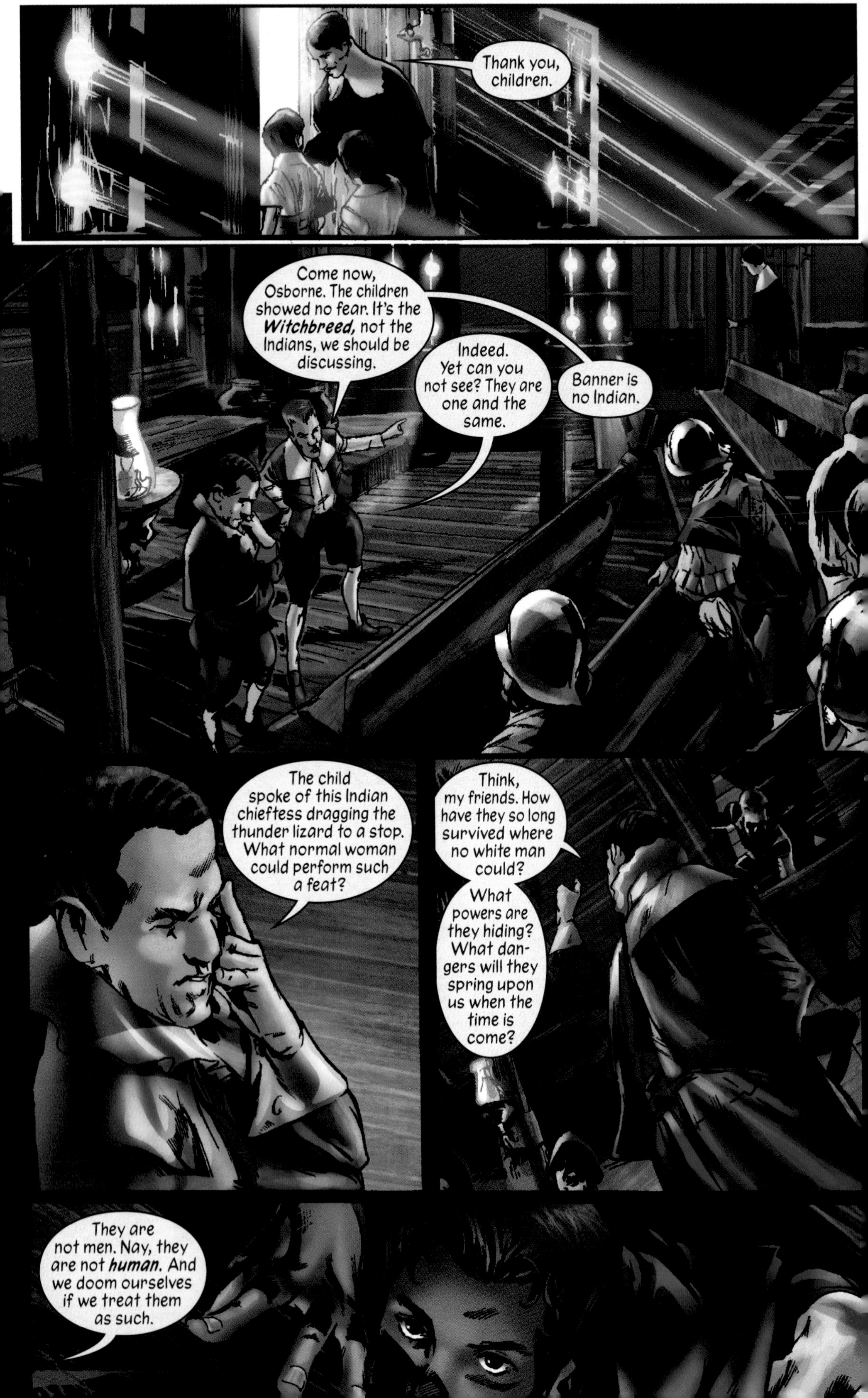
Thank you, children.
Come now, Osborne. The children showed no fear. It's the **Witchbreed,** not the Indians, we should be discussing.
Indeed. Yet can you not see? They are one and the same.
Banner is no Indian.
The child spoke of this Indian chieftess dragging the thunder lizard to a stop. What normal woman could perform such a feat?
Think, my friends. How have they so long survived where no white man could?
What powers are they hiding? What dangers will they spring upon us when the time is come?
They are not men. Nay, they are not **human.** And we doom ourselves if we treat them as such.

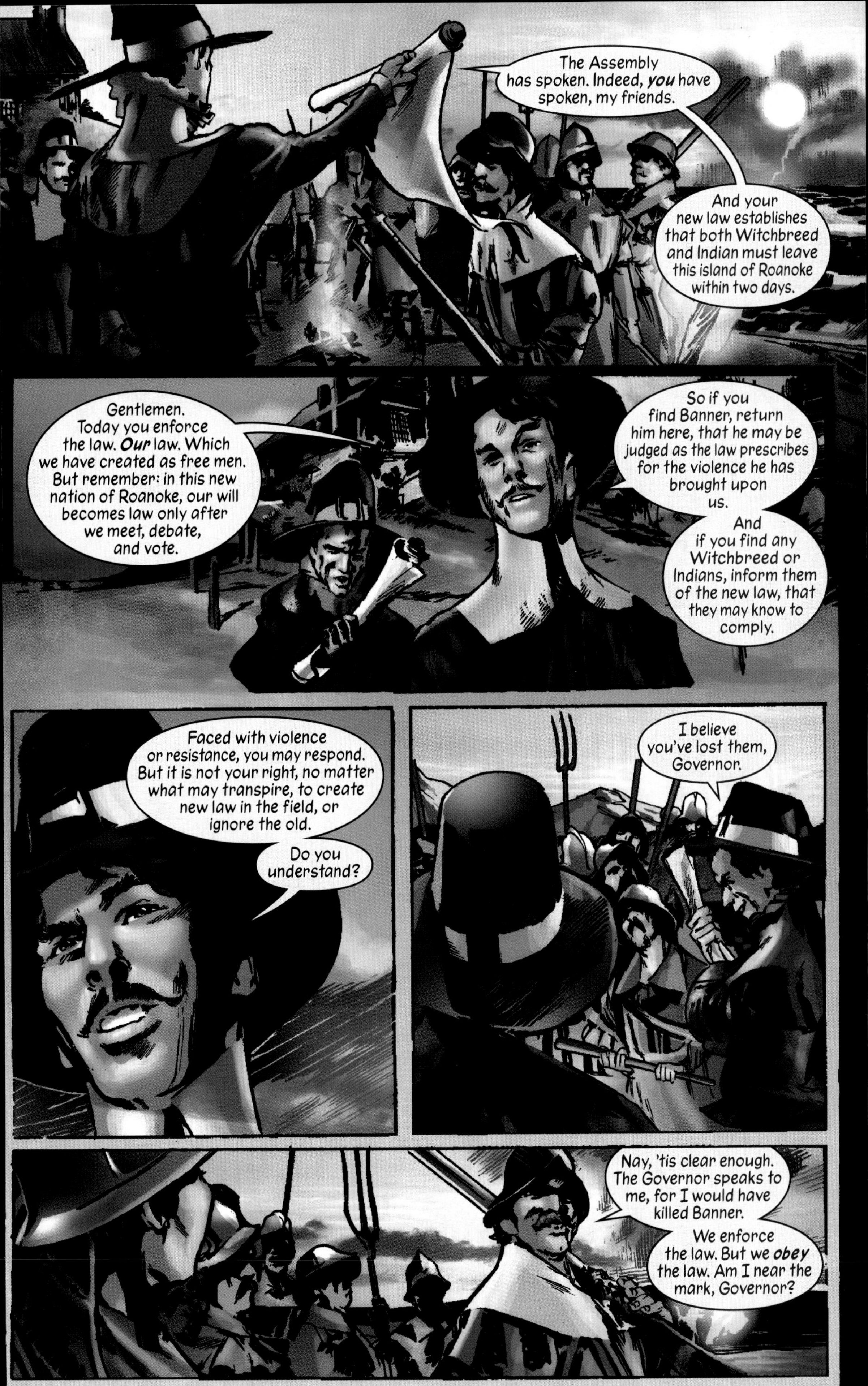

The Assembly has spoken. Indeed, *you* have spoken, my friends.
And your new law establishes that both Witchbreed and Indian must leave this island of Roanoke within two days.
Gentlemen. Today you enforce the law. *Our* law. Which we have created as free men. But remember: in this new nation of Roanoke, our will becomes law only after we meet, debate, and vote.
So if you find Banner, return him here, that he may be judged as the law prescribes for the violence he has brought upon us.
And if you find any Witchbreed or Indians, inform them of the new law, that they may know to comply.
Faced with violence or resistance, you may respond. But it is not your right, no matter what may transpire, to create new law in the field, or ignore the old.
Do you understand?
I believe you've lost them, Governor.
Nay, 'tis clear enough. The Governor speaks to me, for I would have killed Banner.
We enforce the law. But we *obey* the law. Am I near the mark, Governor?

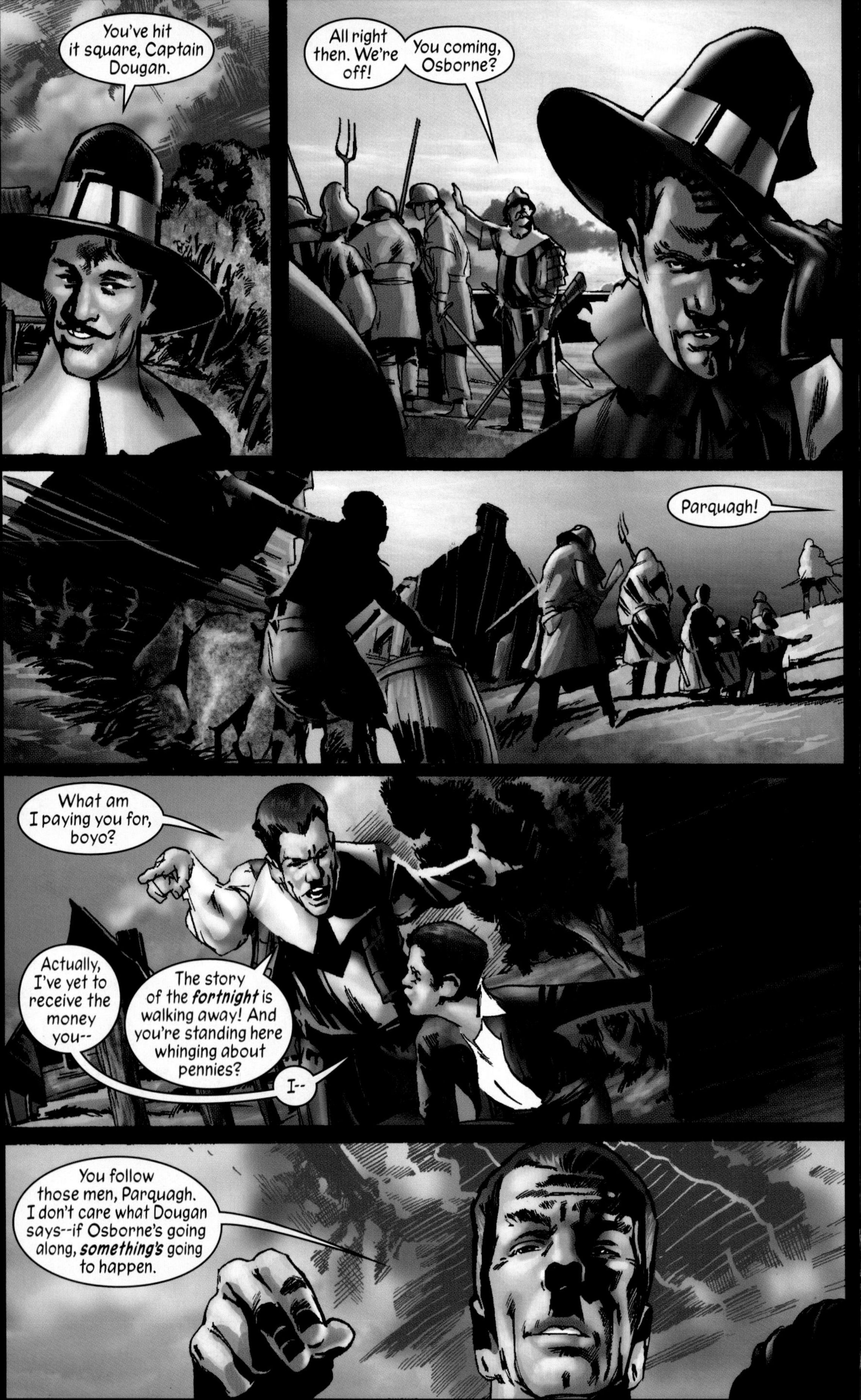
You've hit it square, Captain Dougan.
All right then. We're off!
You coming, Osborne?
Parquagh!
What am I paying you for, boyo?
Actually, I've yet to receive the money you--
The story of the *fortnight* is walking away! And you're standing here whinging about pennies?
I--
You follow those men, Parquagh. I don't care what Dougan says--if Osborne's going along, *something's* going to happen.

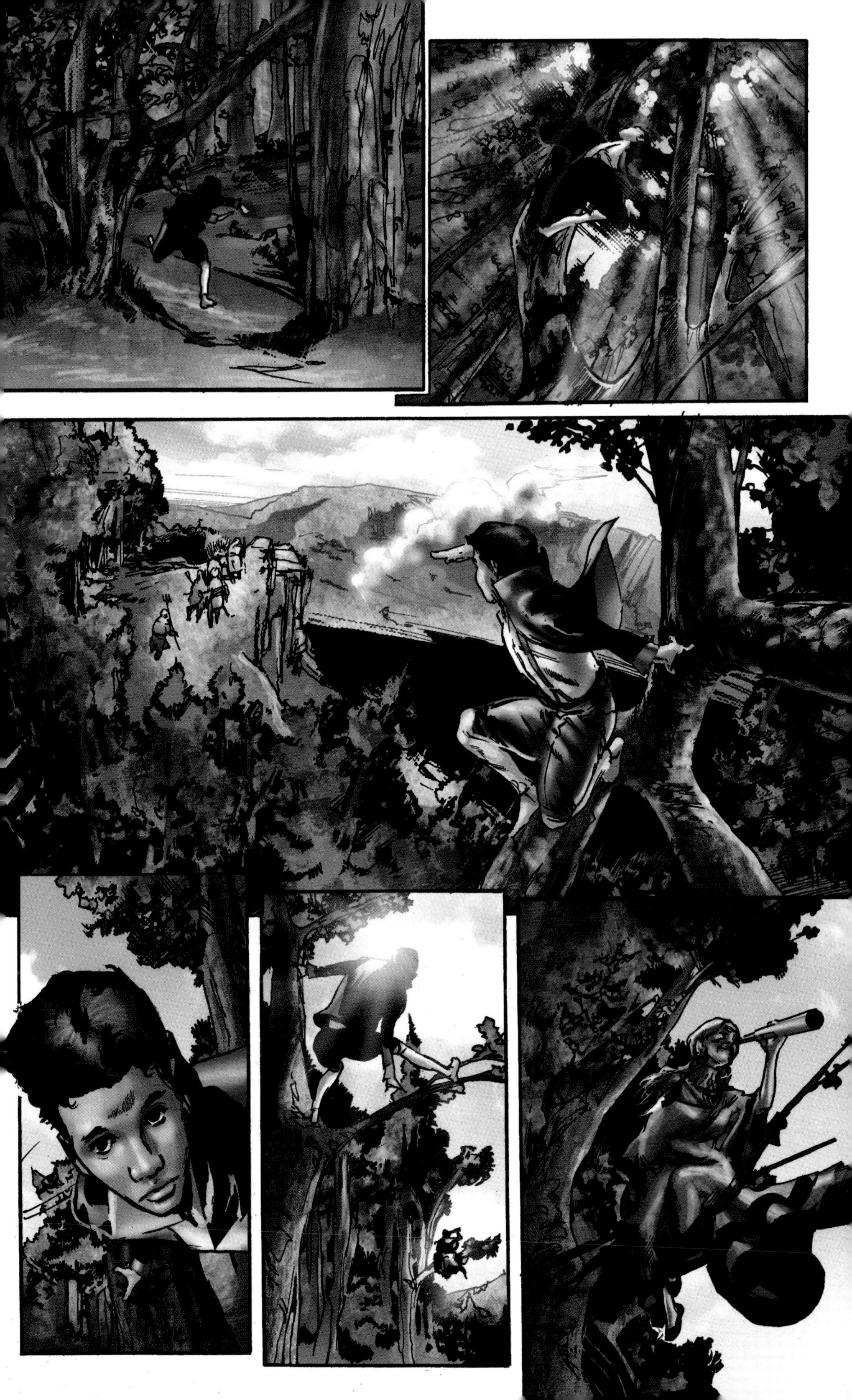

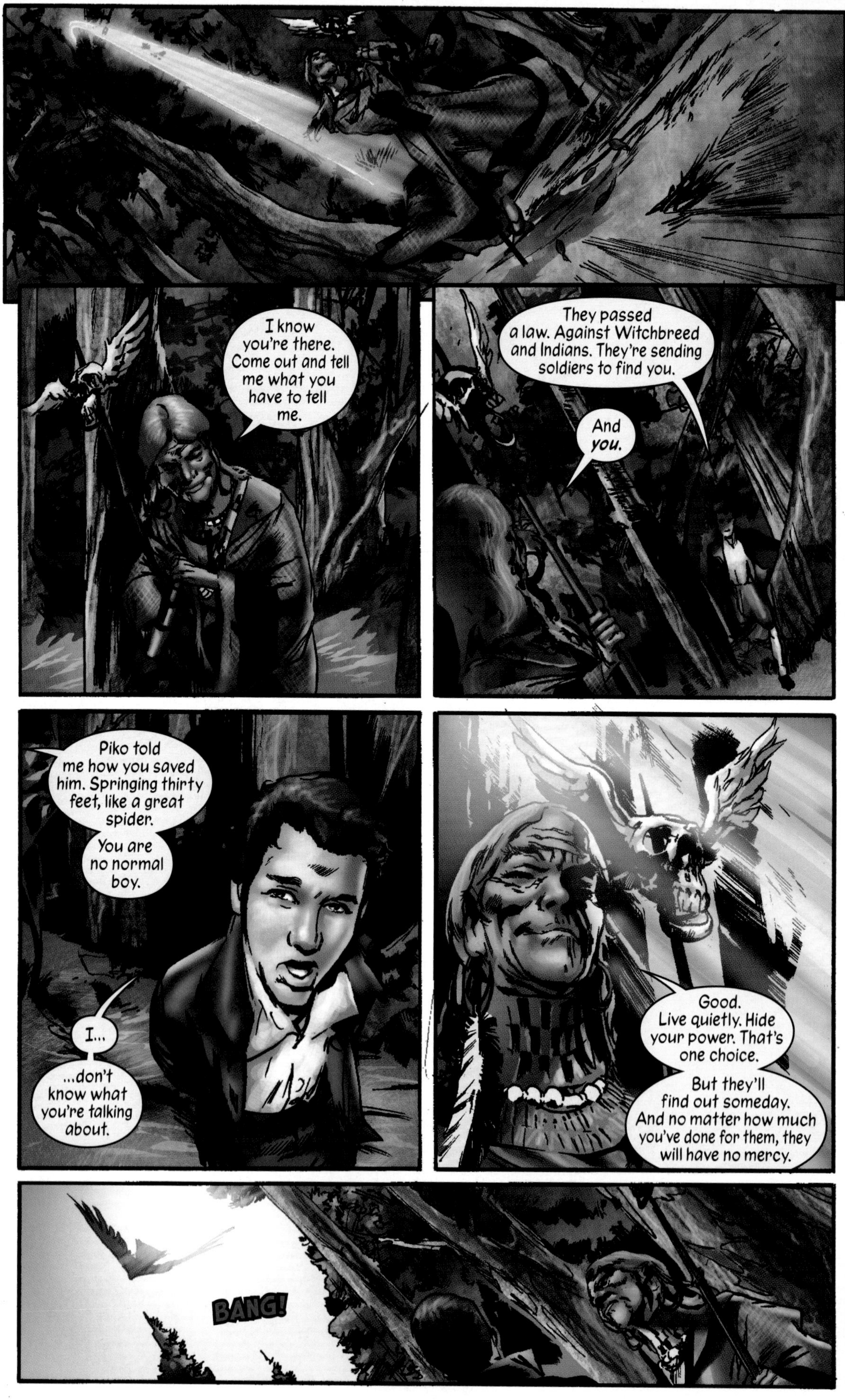
I know you're there. Come out and tell me what you have to tell me.
They passed a law. Against Witchbreed and Indians. They're sending soldiers to find you.
And *you.*
Piko told me how you saved him. Springing thirty feet, like a great spider.
You are no normal boy.
I...
...don't know what you're talking about.
Good. Live quietly. Hide your power. That's one choice.
But they'll find out someday. And no matter how much you've done for them, they will have no mercy.
BANG!

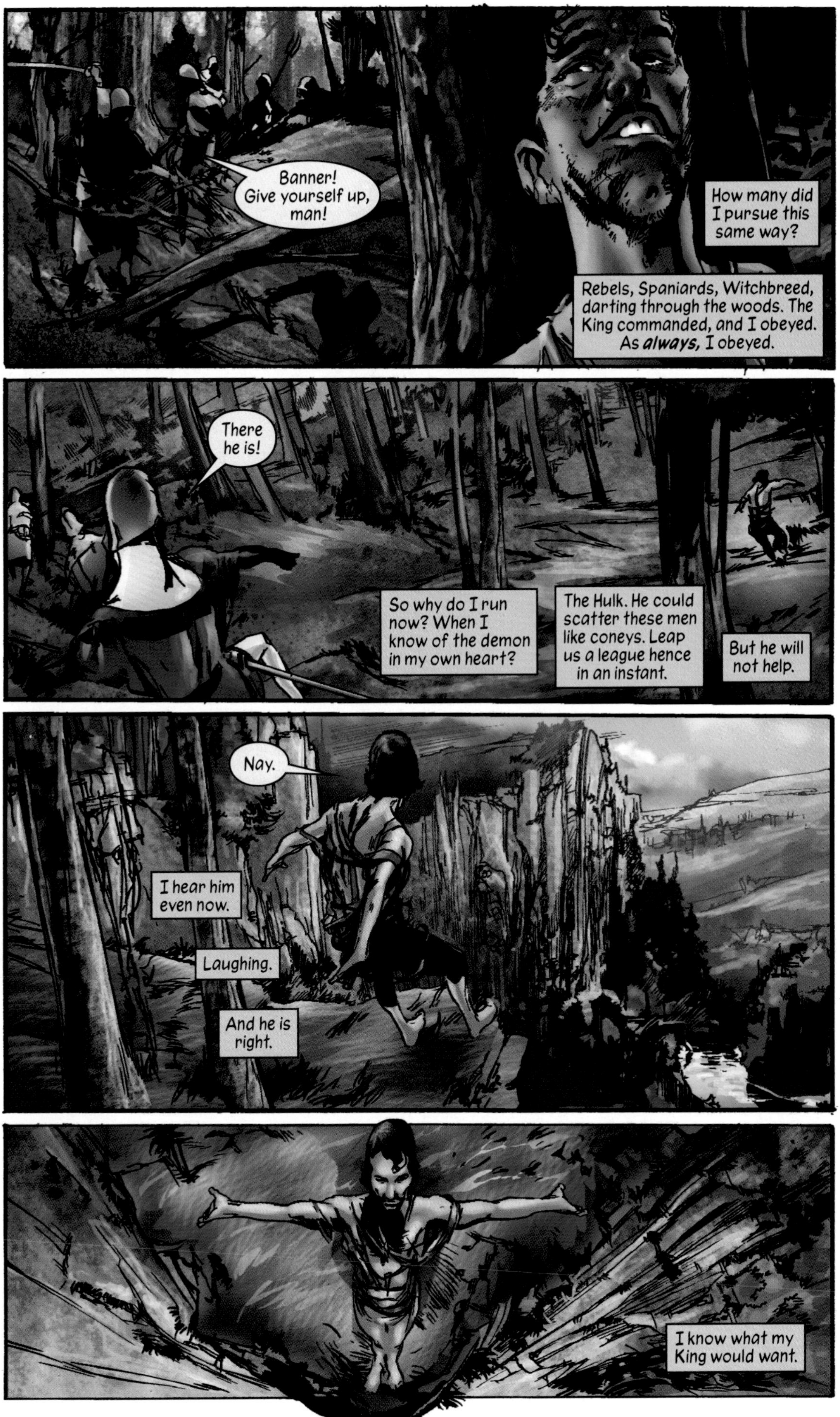
Banner! Give yourself up, man!
How many did I pursue this same way?
Rebels, Spaniards, Witchbreed, darting through the woods. The King commanded, and I obeyed. As *always,* I obeyed.
There he is!
So why do I run now? When I know of the demon in my own heart?
The Hulk. He could scatter these men like coneys. Leap us a league hence in an instant.
But he will not help.
Nay.
I hear him even now.
Laughing.
And he is right.
I know what my King would want.

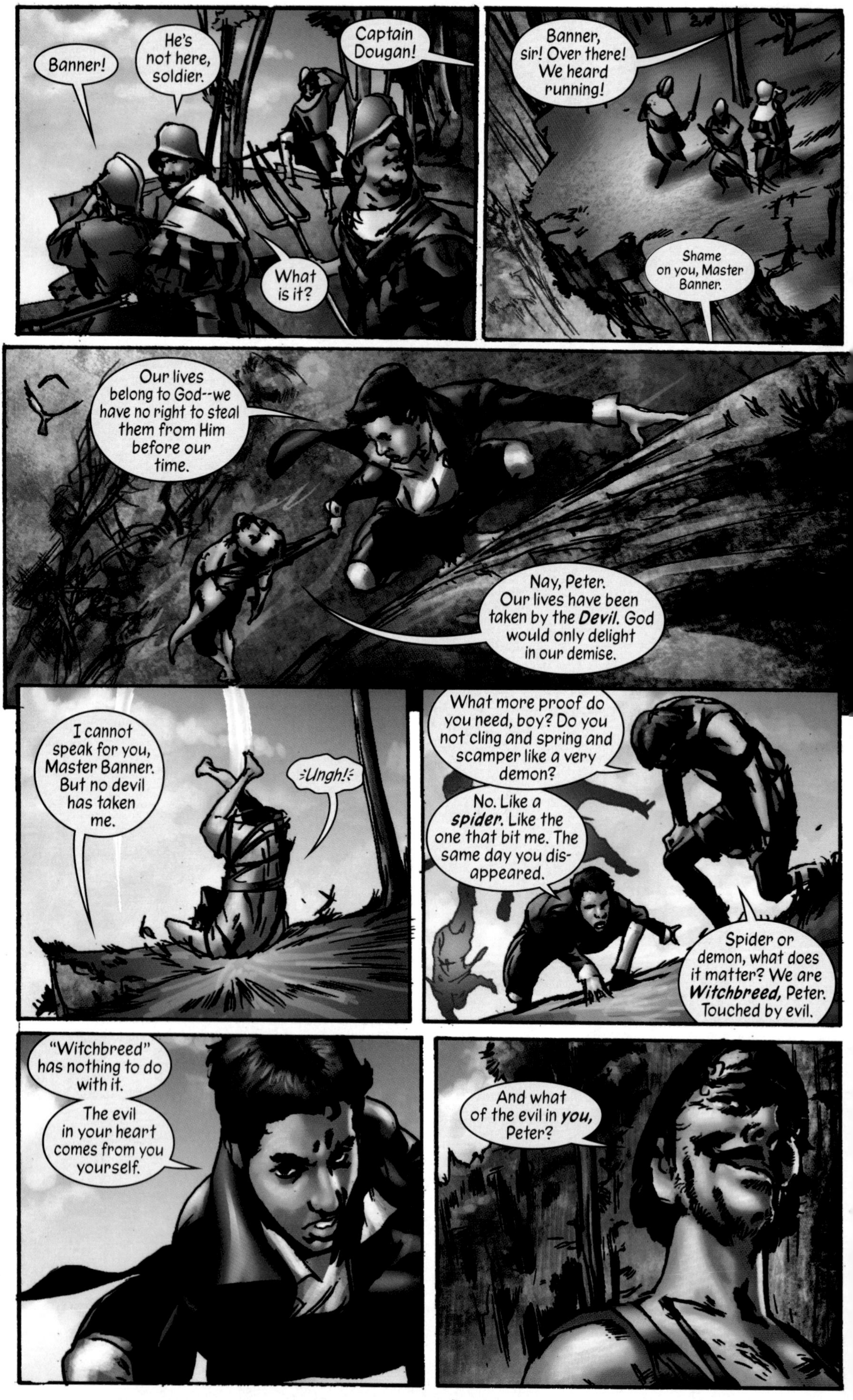

Banner!
He's not here, soldier.
Captain Dougan!
What is it?
Banner, sir! Over there! We heard running!
Shame on you, Master Banner.
Our lives belong to God--we have no right to steal them from Him before our time.
Nay, Peter. Our lives have been taken by the Devil. God would only delight in our demise.
I cannot speak for you, Master Banner. But no devil has taken me.
Ungh!
What more proof do you need, boy? Do you not cling and spring and scamper like a very demon?
No. Like a spider. Like the one that bit me. The same day you disappeared.
Spider or demon, what does it matter? We are Witchbreed, Peter. Touched by evil.
"Witchbreed" has nothing to do with it.
The evil in your heart comes from you yourself.
And what of the evil in you, Peter?

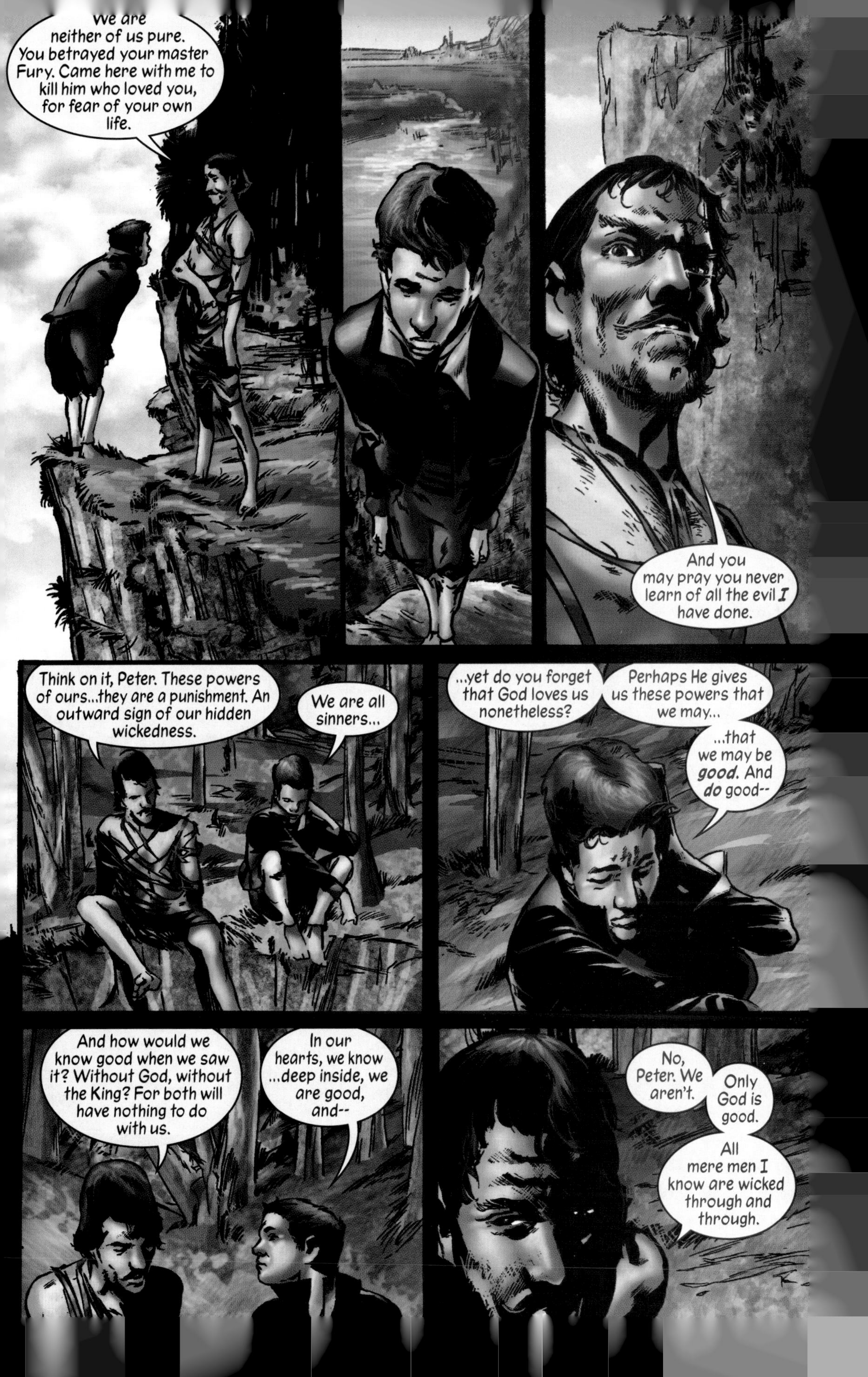
We are neither of us pure. You betrayed your master Fury. Came here with me to kill him who loved you, for fear of your own life.
And you may pray you never learn of all the evil *I* have done.
Think on it, Peter. These powers of ours...they are a punishment. An outward sign of our hidden wickedness.
We are all sinners...
...yet do you forget that God loves us nonetheless?
Perhaps He gives us these powers that we may...
...that we may be **good**. And **do** good--
And how would we know good when we saw it? Without God, without the King? For both will have nothing to do with us.
In our hearts, we know ...deep inside, we are good, and--
No, Peter. We aren't.
Only God is good.
All mere men I know are wicked through and through.

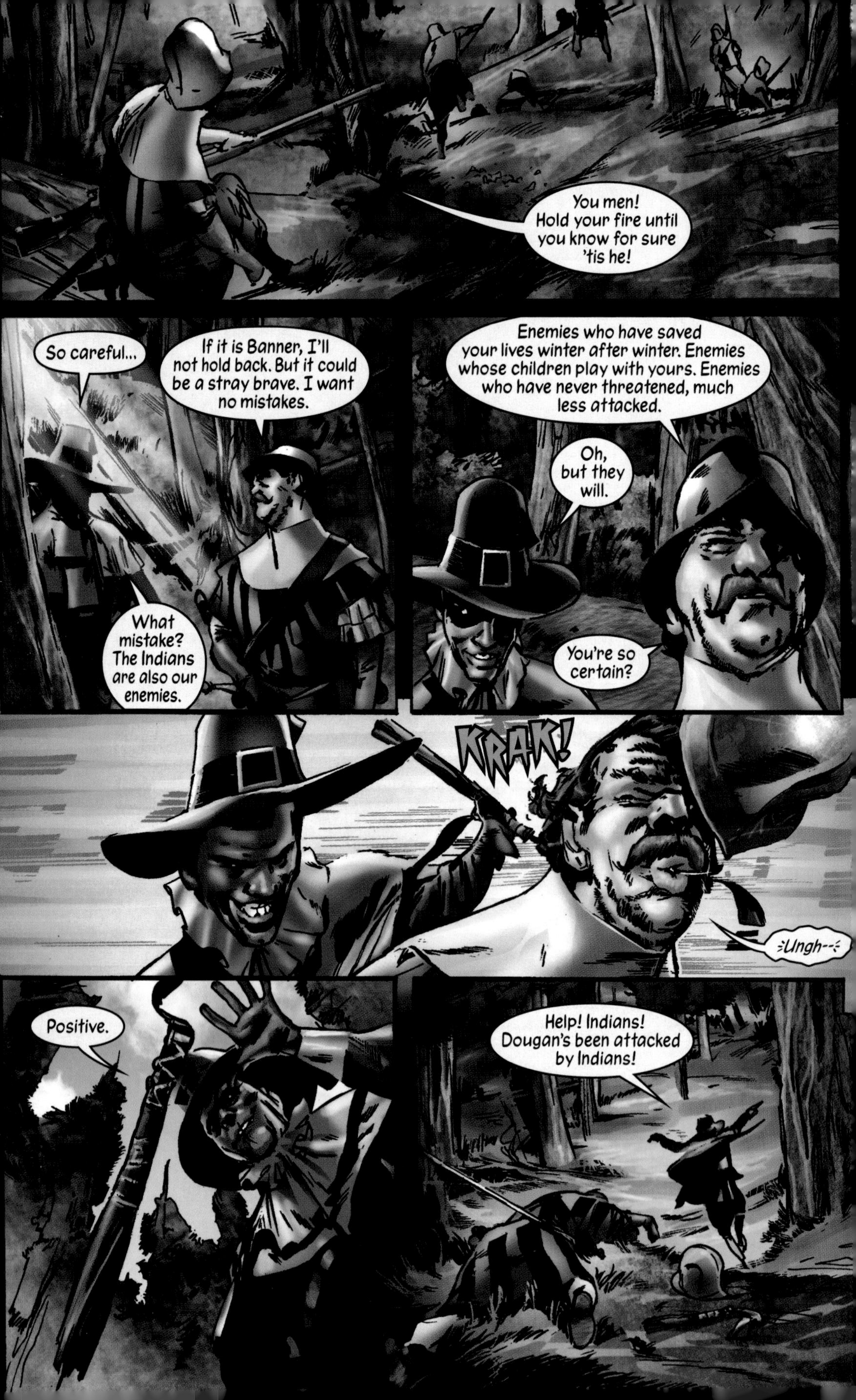
You men! Hold your fire until you know for sure 'tis he!
So careful...
If it is Banner, I'll not hold back. But it could be a stray brave. I want no mistakes.
What mistake? The Indians are also our enemies.
Enemies who have saved your lives winter after winter. Enemies whose children play with yours. Enemies who have never threatened, much less attacked.
Oh, but they will.
You're so certain?
KRAK!
Ungh--
Positive.
Help! Indians! Dougan's been attacked by Indians!

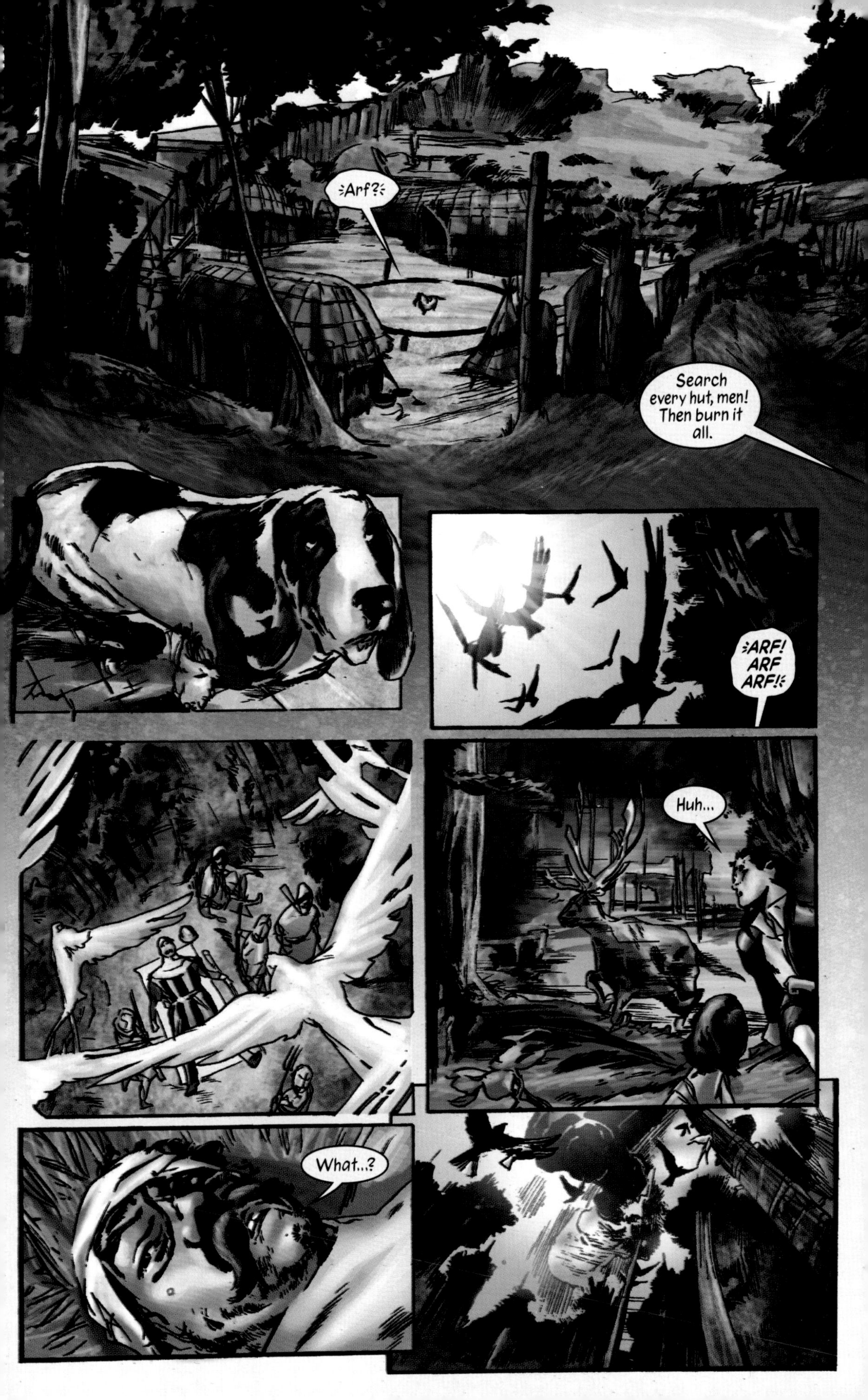
Arf?
Search every hut, men! Then burn it all.
ARF! ARF ARF!
Huh...
What...?

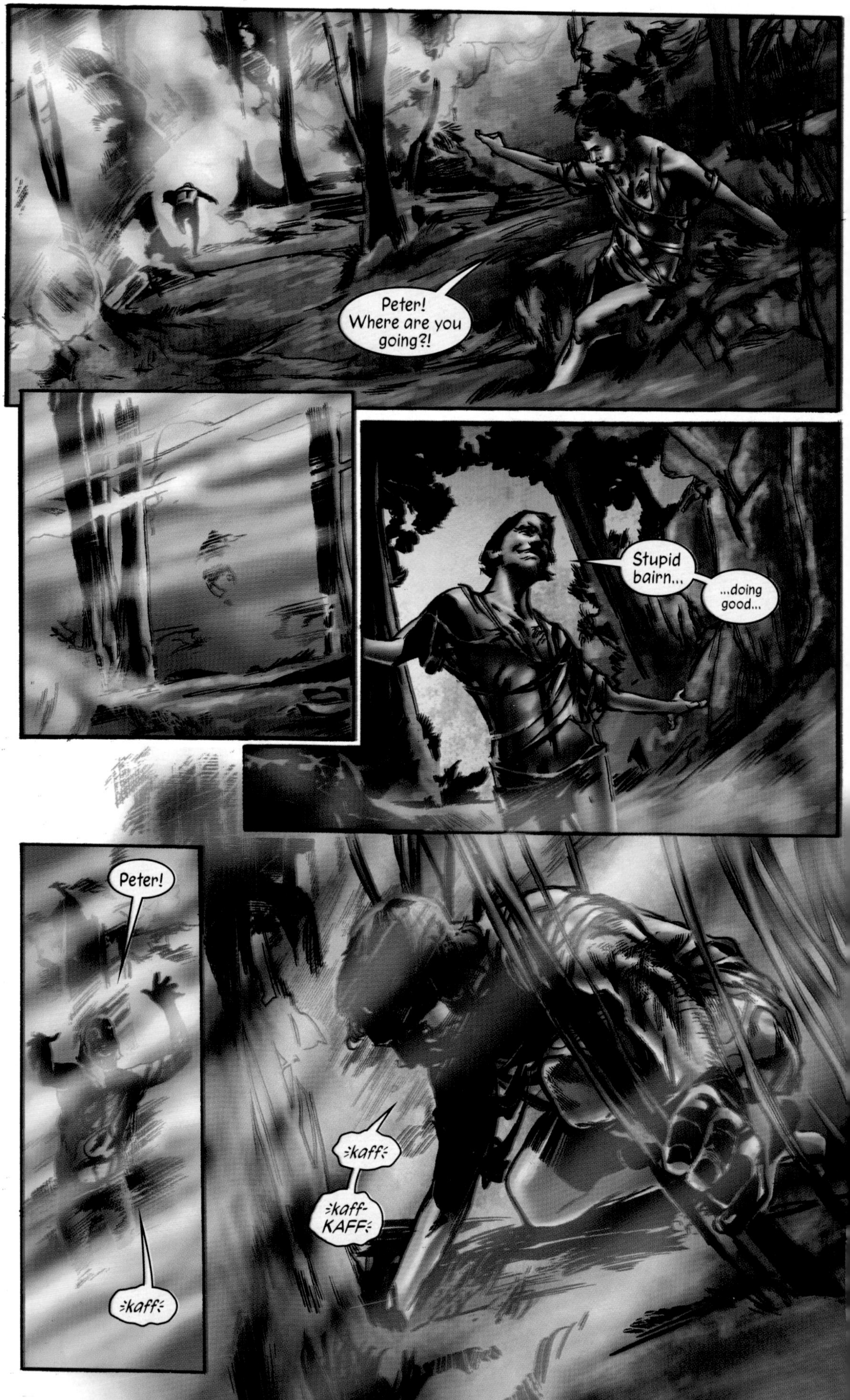
Peter! Where are you going?!
Stupid bairn...
...doing good...
Peter!
kaff
kaff
kaff-KAFF

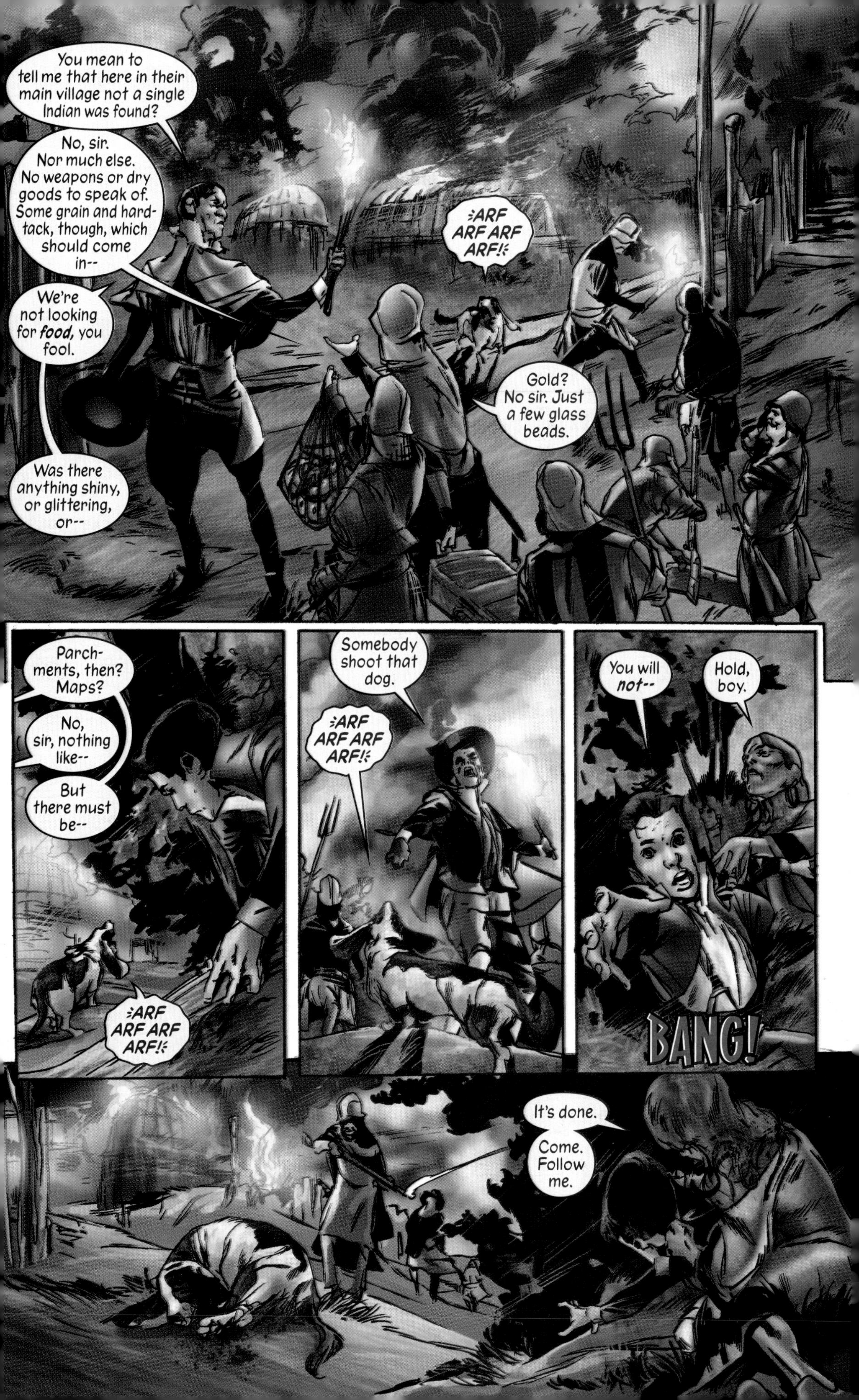
You mean to tell me that here in their main village not a single Indian was found?
No, sir. Nor much else. No weapons or dry goods to speak of. Some grain and hard-tack, though, which should come in--
We're not looking for *food*, you fool.
ARF ARF ARF ARF!
Gold? No sir. Just a few glass beads.
Was there anything shiny, or glittering, or--
Parchments, then? Maps?
No, sir, nothing like--
But there must be--
ARF ARF ARF ARF!
Somebody shoot that dog.
ARF ARF ARF ARF!
You will *not*--
Hold, boy.
BANG!
It's done.
Come. Follow me.

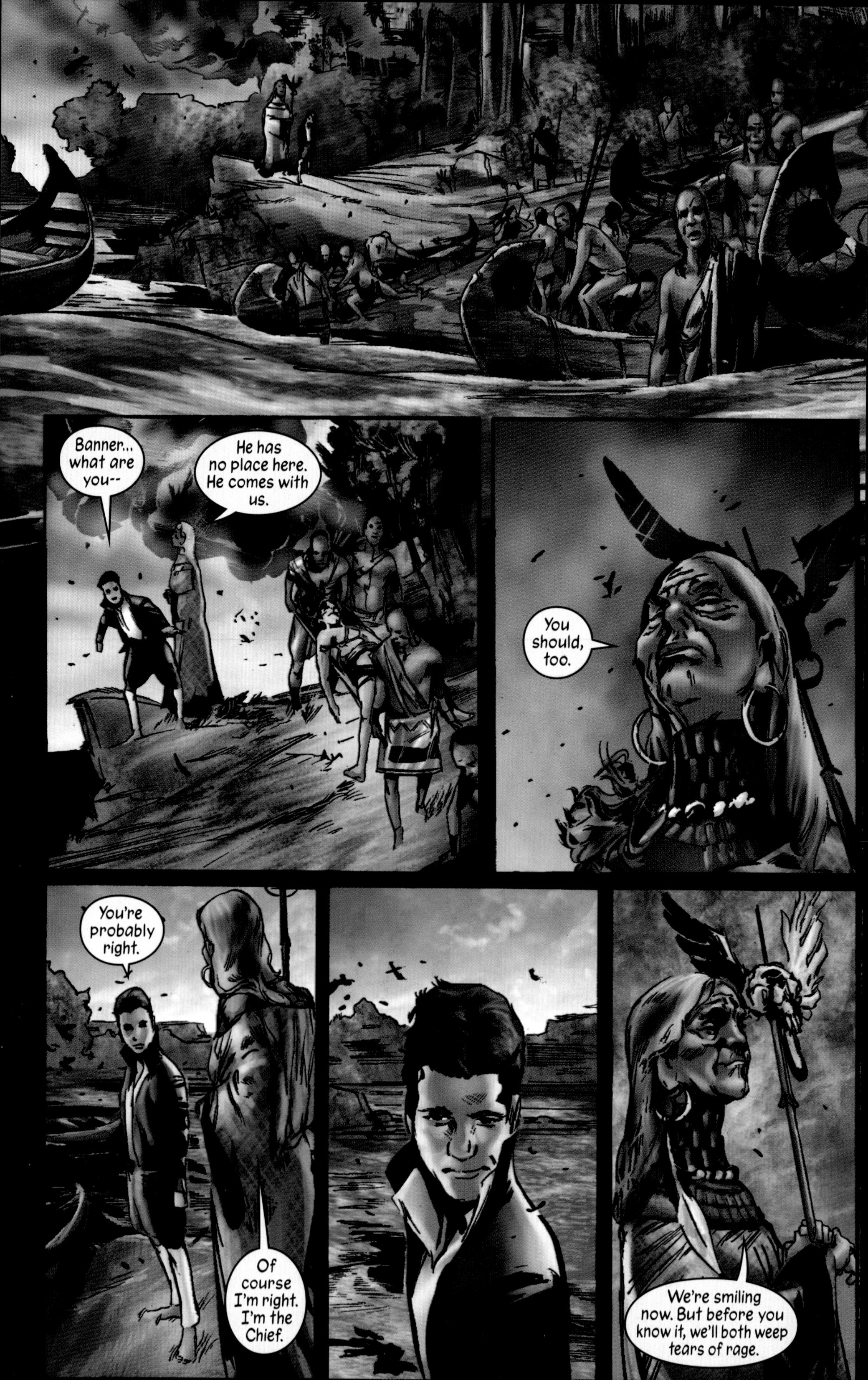
Banner... what are you--
He has no place here. He comes with us.
You should, too.
You're probably right.
Of course I'm right. I'm the Chief.
We're smiling now. But before you know it, we'll both weep tears of rage.

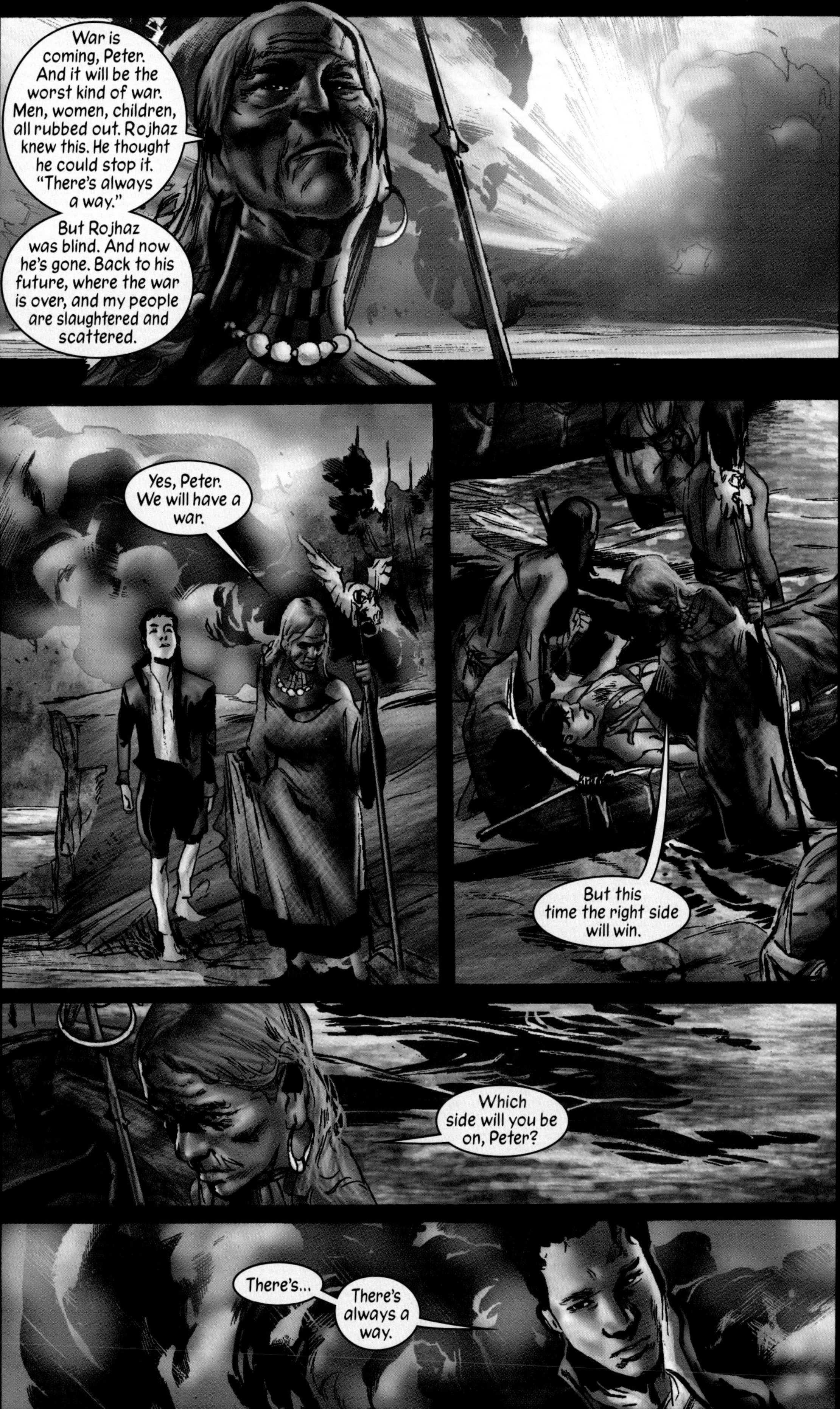
War is coming, Peter. And it will be the worst kind of war. Men, women, children, all rubbed out. Rojhaz knew this. He thought he could stop it. "There's always a way."
But Rojhaz was blind. And now he's gone. Back to his future, where the war is over, and my people are slaughtered and scattered.
Yes, Peter. We will have a war.
But this time the right side will win.
Which side will you be on, Peter?
There's...
There's always a way.

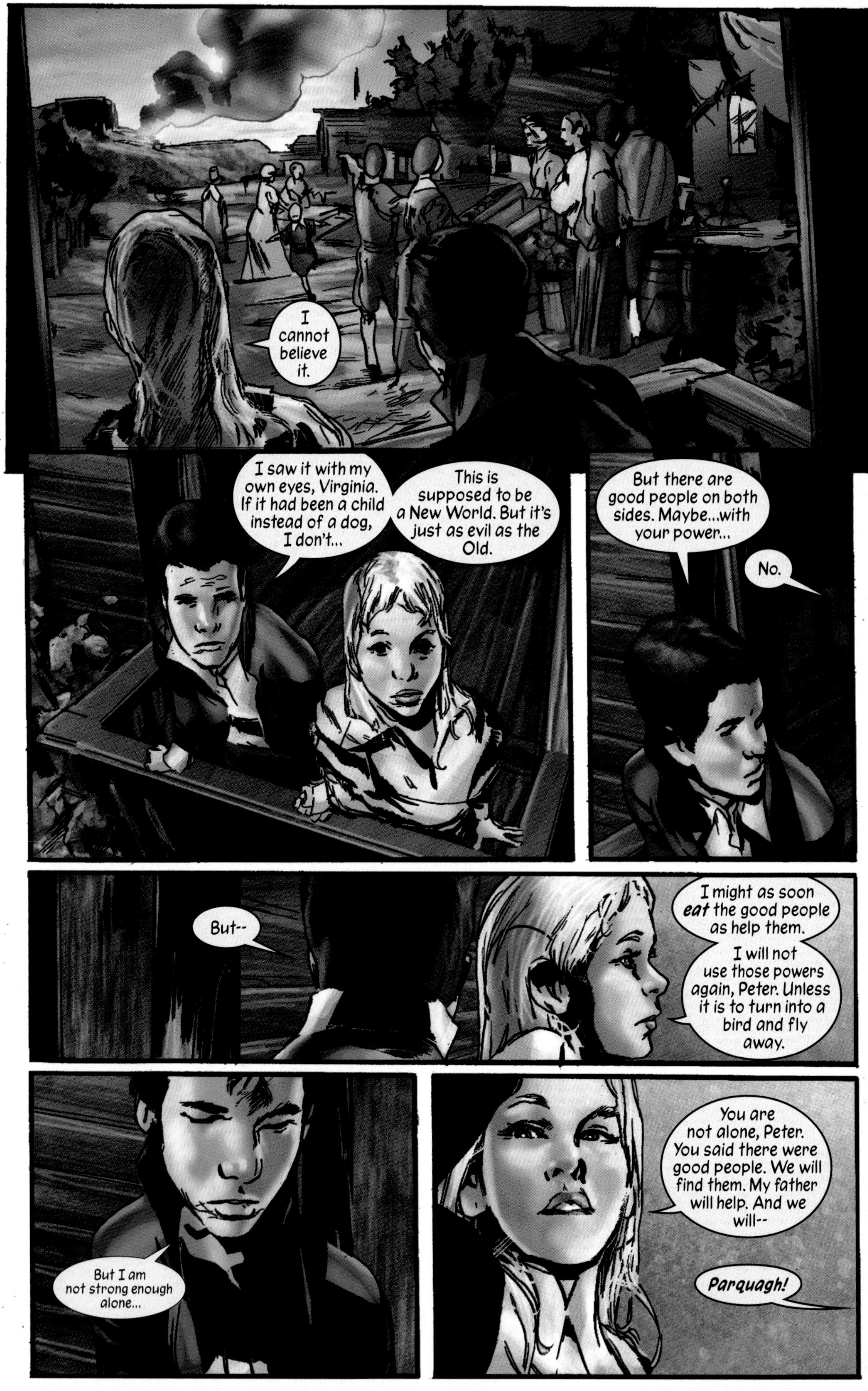
I cannot believe it.
I saw it with my own eyes, Virginia. If it had been a child instead of a dog, I don't...
This is supposed to be a New World. But it's just as evil as the Old.
But there are good people on both sides. Maybe...with your power...
No.
But--
I might as soon *eat* the good people as help them.
I will not use those powers again, Peter. Unless it is to turn into a bird and fly away.
But I am not strong enough alone...
You are not alone, Peter. You said there were good people. We will find them. My father will help. And we will--
Parquagh!

Where the devil have you been?

You told me to follow the soldiers. I--

Don't give me your excuses, boyo! The story of the *year* sails up to the port and you're nowhere to be found?

Whoa.

A broadsheet man develops instincts, Parquagh. A special sense, like the tingling when something's going to happen. You don't have any idea what I'm talking about, do you?

Actually, sir...

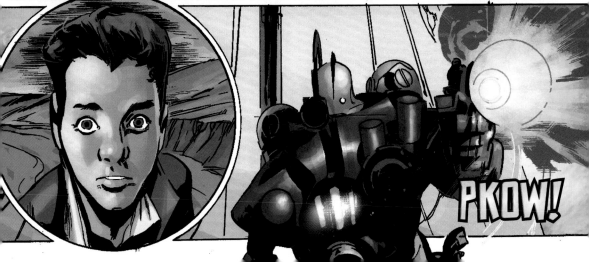

PKOW!

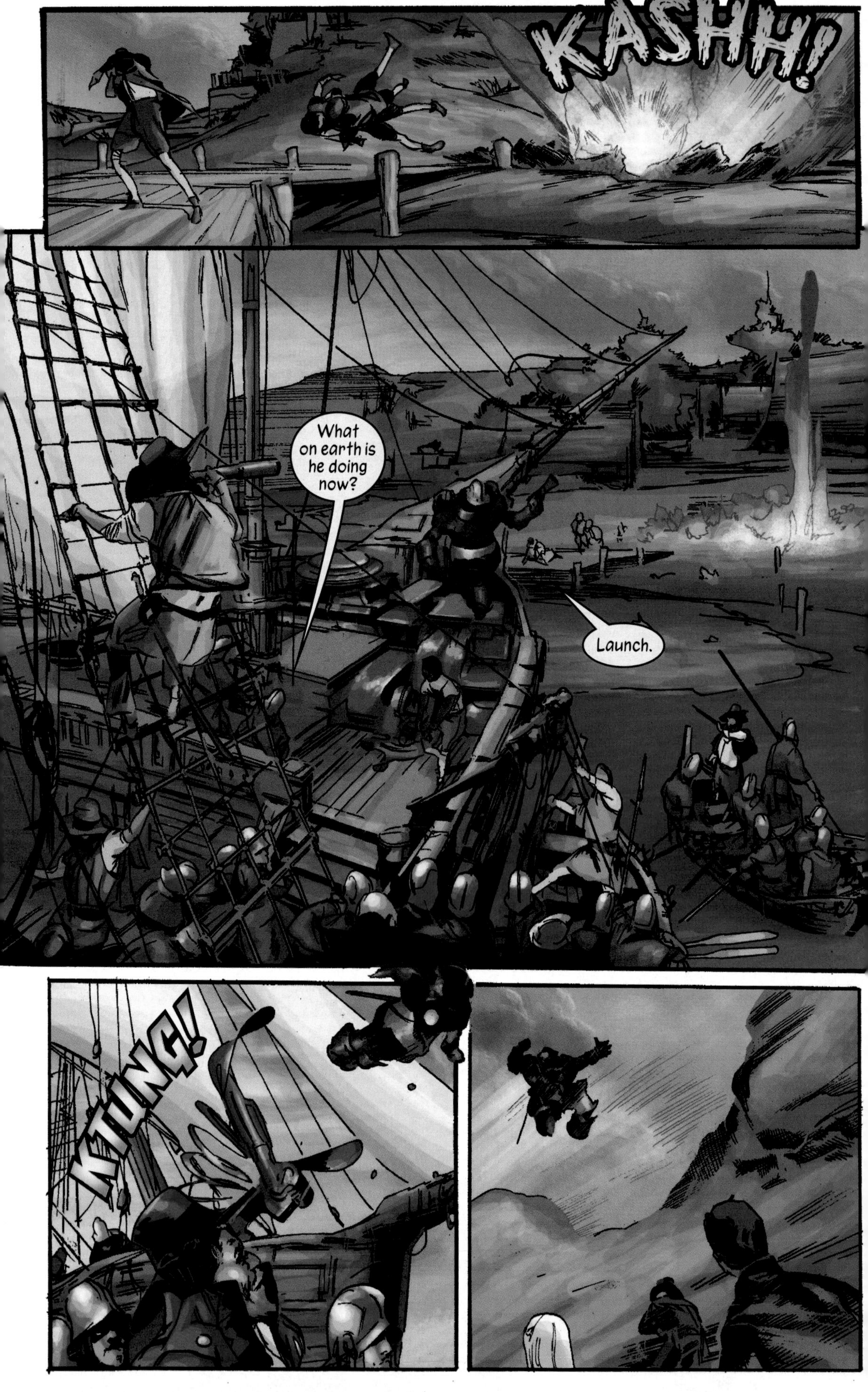
KASHH!
What on earth is he doing now?
Launch.
KTUNG!

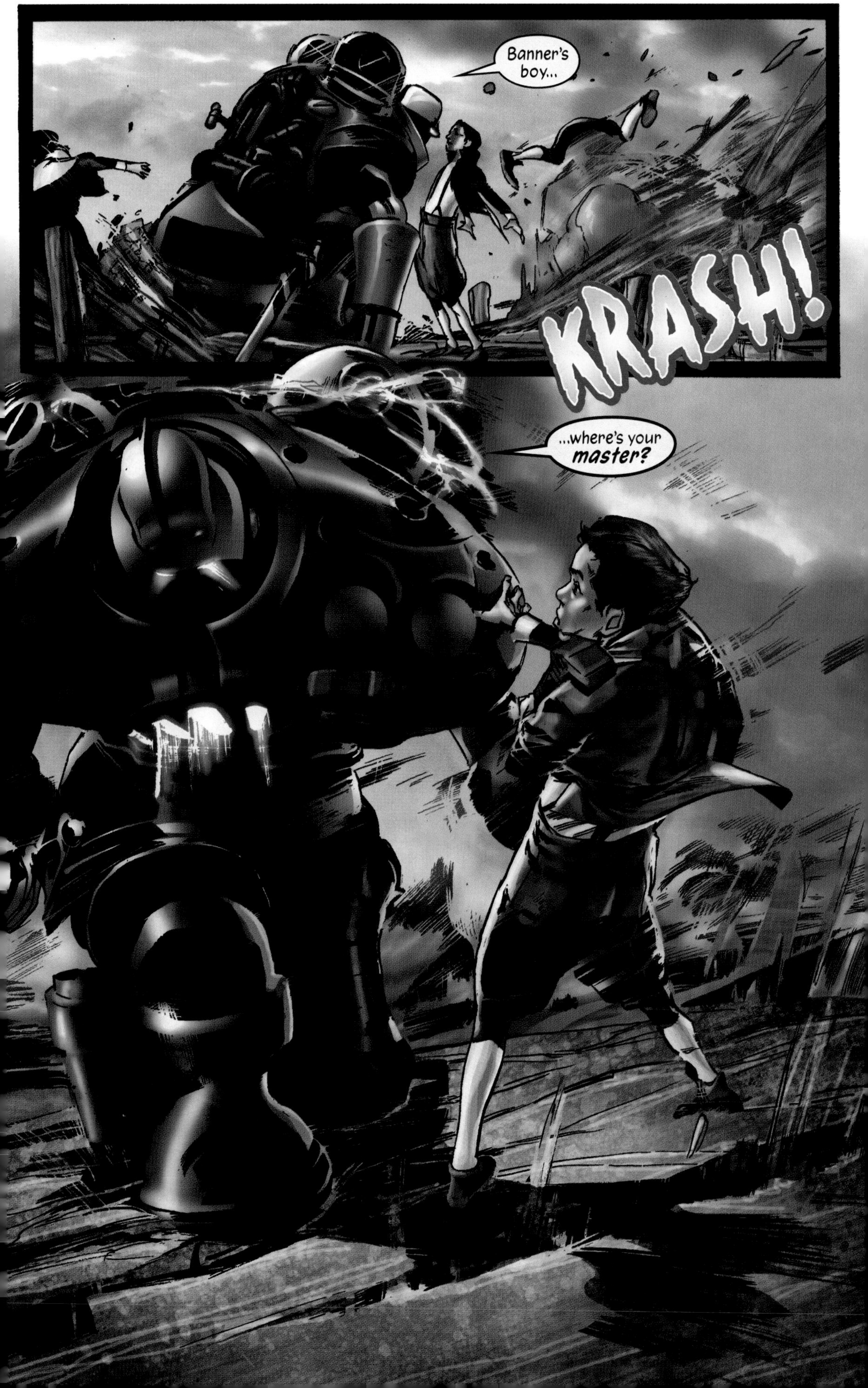
Banner's boy...
KRASH!
...where's your *master?*

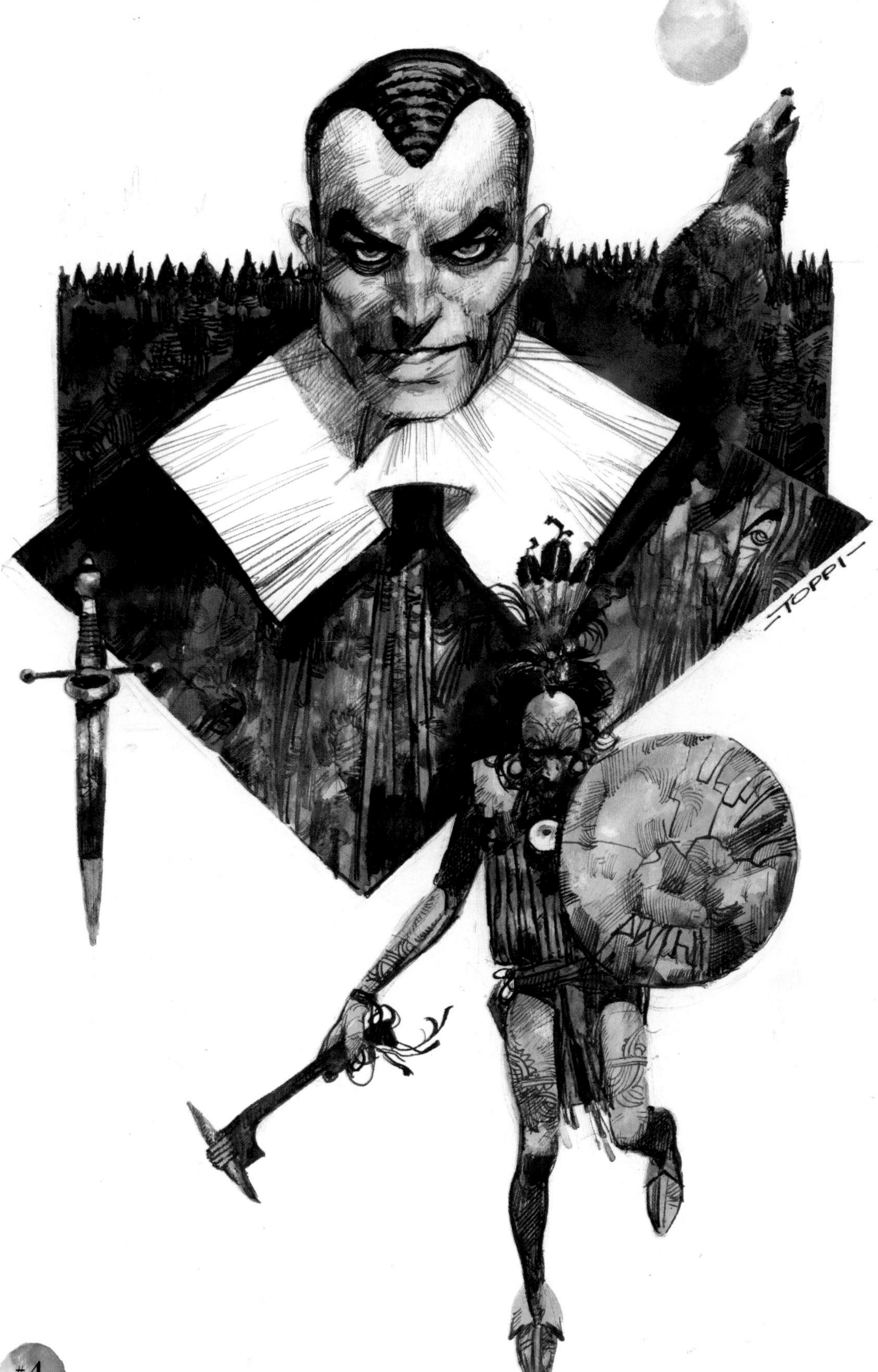
TOPPI

#4

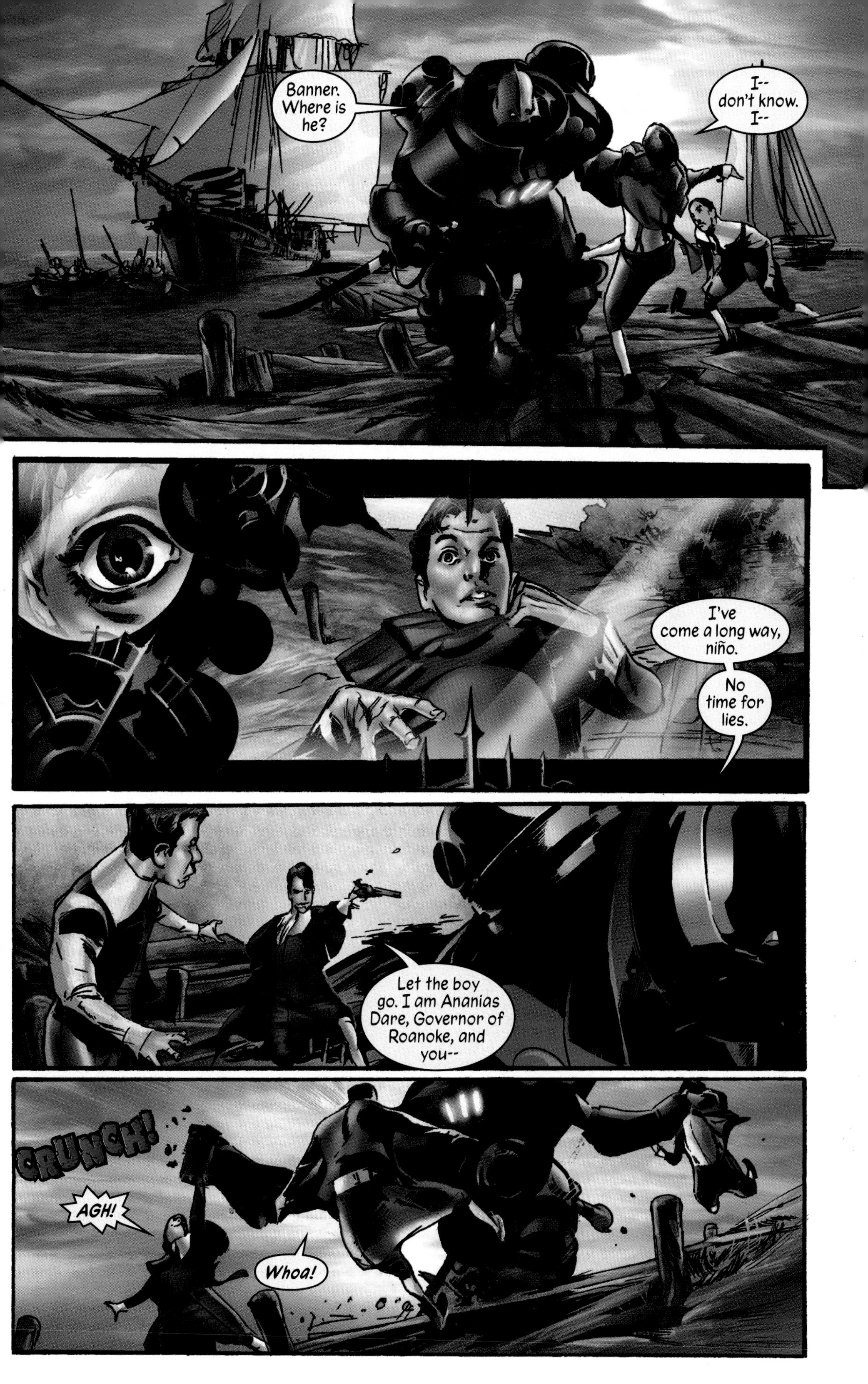
Banner. Where is he?
I-- don't know. I--
I've come a long way, niño.
No time for lies.
Let the boy go. I am Ananias Dare, Governor of Roanoke, and you--
CRUNCH!
AGH!
Whoa!

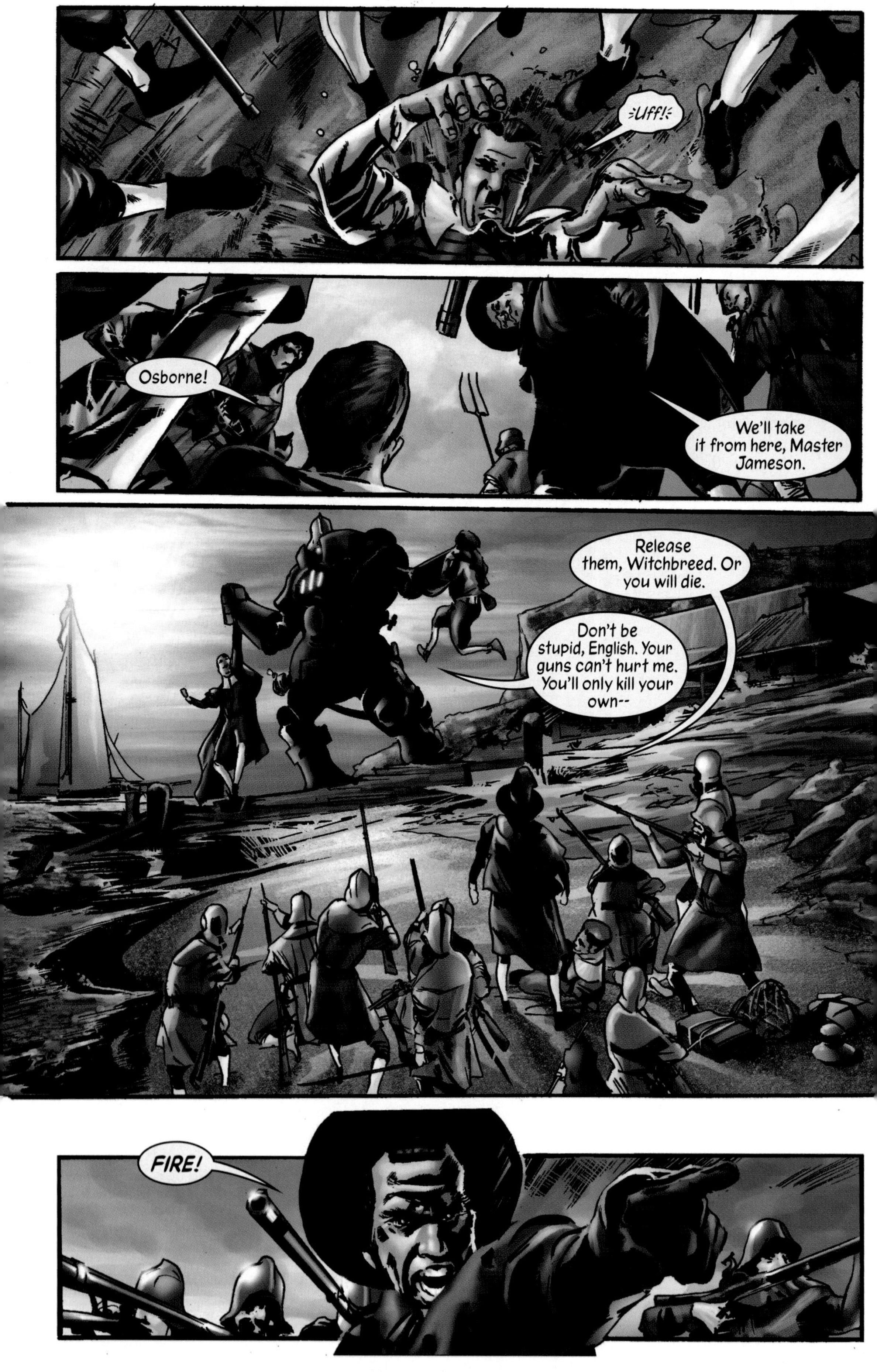

Uff!
Osborne!
We'll take it from here, Master Jameson.
Release them, Witchbreed. Or you will die.
Don't be stupid, English. Your guns can't hurt me. You'll only kill your own--
FIRE!

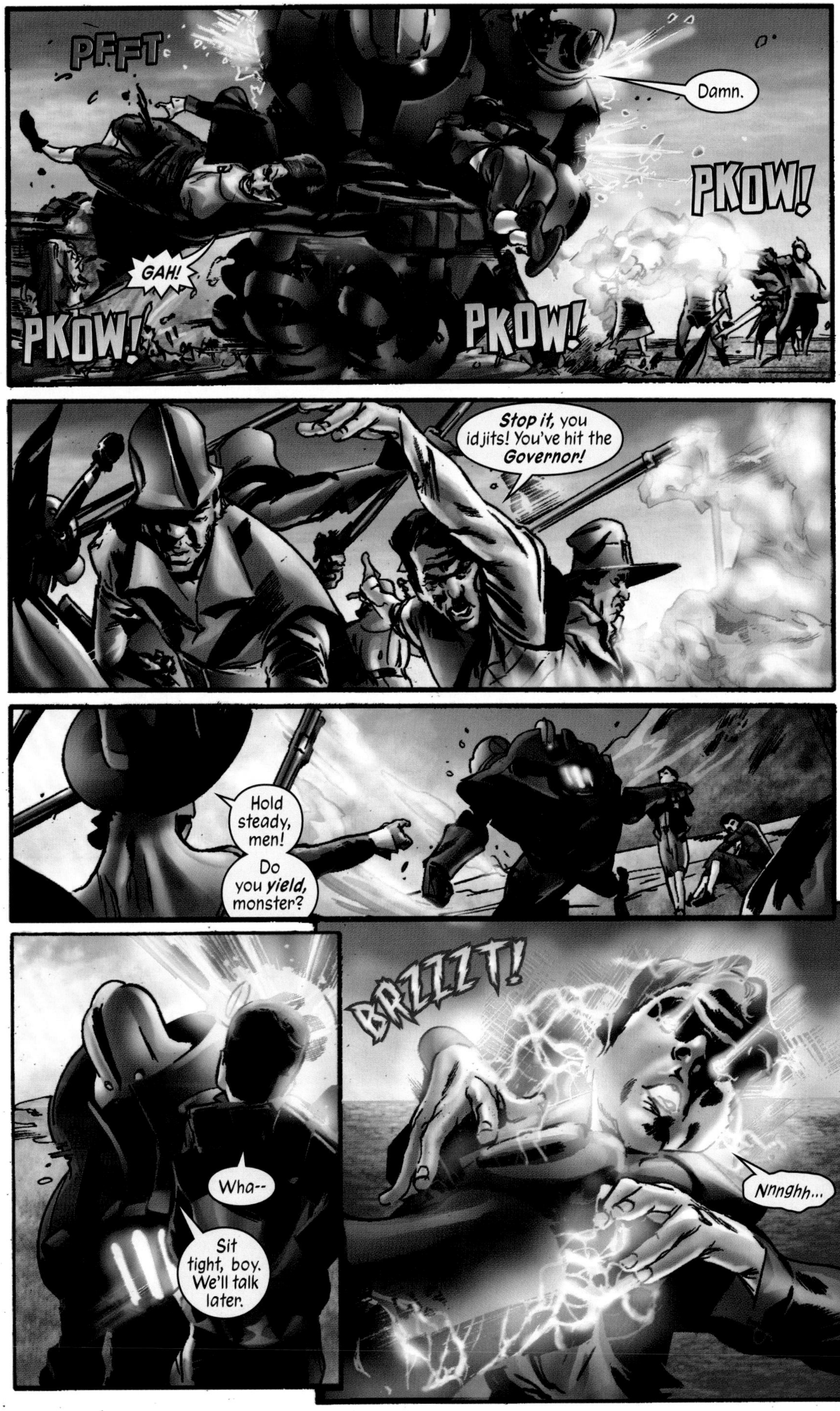
PFFT
Damn.
PKOW!
GAH!
PKOW!
PKOW!
Stop it, you idjits! You've hit the Governor!
Hold steady, men!
Do you yield, monster?
BRZZZT!
Wha--
Sit tight, boy. We'll talk later.
Nnnghh...

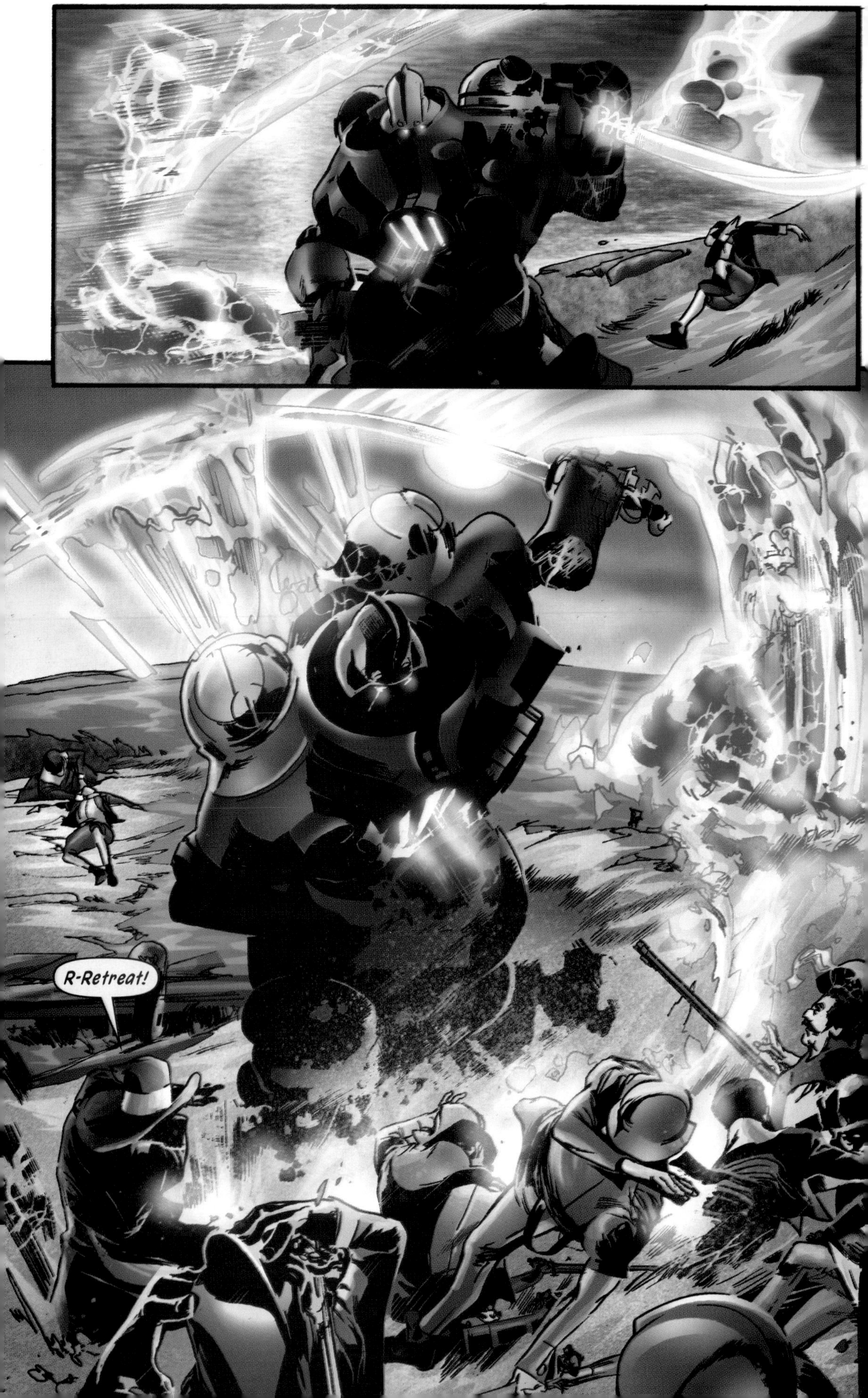
R-Retreat!

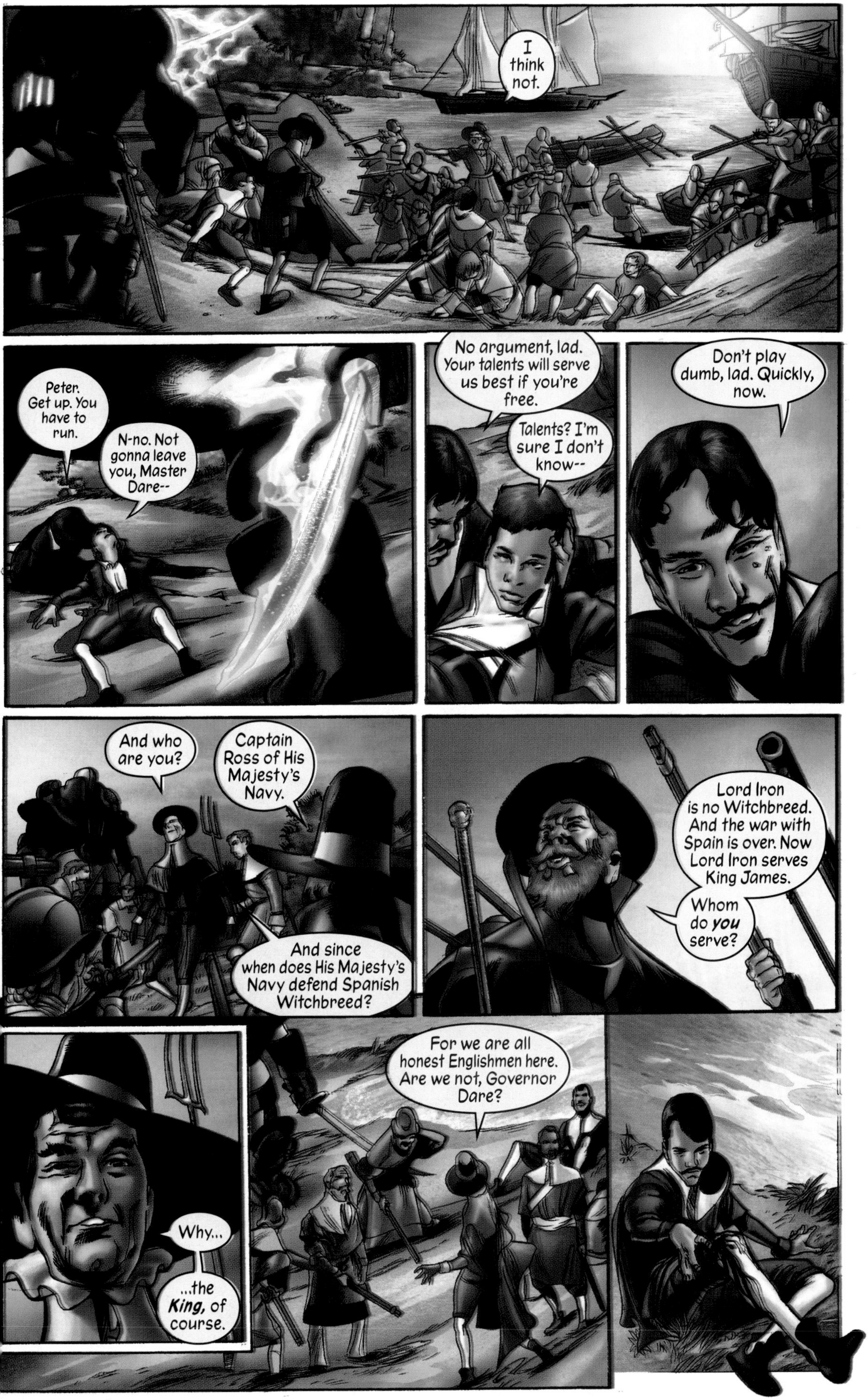
I think not.
Peter. Get up. You have to run.
N-no. Not gonna leave you, Master Dare--
No argument, lad. Your talents will serve us best if you're free.
Talents? I'm sure I don't know--
Don't play dumb, lad. Quickly, now.
And who are you?
Captain Ross of His Majesty's Navy.
And since when does His Majesty's Navy defend Spanish Witchbreed?
Lord Iron is no Witchbreed. And the war with Spain is over. Now Lord Iron serves King James.
Whom do *you* serve?
Why...
...the *King,* of course.
For we are all honest Englishmen here. Are we not, Governor Dare?

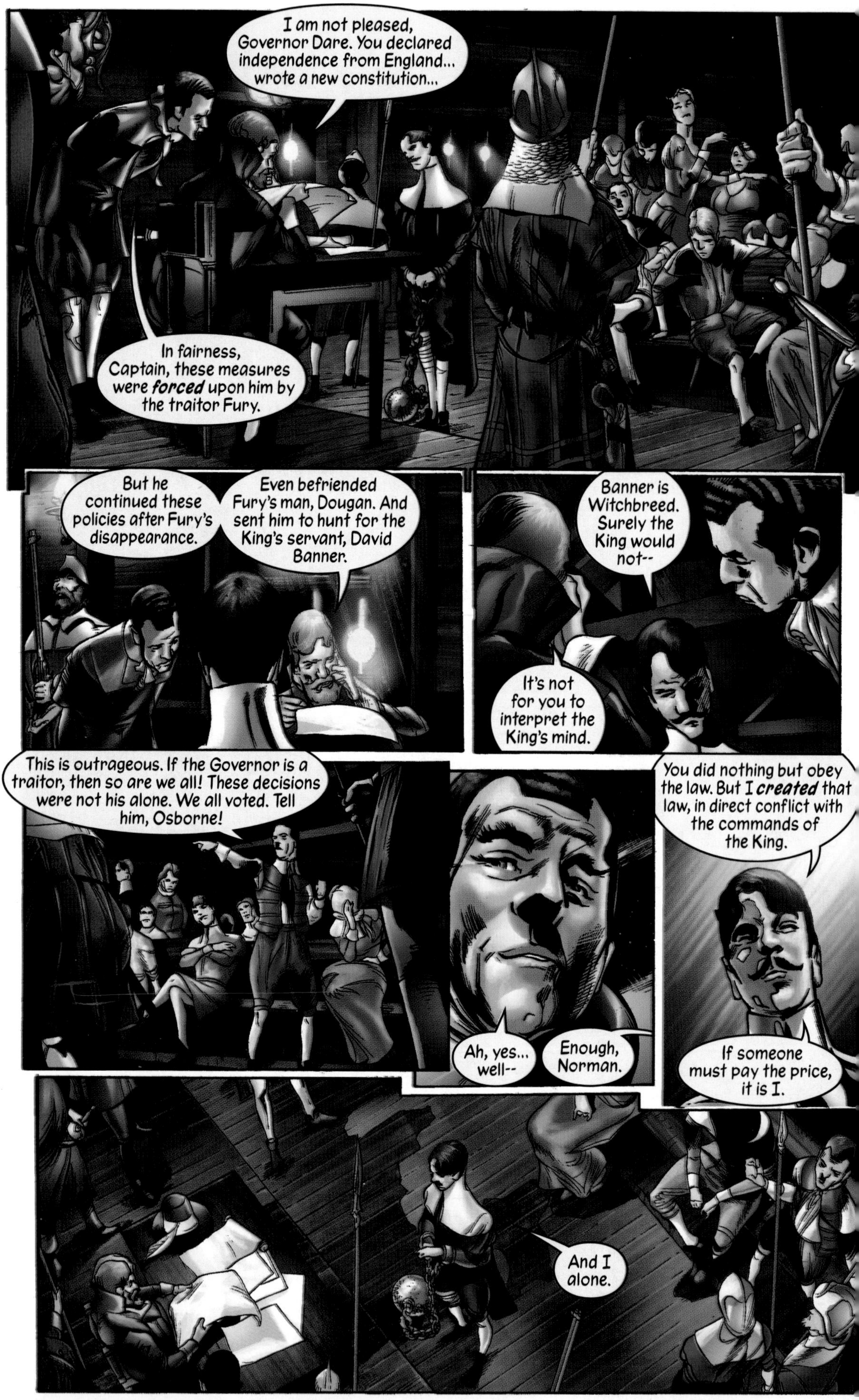
I am not pleased, Governor Dare. You declared independence from England... wrote a new constitution...
In fairness, Captain, these measures were *forced* upon him by the traitor Fury.
But he continued these policies after Fury's disappearance.
Even befriended Fury's man, Dougan. And sent him to hunt for the King's servant, David Banner.
Banner is Witchbreed. Surely the King would not--
It's not for you to interpret the King's mind.
This is outrageous. If the Governor is a traitor, then so are we all! These decisions were not his alone. We all voted. Tell him, Osborne!
Ah, yes... well--
Enough, Norman.
You did nothing but obey the law. But I *created* that law, in direct conflict with the commands of the King.
If someone must pay the price, it is I.
And I alone.

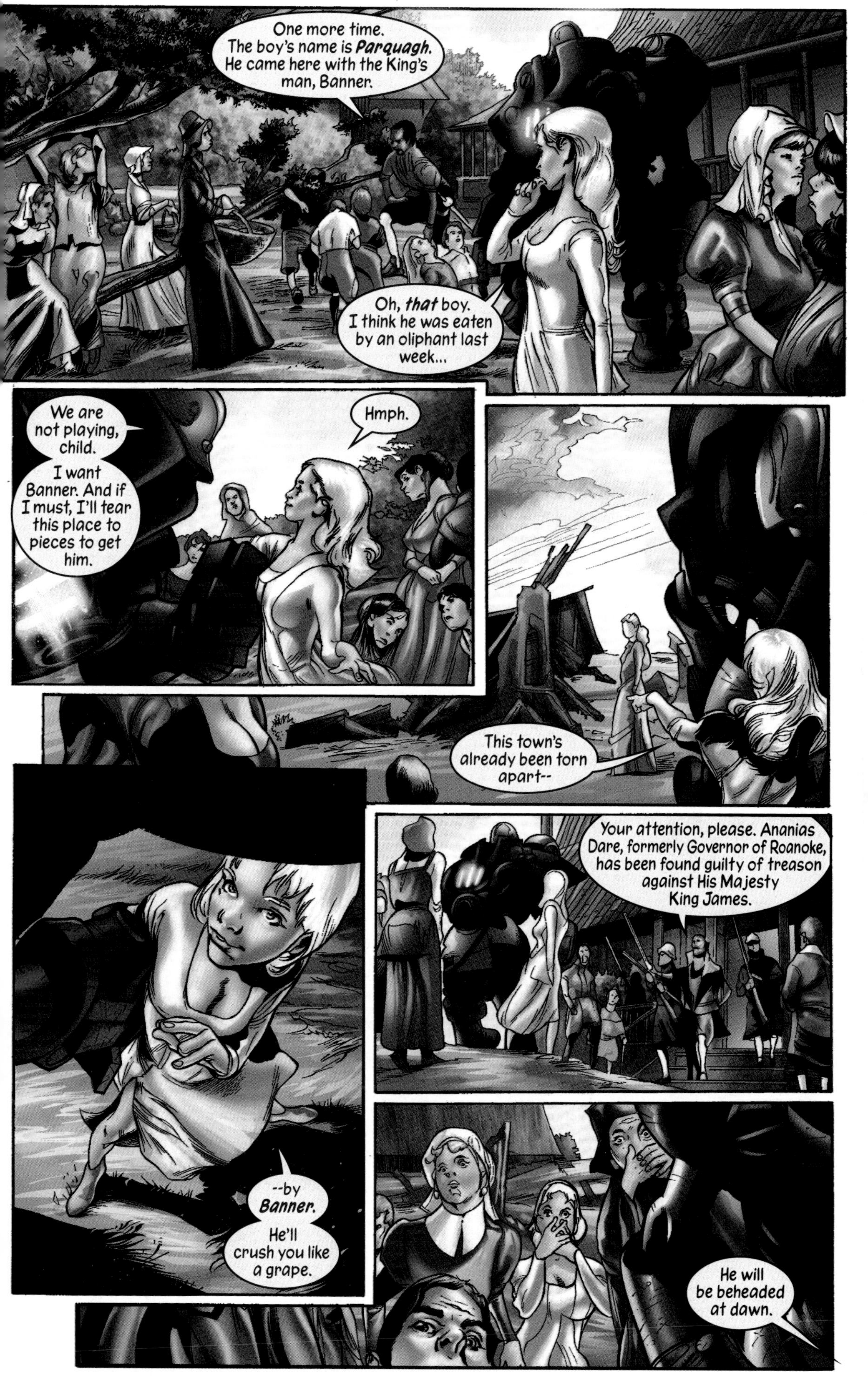

One more time. The boy's name is ***Parquagh.*** He came here with the King's man, Banner.
Oh, ***that*** boy. I think he was eaten by an oliphant last week...
We are not playing, child.
Hmph.
I want Banner. And if I must, I'll tear this place to pieces to get him.
This town's already been torn apart--
--by ***Banner.***
He'll crush you like a grape.
Your attention, please. Ananias Dare, formerly Governor of Roanoke, has been found guilty of treason against His Majesty King James.
He will be beheaded at dawn.

Mercy, Captain Ross! **Mercy!**

It is not mine to grant.

Then you shall have none from **ME.**

NO, Virginia!

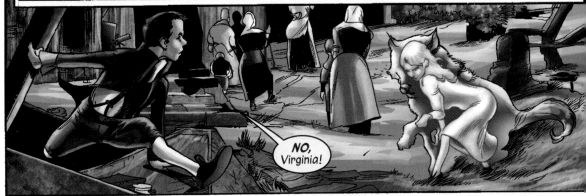

You must not transform.

You said it yourself--you have no control. You might **kill** your father rather than **rescue** him.

NGgahh...

Then... then who will save him, Peter?

I will.

You'll need help.

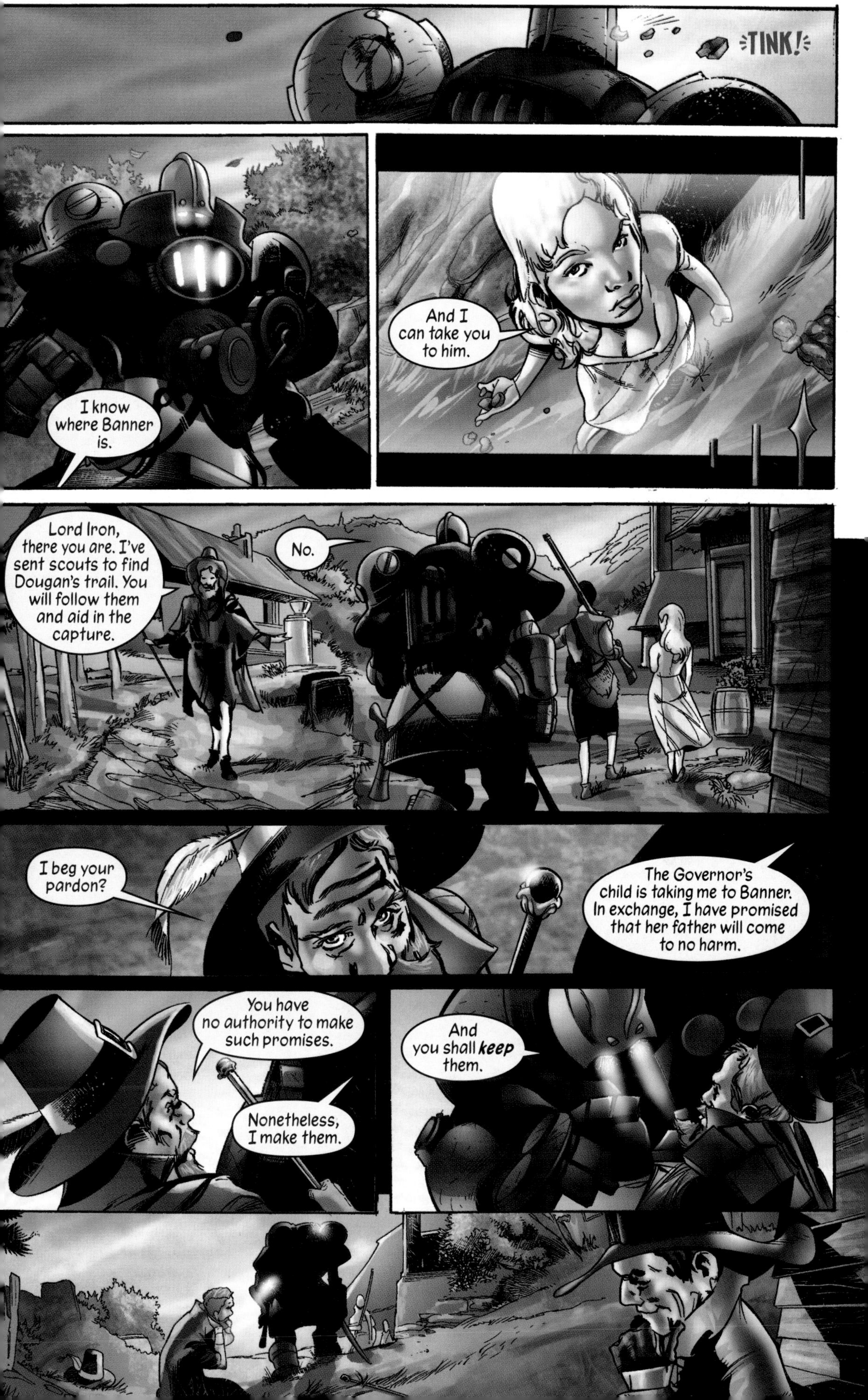
TINK!
I know where Banner is.
And I can take you to him.
Lord Iron, there you are. I've sent scouts to find Dougan's trail. You will follow them and aid in the capture.
No.
I beg your pardon?
The Governor's child is taking me to Banner. In exchange, I have promised that her father will come to no harm.
You have no authority to make such promises.
Nonetheless, I make them.
And you shall *keep* them.

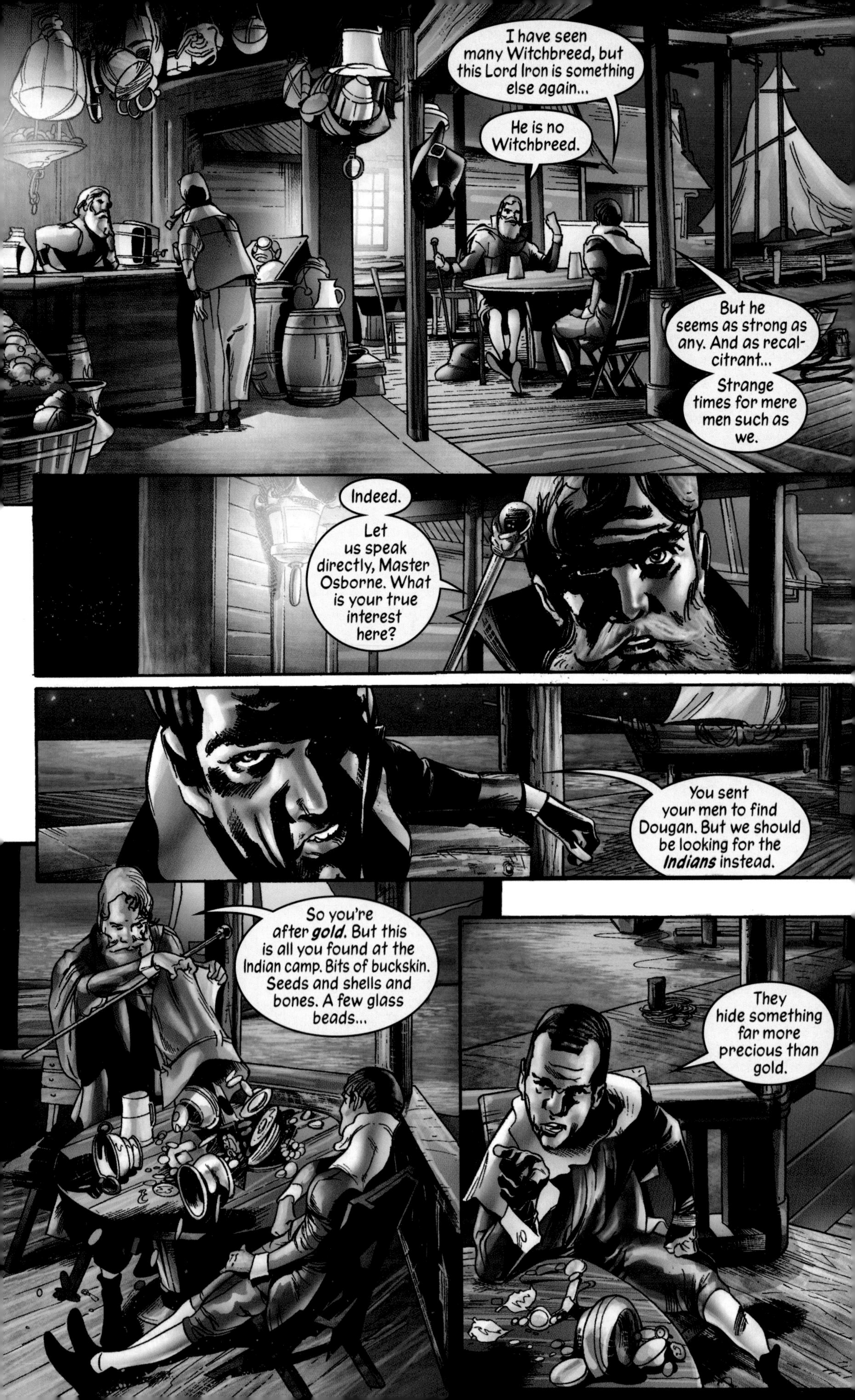

I have seen many Witchbreed, but this Lord Iron is something else again...
He is no Witchbreed.
But he seems as strong as any. And as recal-citrant...
Strange times for mere men such as we.
Indeed.
Let us speak directly, Master Osborne. What is your true interest here?
You sent your men to find Dougan. But we should be looking for the *Indians* instead.
So you're after **gold**. But this is all you found at the Indian camp. Bits of buckskin. Seeds and shells and bones. A few glass beads...
They hide something far more precious than gold.

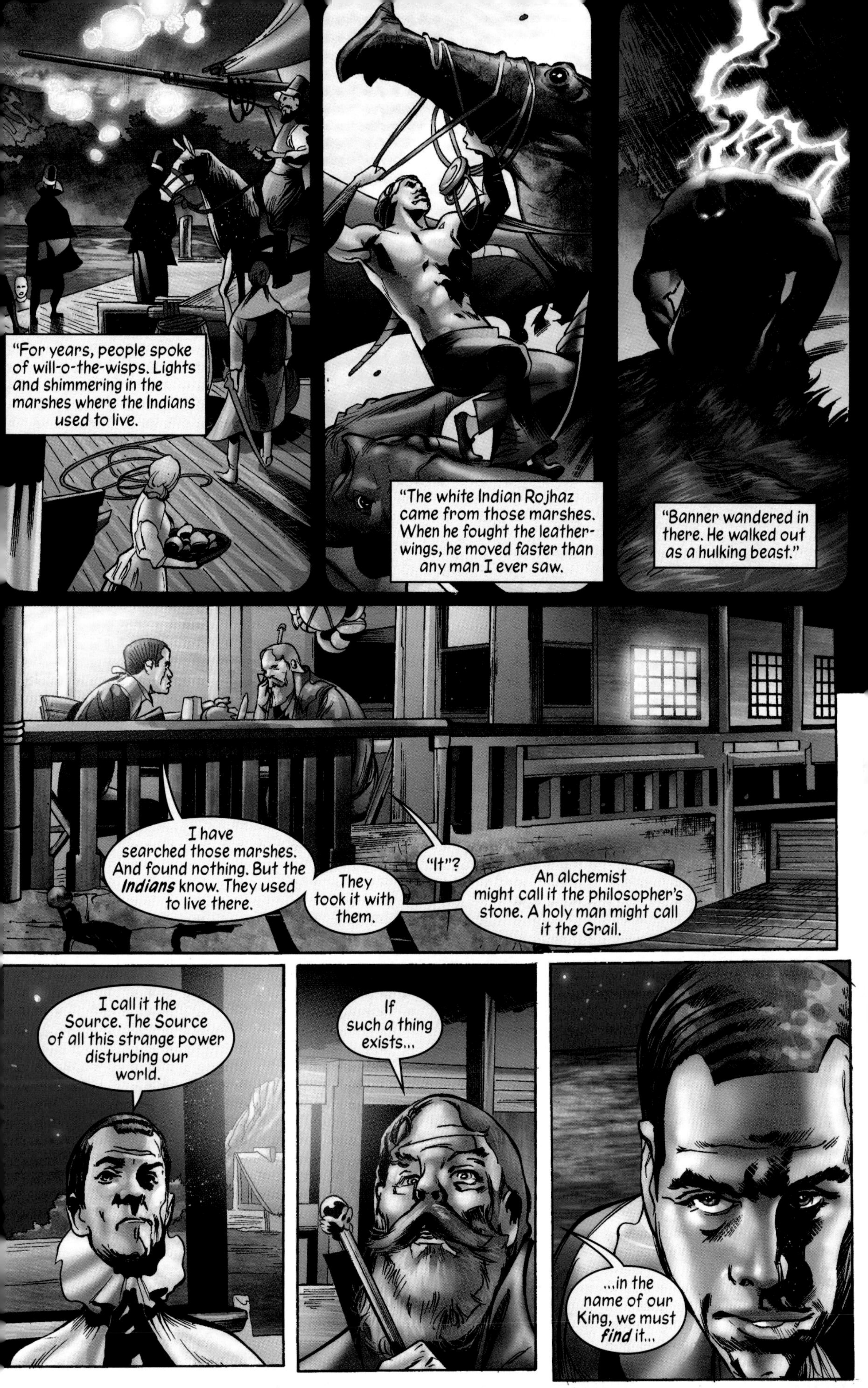
"For years, people spoke of will-o-the-wisps. Lights and shimmering in the marshes where the Indians used to live.
"The white Indian Rojhaz came from those marshes. When he fought the leather-wings, he moved faster than any man I ever saw.
"Banner wandered in there. He walked out as a hulking beast."
I have searched those marshes. And found nothing. But the *Indians* know. They used to live there.
They took it with them.
"It"?
An alchemist might call it the philosopher's stone. A holy man might call it the Grail.
I call it the Source. The Source of all this strange power disturbing our world.
If such a thing exists...
...in the name of our King, we must *find* it...

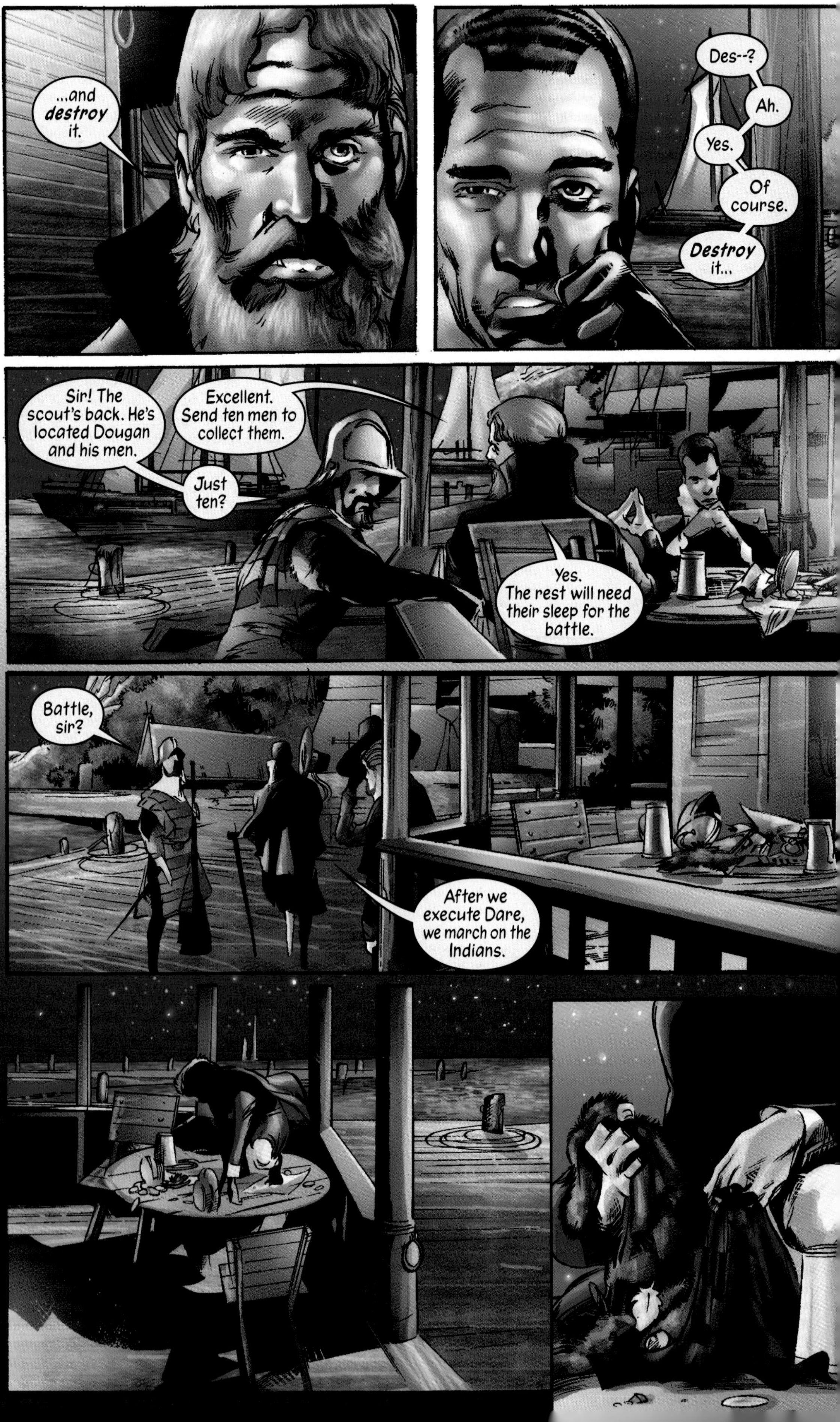
...and *destroy* it.
Des--?
Ah.
Yes.
Of course.
Destroy it...
Sir! The scout's back. He's located Dougan and his men.
Excellent. Send ten men to collect them.
Just ten?
Yes. The rest will need their sleep for the battle.
Battle, sir?
After we execute Dare, we march on the Indians.

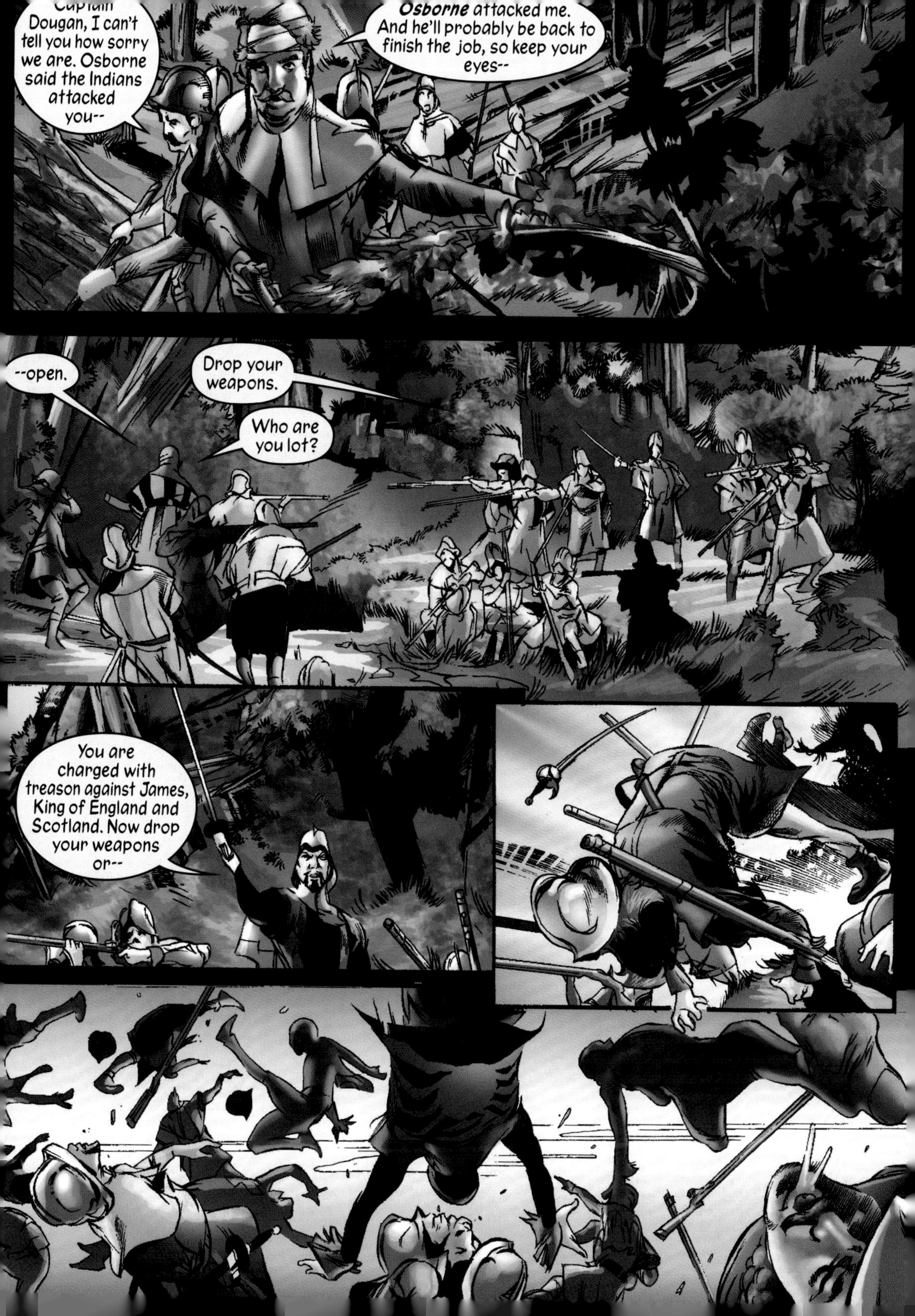
Captain Dougan, I can't tell you how sorry we are. Osborne said the Indians attacked you--
Osborne attacked me. And he'll probably be back to finish the job, so keep your eyes--
--open.
Drop your weapons.
Who are you lot?
You are charged with treason against James, King of England and Scotland. Now drop your weapons or--

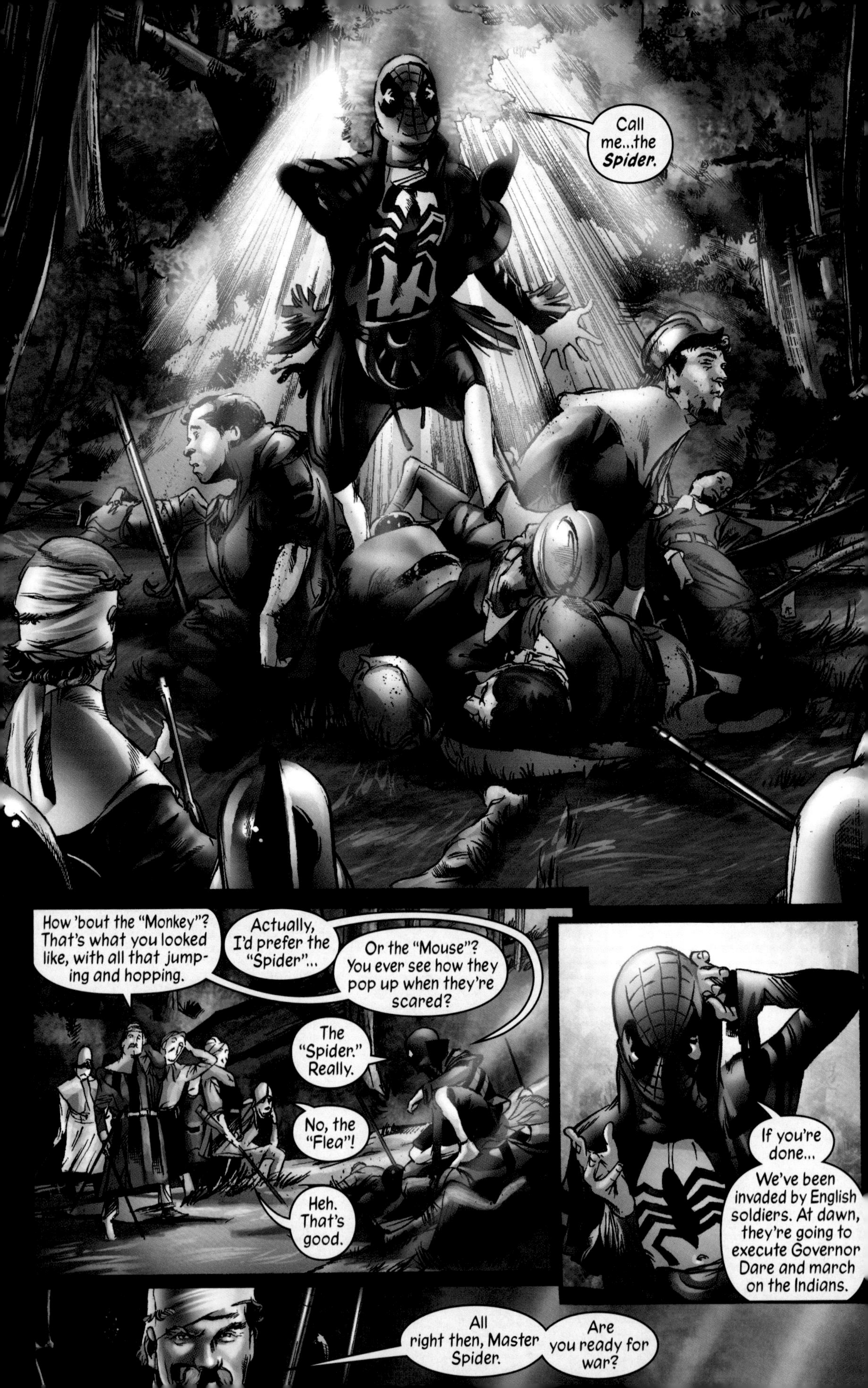

Call me...the *Spider.*
How 'bout the "Monkey"? That's what you looked like, with all that jumping and hopping.
Actually, I'd prefer the "Spider"...
Or the "Mouse"? You ever see how they pop up when they're scared?
The "Spider." Really.
No, the "Flea"!
Heh. That's good.
If you're done...
We've been invaded by English soldiers. At dawn, they're going to execute Governor Dare and march on the Indians.
All right then, Master Spider.
Are you ready for war?

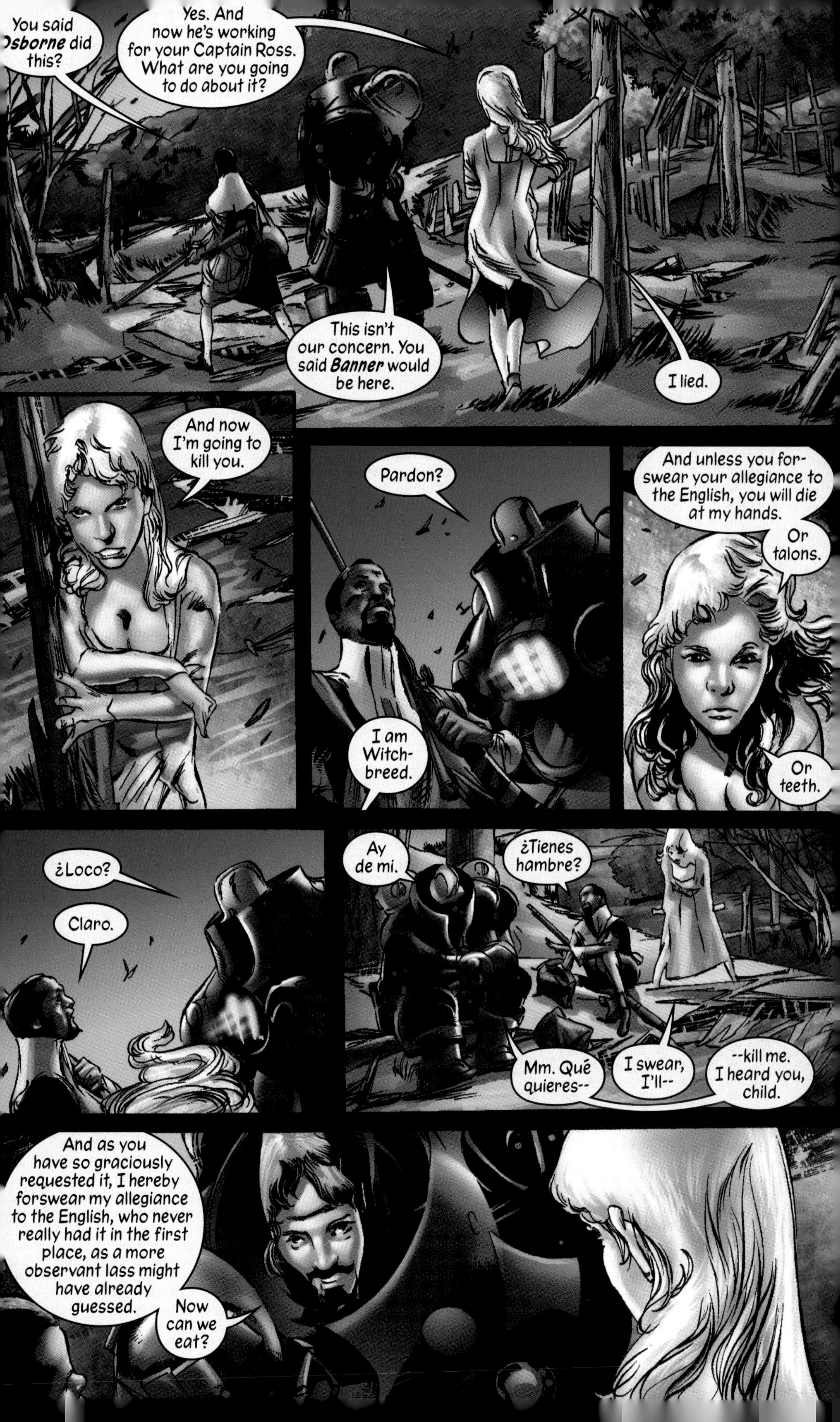
You said Osborne did this?
Yes. And now he's working for your Captain Ross. What are you going to do about it?
This isn't our concern. You said Banner would be here.
I lied.
And now I'm going to kill you.
Pardon?
I am Witch-breed.
And unless you for-swear your allegiance to the English, you will die at my hands.
Or talons.
Or teeth.
¿Loco?
Claro.
Ay de mi.
¿Tienes hambre?
Mm. Qué quieres--
I swear, I'll--
--kill me. I heard you, child.
And as you have so graciously requested it, I hereby forswear my allegiance to the English, who never really had it in the first place, as a more observant lass might have already guessed.
Now can we eat?

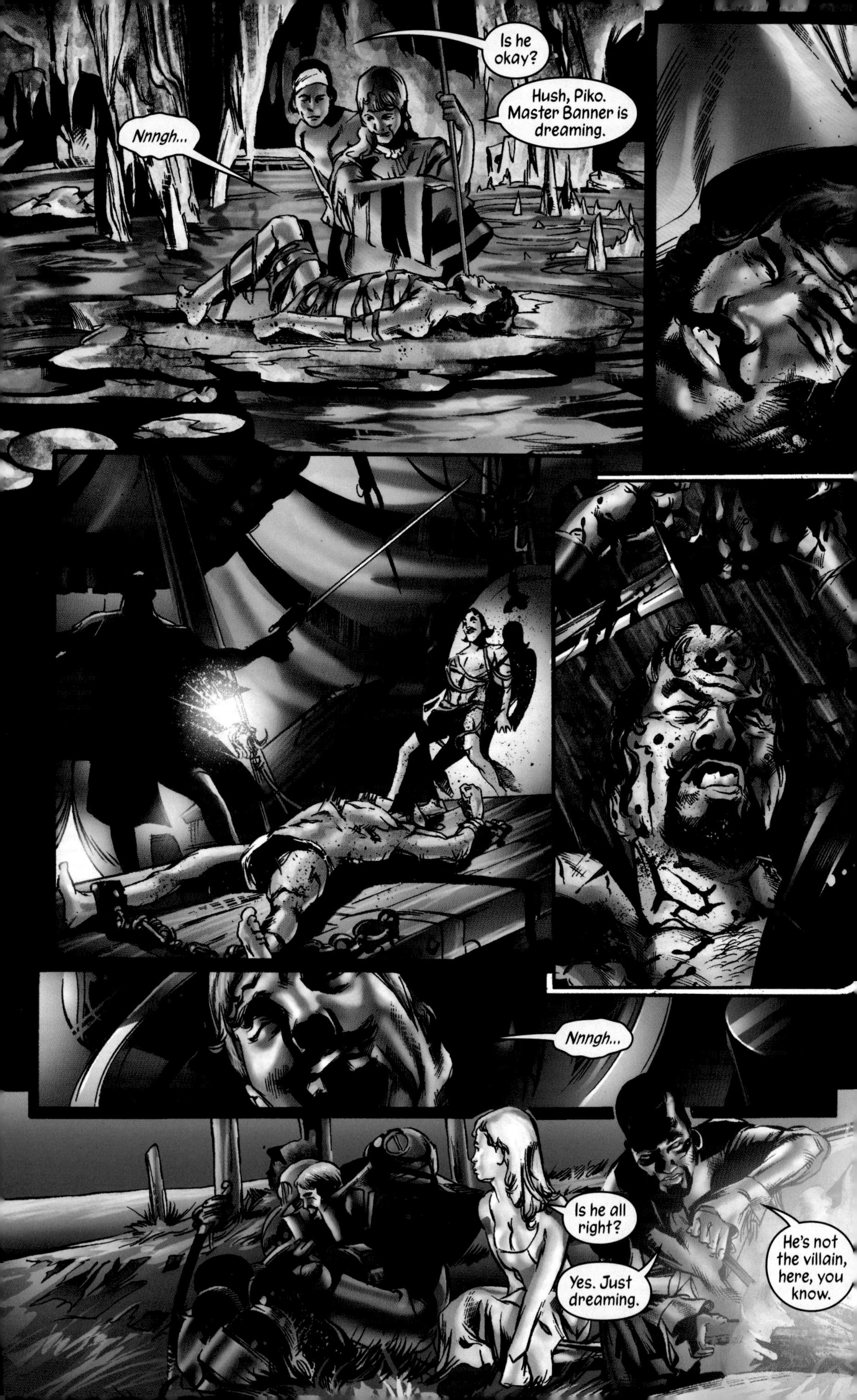
Is he okay?
Hush, Piko. Master Banner is dreaming.
Nnngh...
Nnngh...
Is he all right?
Yes. Just dreaming.
He's not the villain, here, you know.

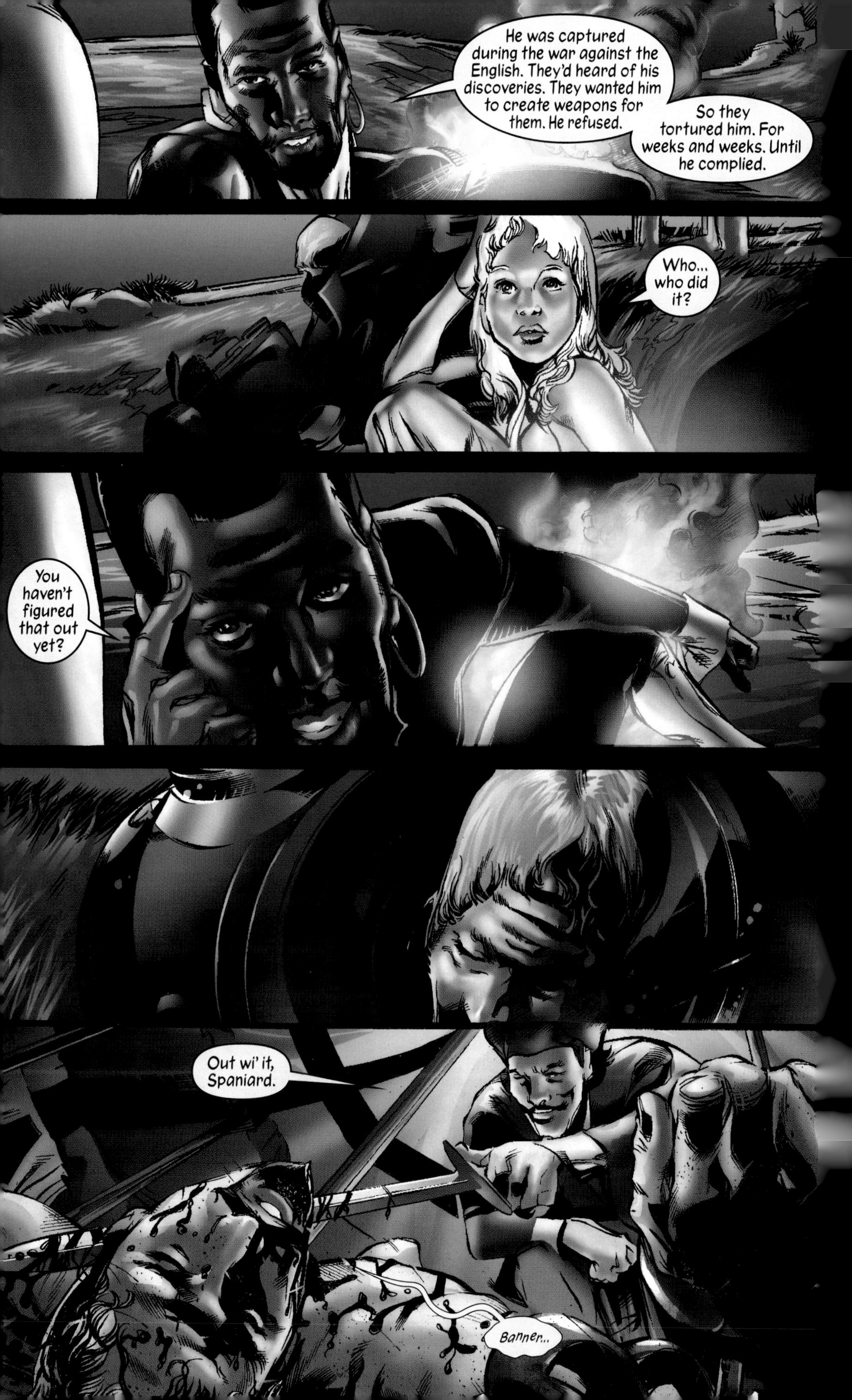
He was captured during the war against the English. They'd heard of his discoveries. They wanted him to create weapons for them. He refused.
So they tortured him. For weeks and weeks. Until he complied.
Who... who did it?
You haven't figured that out yet?
Out wi' it, Spaniard.
Banner...

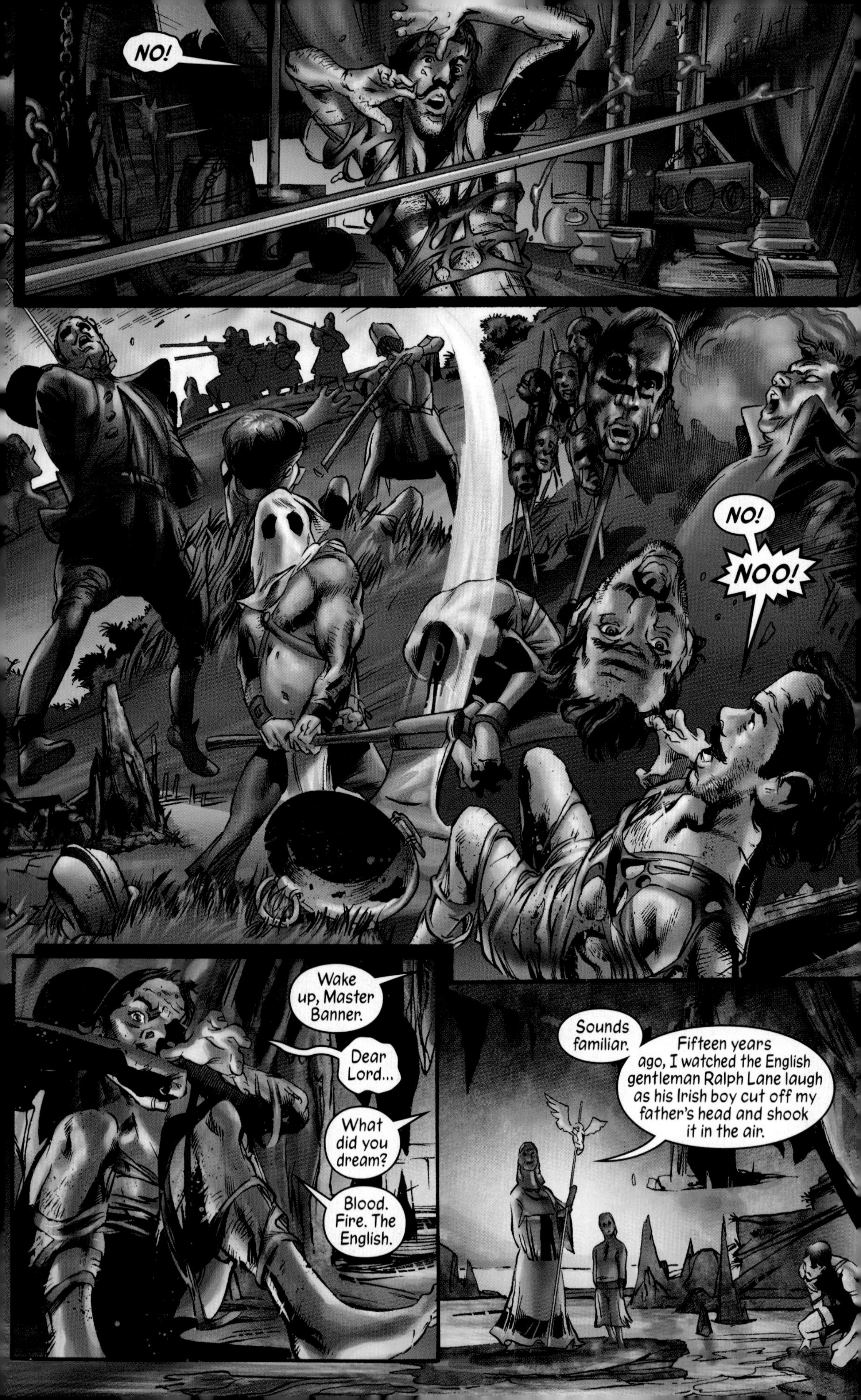
NO!
NO!
NOO!
Wake up, Master Banner.
Dear Lord...
What did you dream?
Blood. Fire. The English.
Sounds familiar.
Fifteen years ago, I watched the English gentleman Ralph Lane laugh as his Irish boy cut off my father's head and shook it in the air.

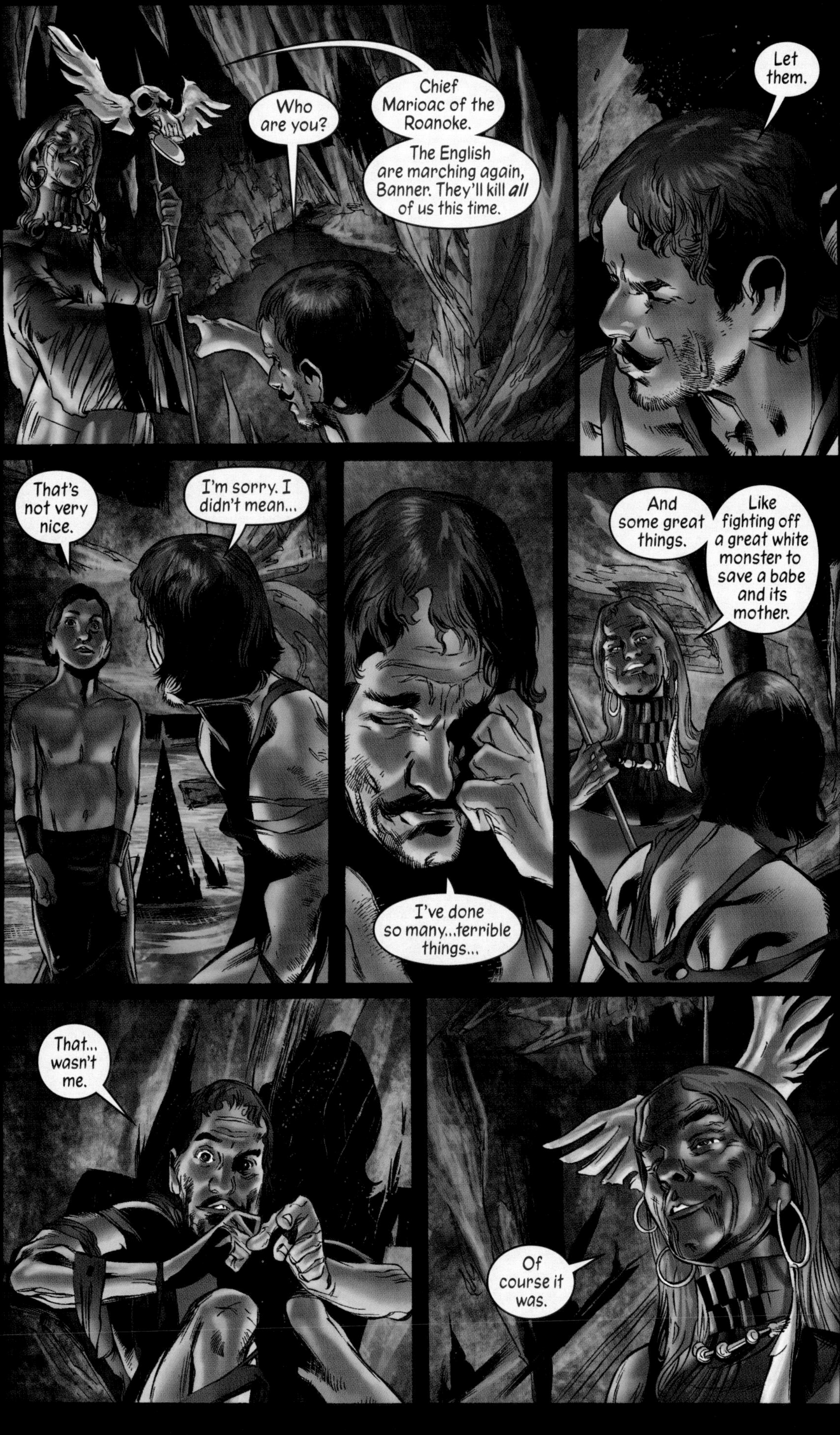
Who are you?
Chief Marioac of the Roanoke.
The English are marching again, Banner. They'll kill *all* of us this time.
Let them.
That's not very nice.
I'm sorry. I didn't mean...
I've done so many...terrible things...
And some great things.
Like fighting off a great white monster to save a babe and its mother.
That... wasn't me.
Of course it was.

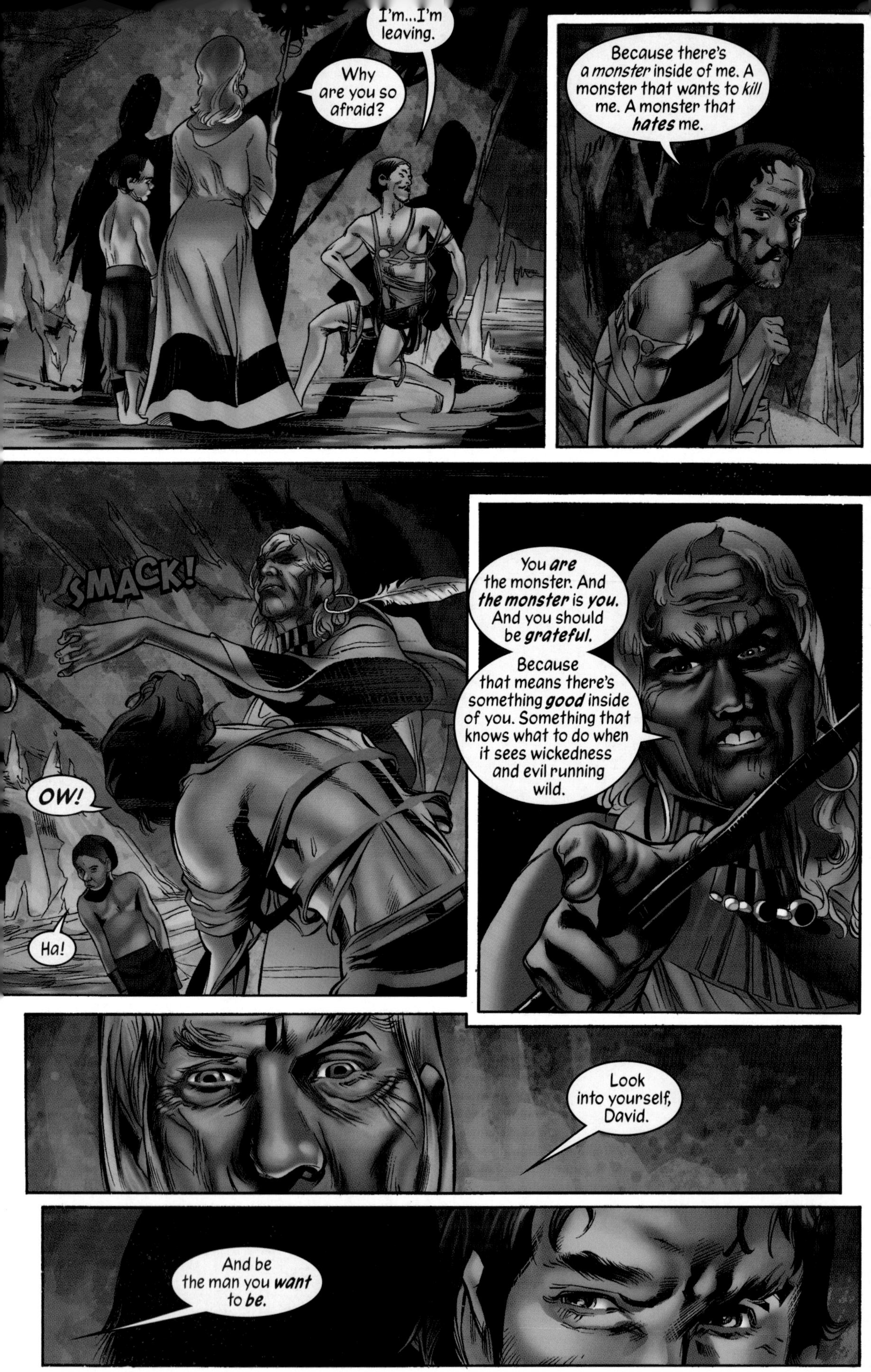

Why are you so afraid?
I'm...I'm leaving.
Because there's a *monster* inside of me. A monster that wants to *kill* me. A monster that ***hates*** me.
SMACK!
OW!
Ha!
You ***are*** the monster. And ***the monster*** is ***you.*** And you should be ***grateful.***
Because that means there's something ***good*** inside of you. Something that knows what to do when it sees wickedness and evil running wild.
Look into yourself, David.
And be the man you ***want*** to ***be.***

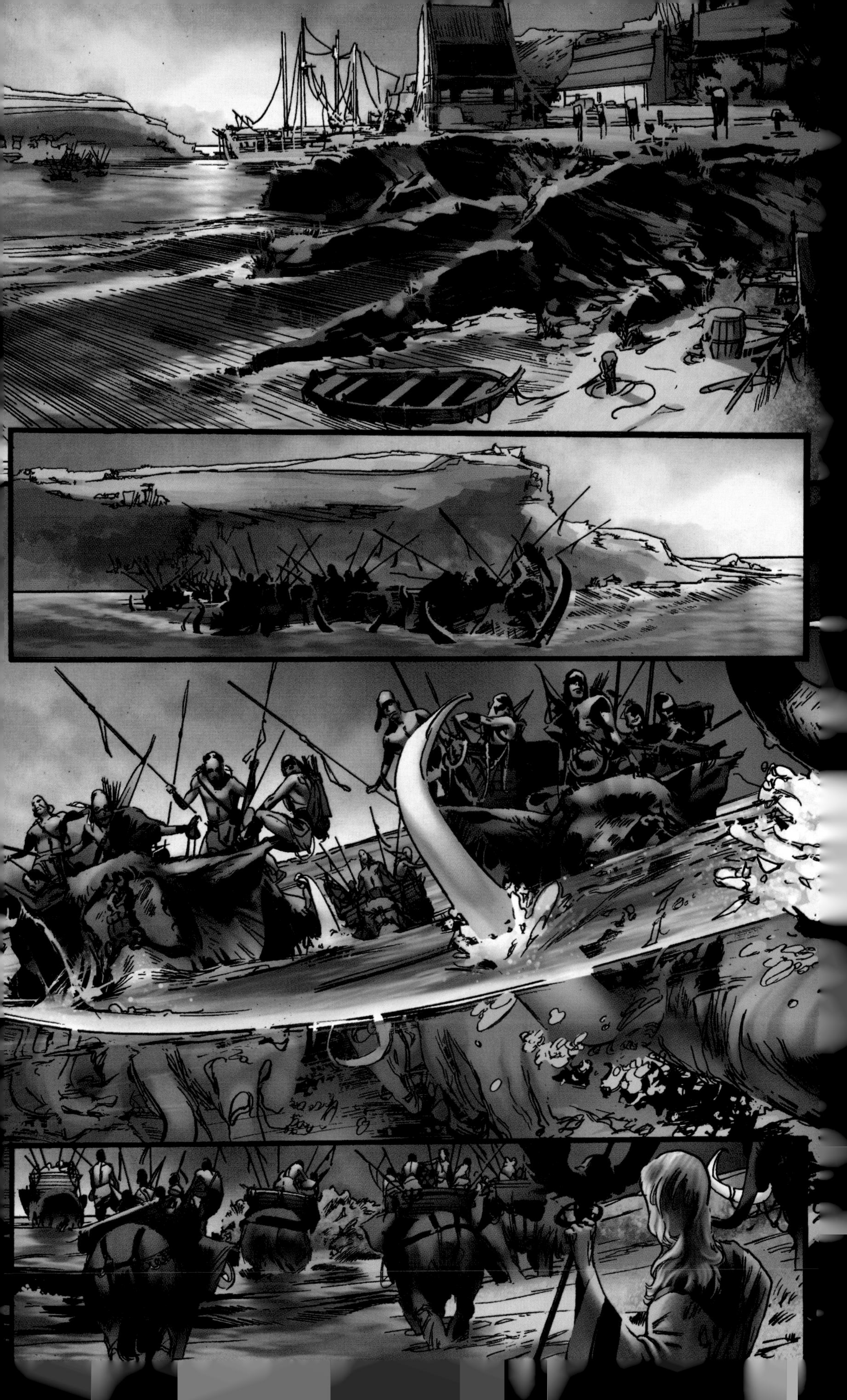

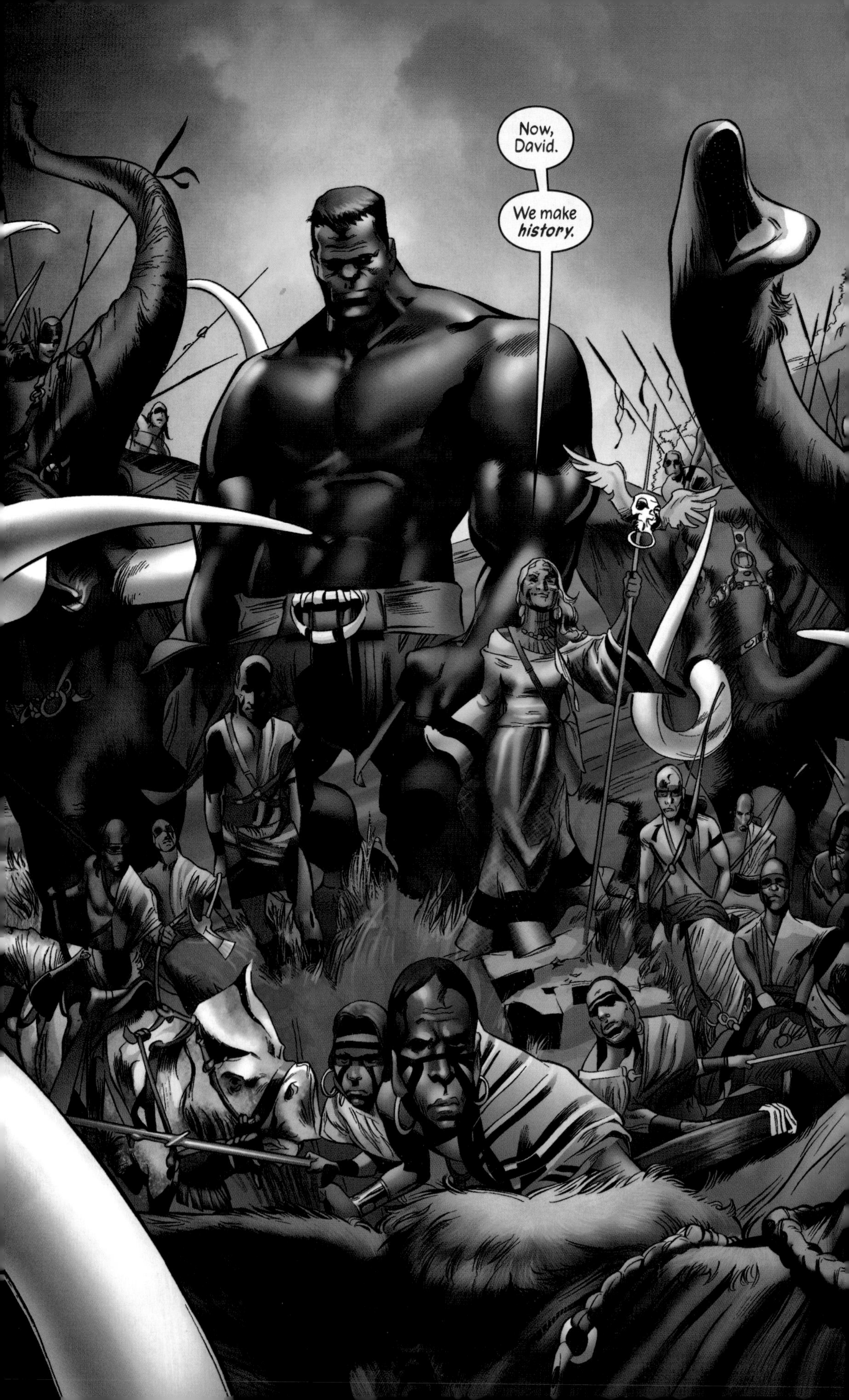
Now, David.
We make *history*.

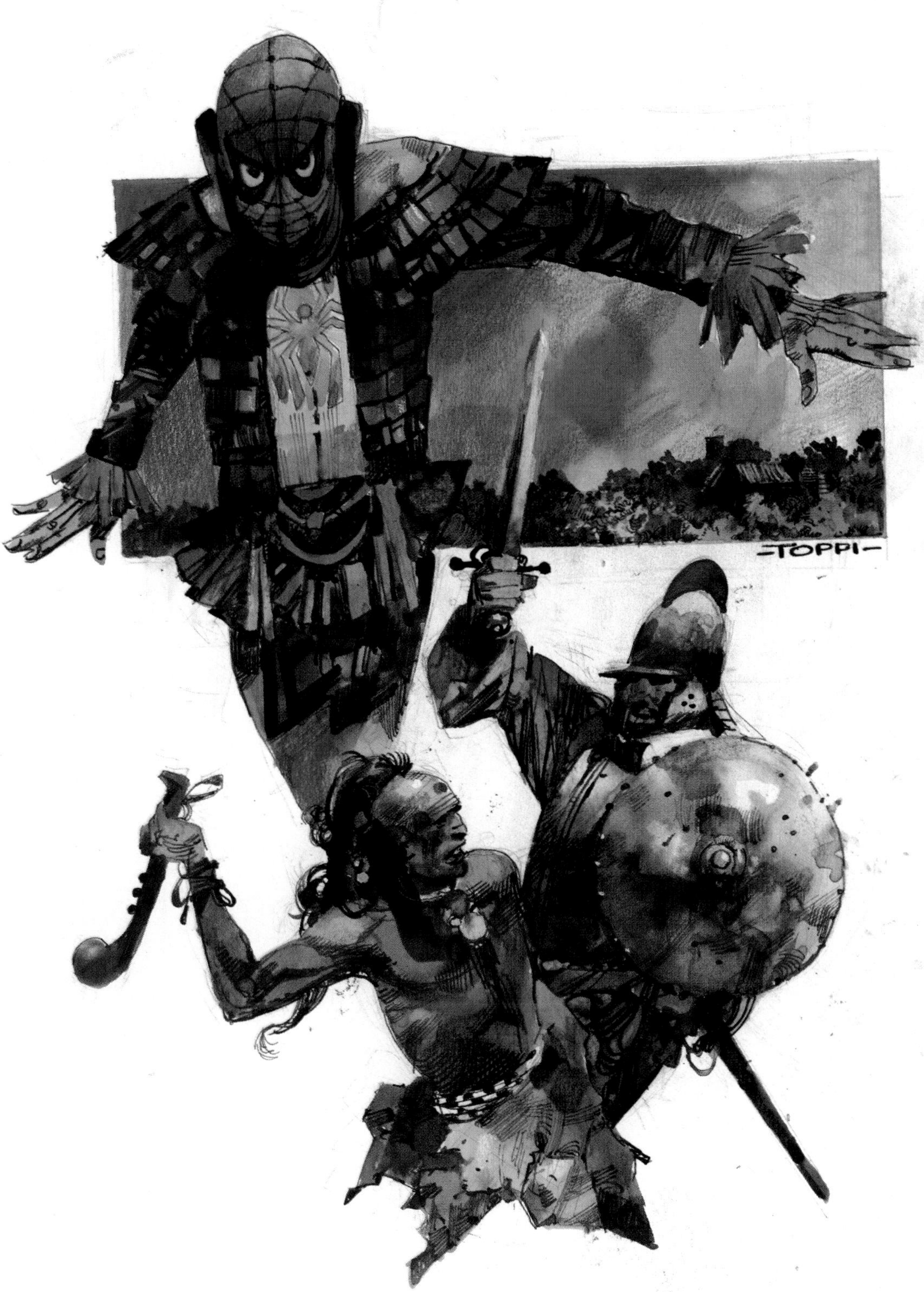
-TOPPI-

#5

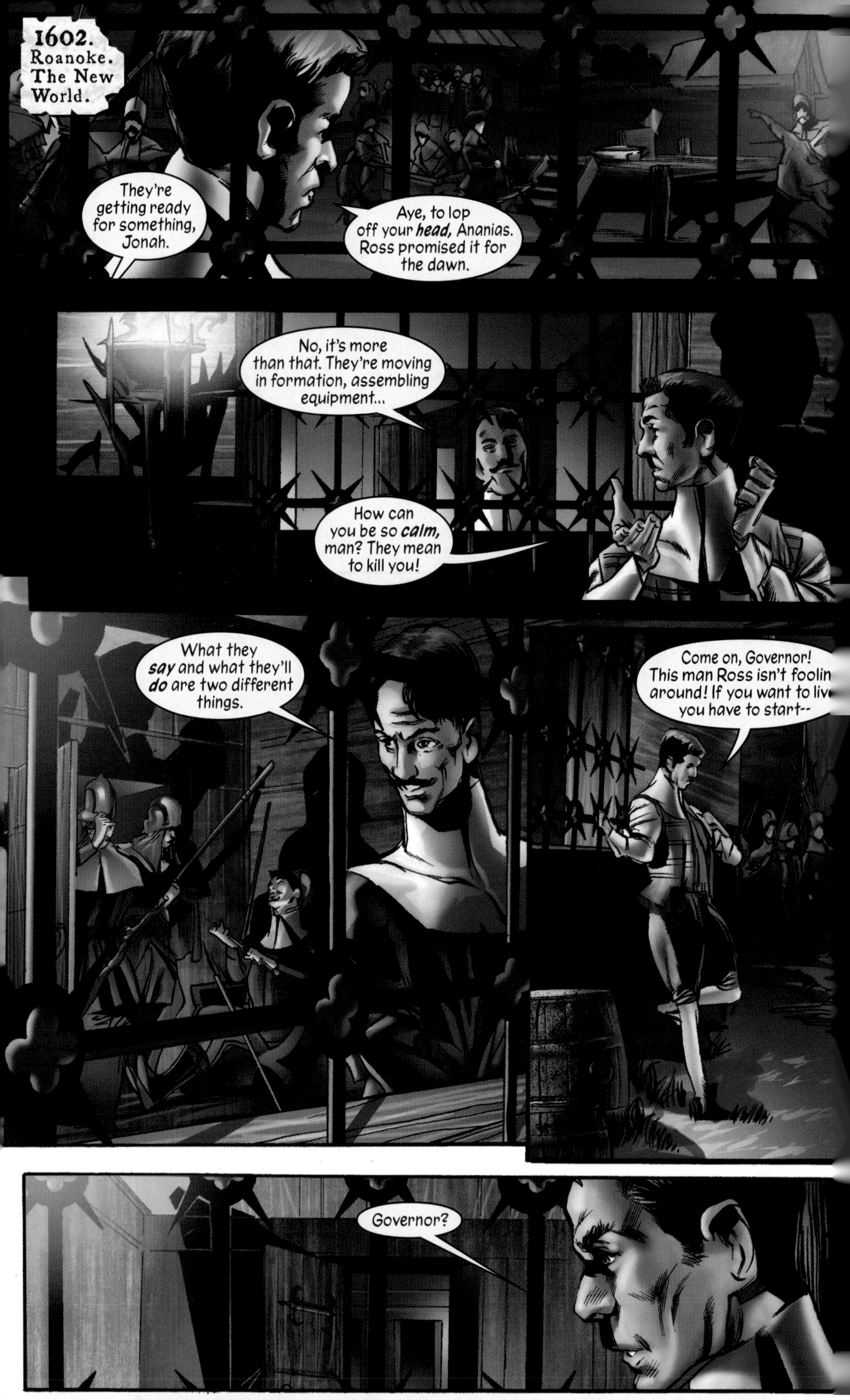

1602. Roanoke. The New World.
They're getting ready for something, Jonah.
Aye, to lop off your *head,* Ananias. Ross promised it for the dawn.
No, it's more than that. They're moving in formation, assembling equipment...
How can you be so *calm,* man? They mean to kill you!
What they *say* and what they'll *do* are two different things.
Come on, Governor! This man Ross isn't foolin around! If you want to liv you have to start--
Governor?

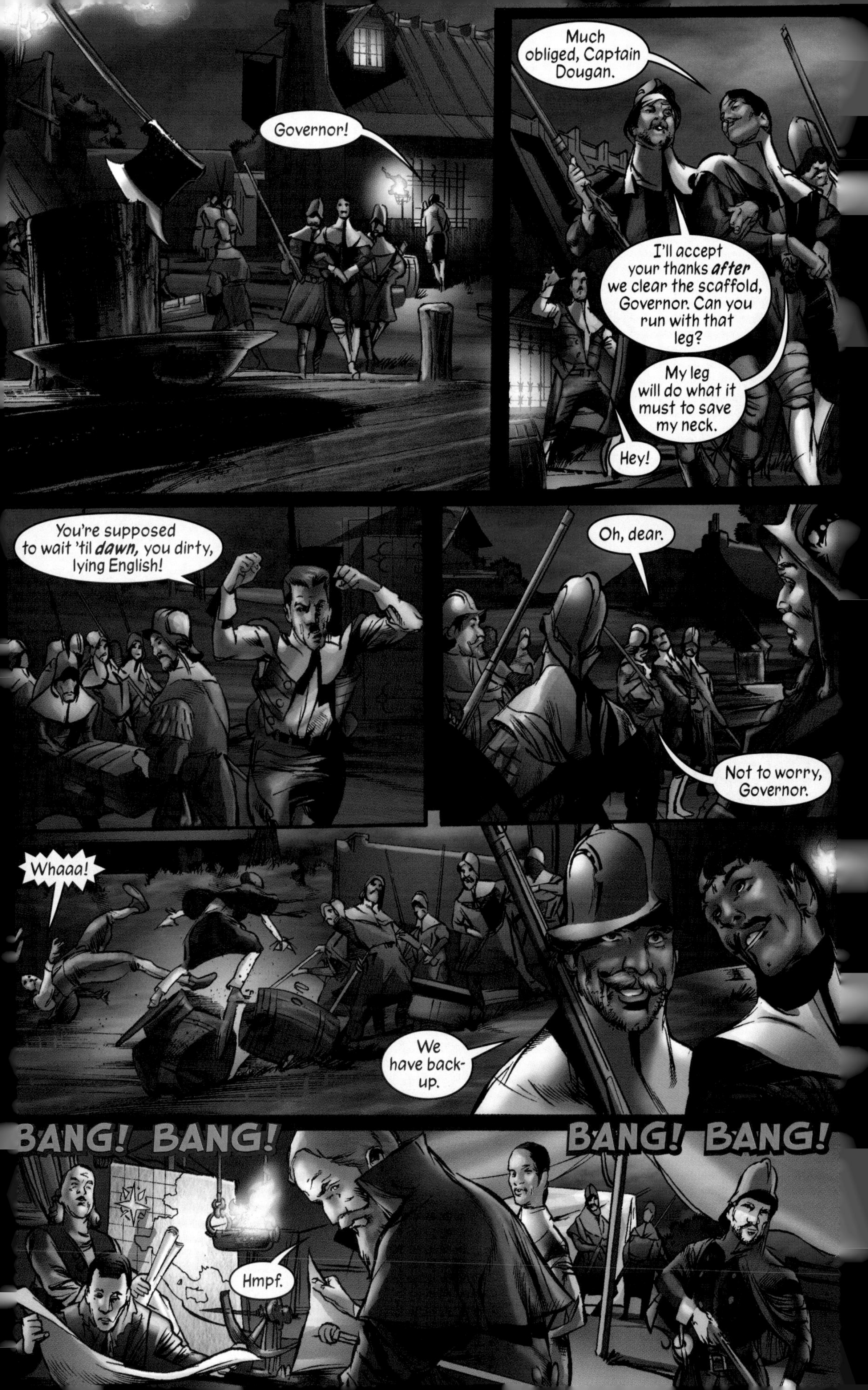
Governor!
Much obliged, Captain Dougan.
I'll accept your thanks *after* we clear the scaffold, Governor. Can you run with that leg?
My leg will do what it must to save my neck.
Hey!
You're supposed to wait 'til *dawn,* you dirty, lying English!
Oh, dear.
Not to worry, Governor.
Whaaa!
We have back-up.
BANG! BANG!
BANG! BANG!
Hmpf.

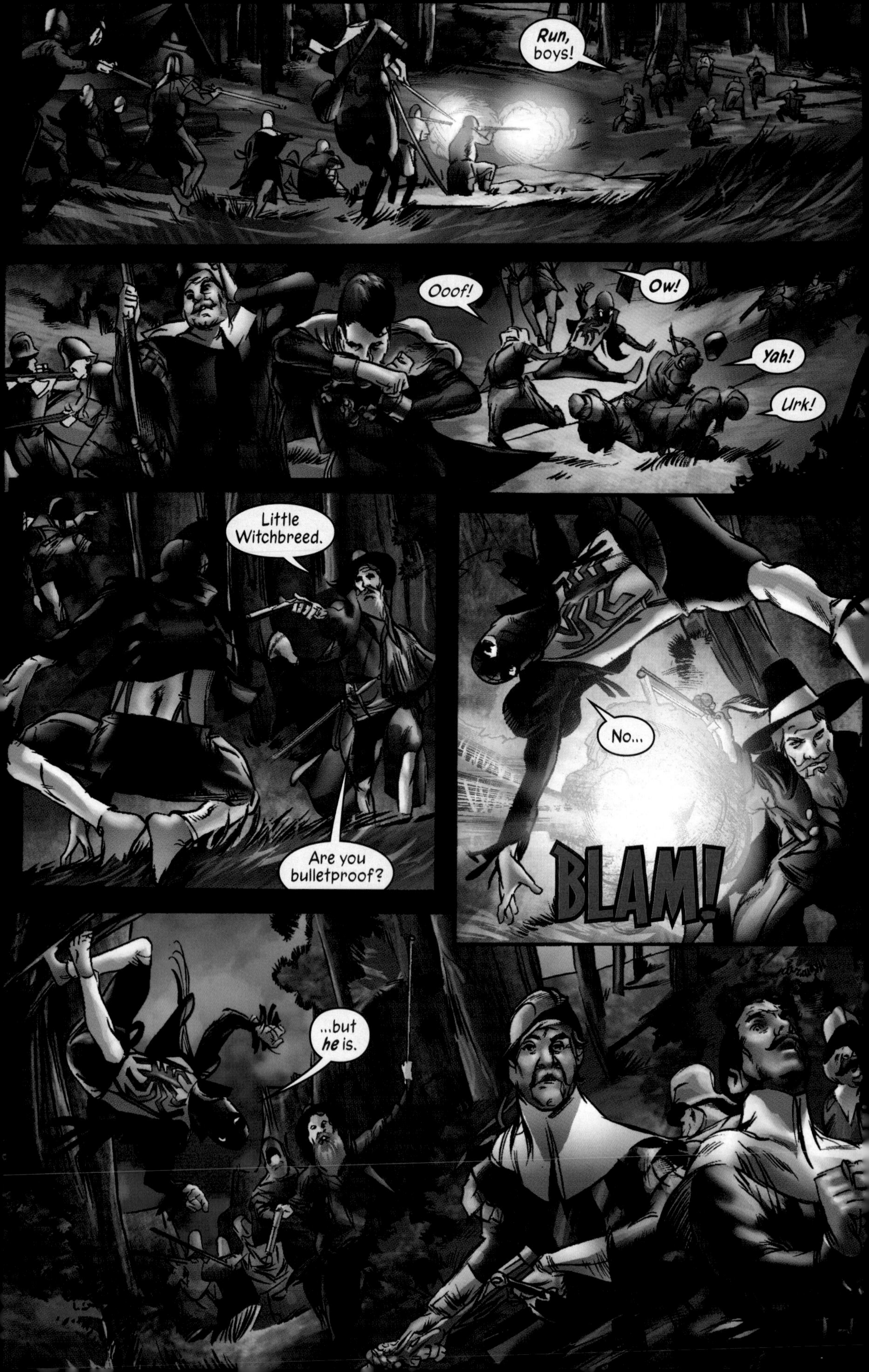
Run, boys!
Ooof!
Ow!
Yah!
Urk!
Little Witchbreed.
Are you bulletproof?
No...
BLAM!
...but he is.

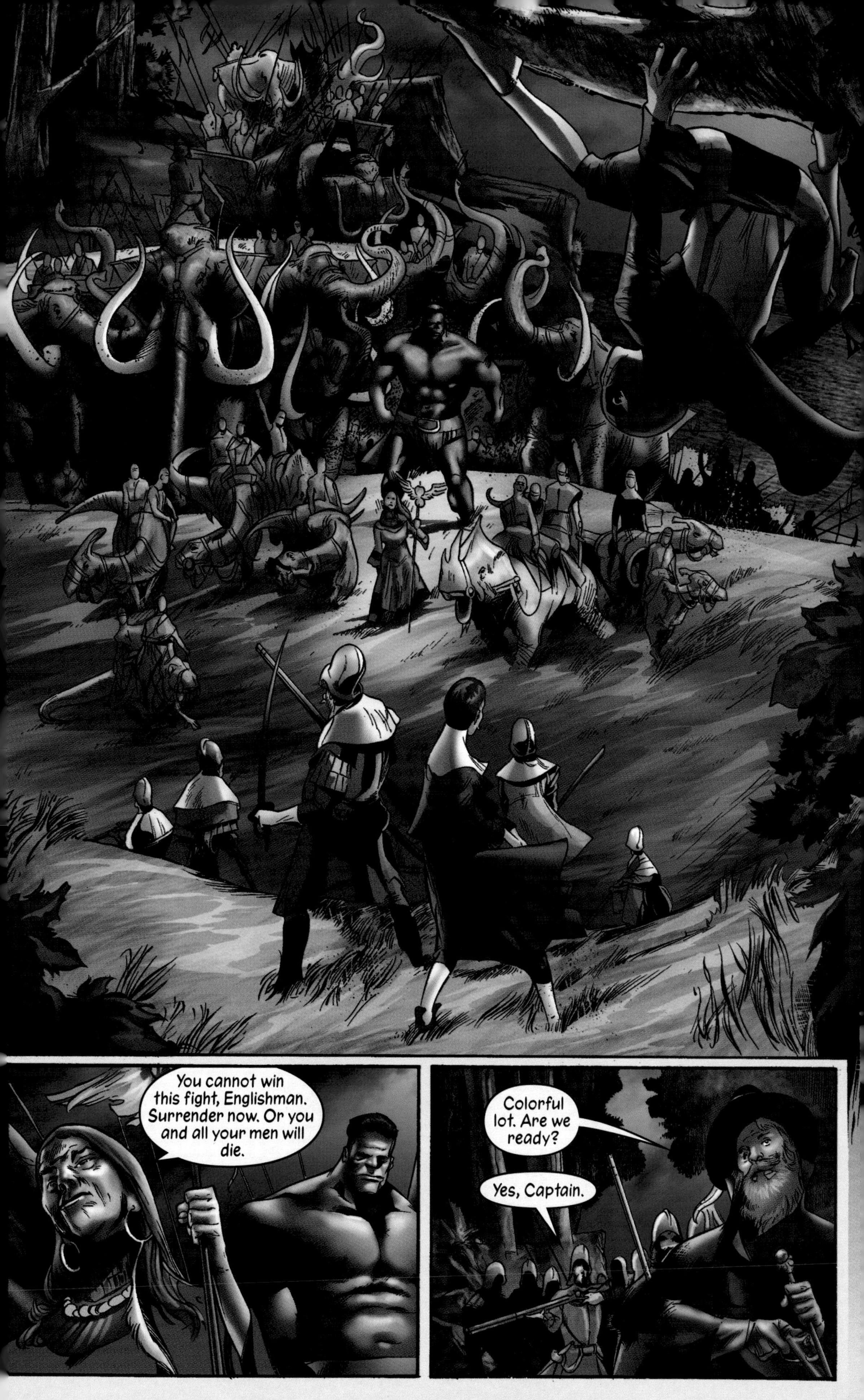
You cannot win this fight, Englishman. Surrender now. Or you and all your men will die.
Colorful lot. Are we ready?
Yes, Captain.

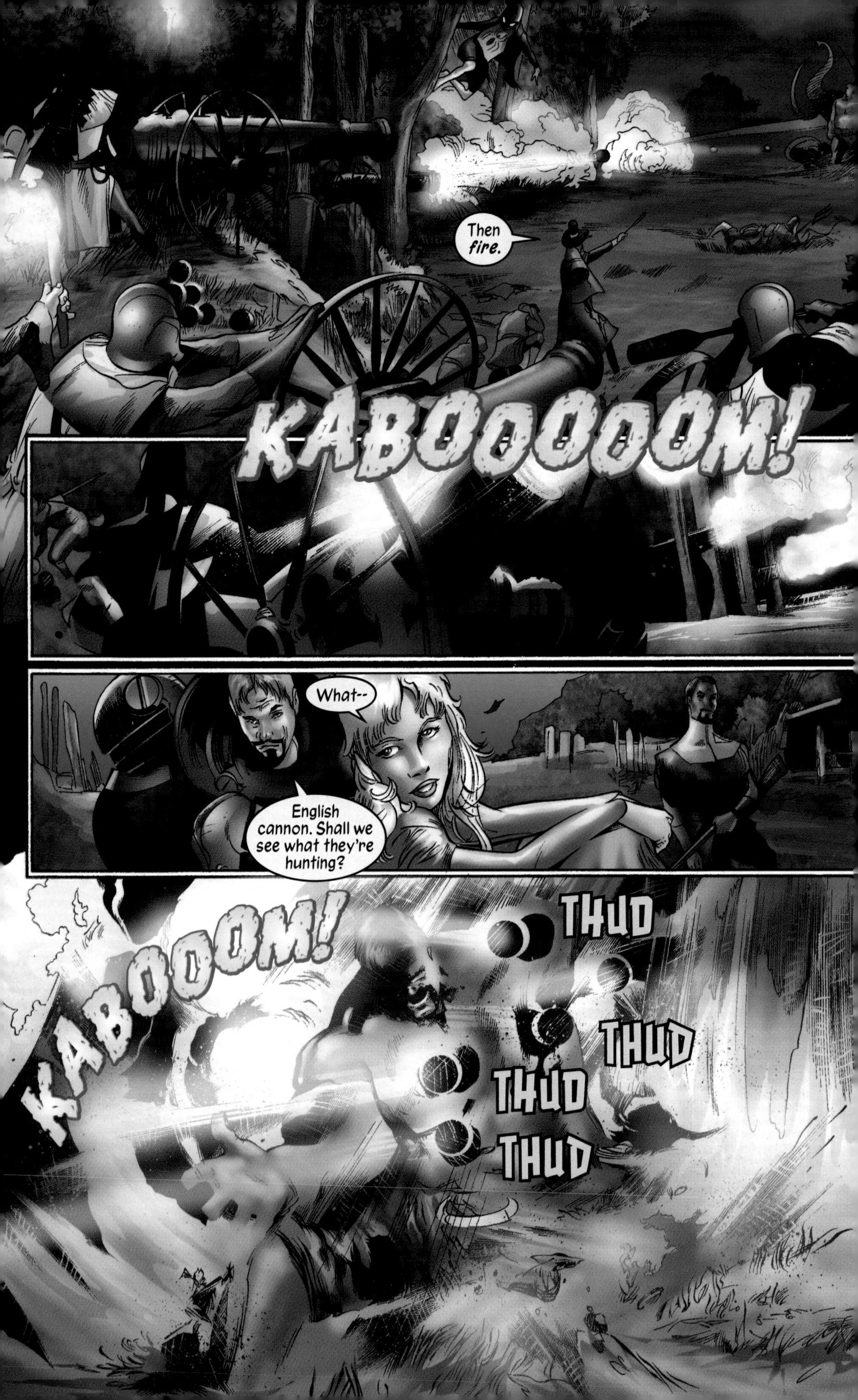

Then fire.
KABOOOOOOM!
What--
English cannon. Shall we see what they're hunting?
KABOOOM!
THUD
THUD
THUD
THUD

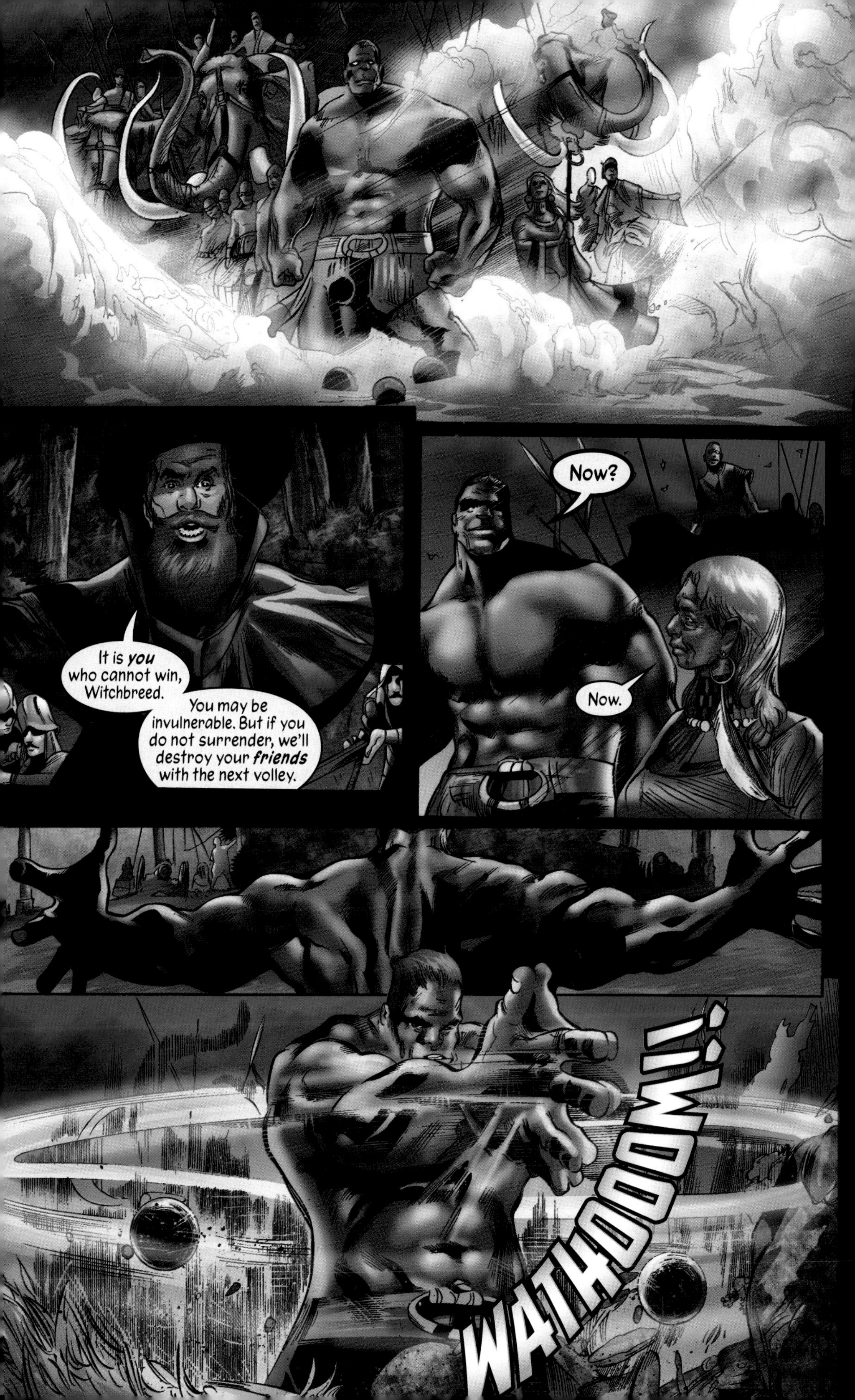
It is *you* who cannot win, Witchbreed.
You may be invulnerable. But if you do not surrender, we'll destroy your *friends* with the next volley.
Now?
Now.
WATHOOOM!!

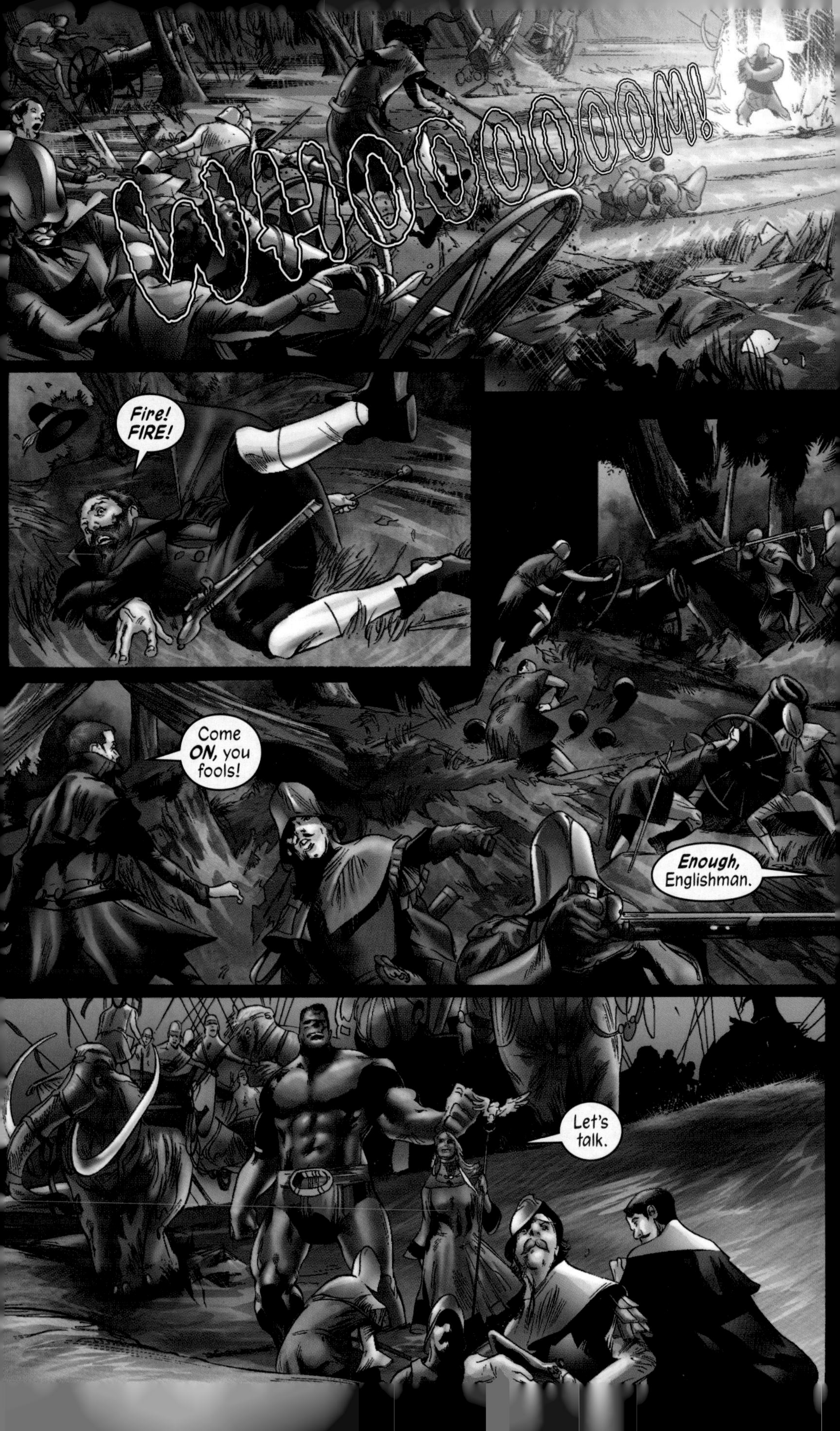
WHOOOOOOOOM!
Fire! FIRE!
Come ON, you fools!
Enough, Englishman.
Let's talk.

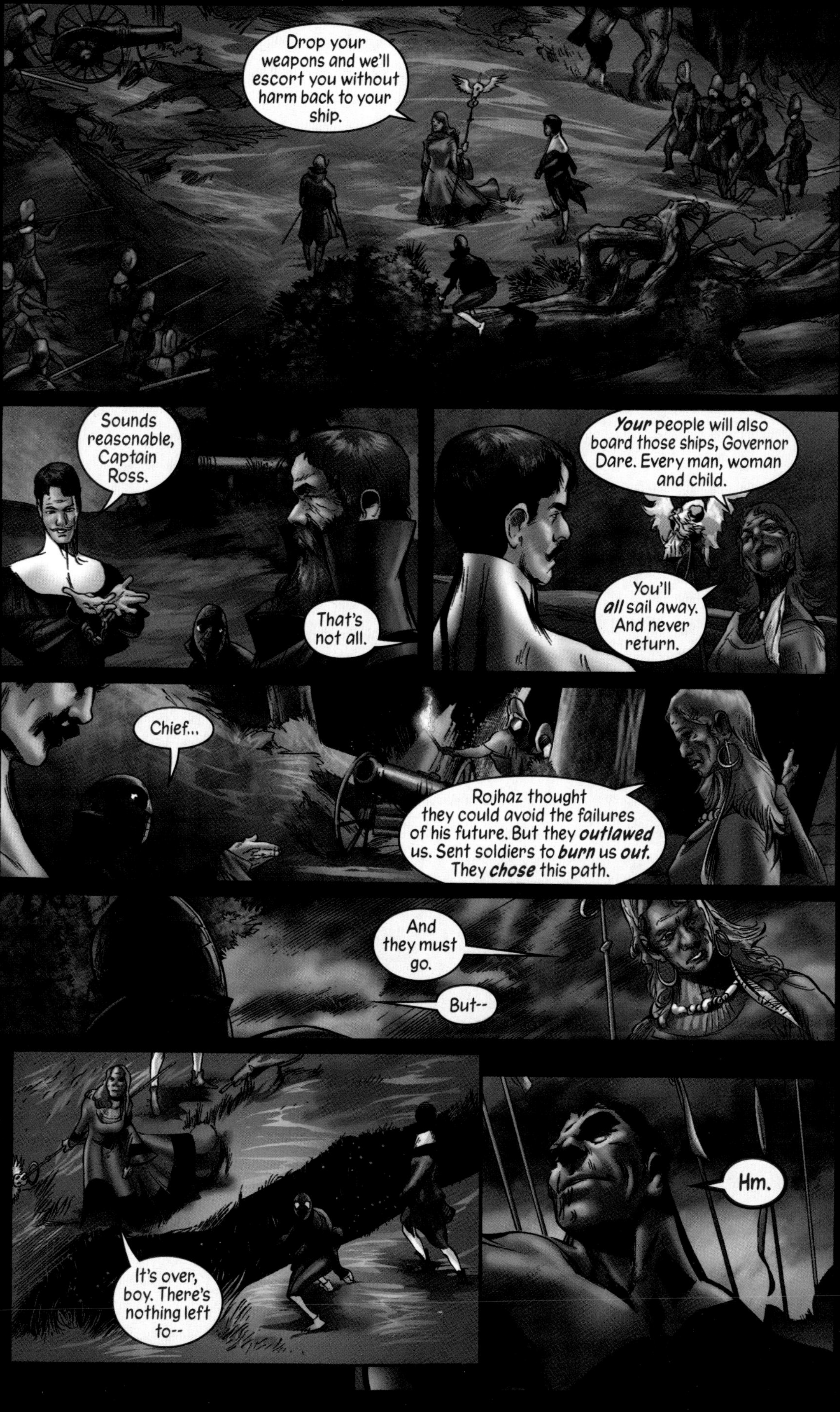
Drop your weapons and we'll escort you without harm back to your ship.
Sounds reasonable, Captain Ross.
That's not all.
Your people will also board those ships, Governor Dare. Every man, woman and child.
You'll all sail away. And never return.
Chief...
Rojhaz thought they could avoid the failures of his future. But they outlawed us. Sent soldiers to burn us out. They chose this path.
And they must go.
But--
It's over, boy. There's nothing left to--
Hm.

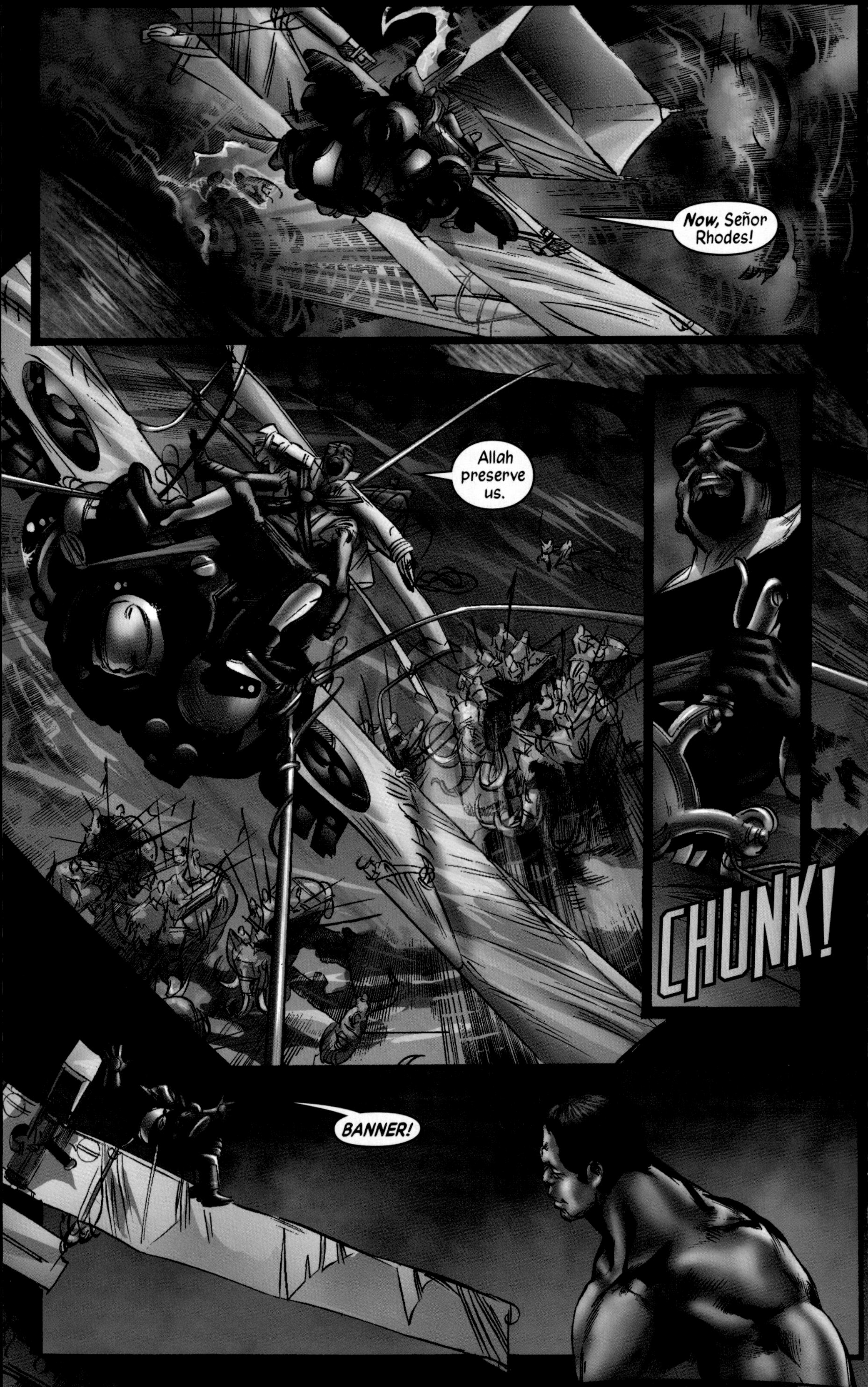
Now, Señor Rhodes!
Allah preserve us.
CHUNK!
BANNER!

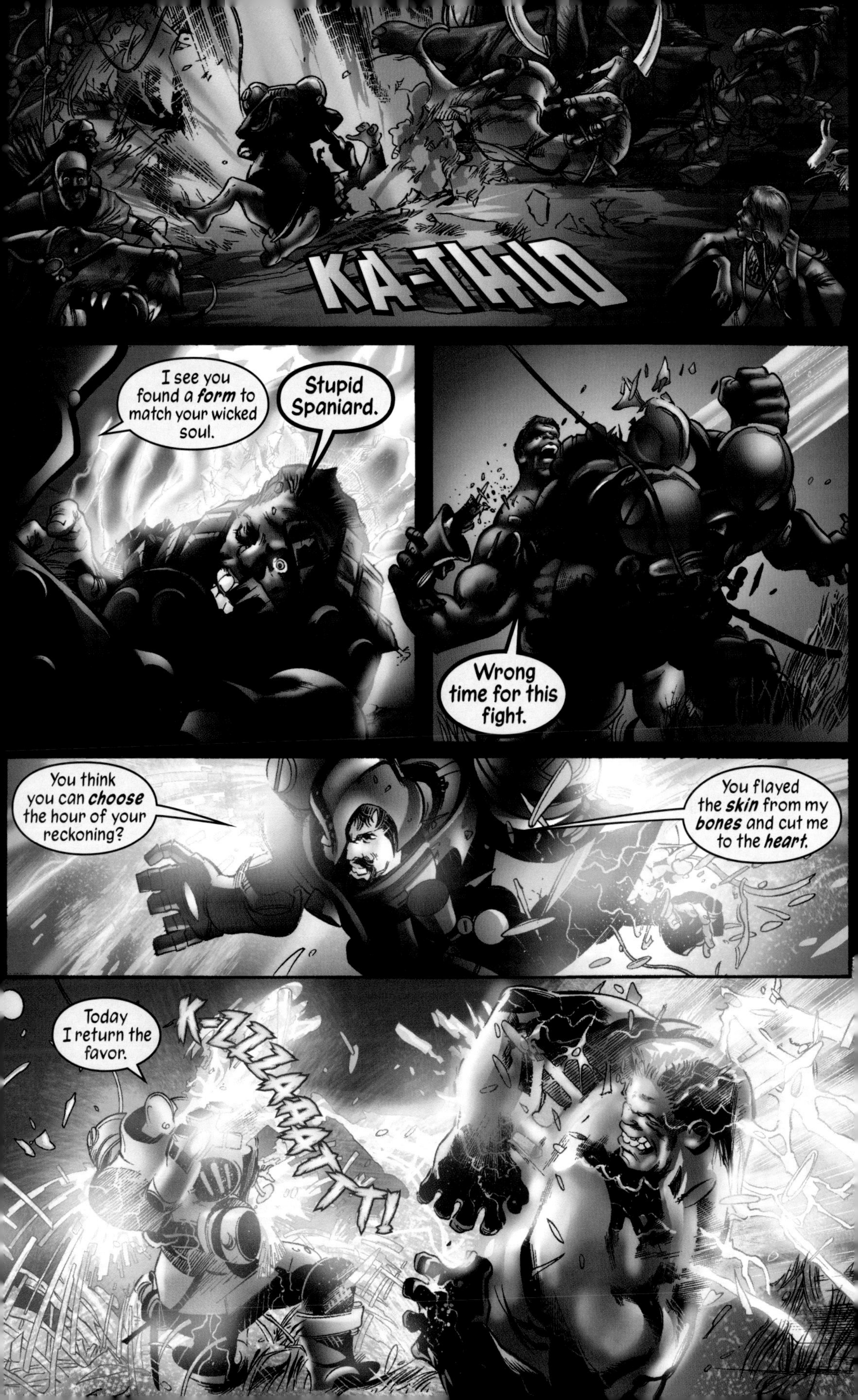
KA-THUD
I see you found a form to match your wicked soul.
Stupid Spaniard.
Wrong time for this fight.
You think you can choose the hour of your reckoning?
You flayed the skin from my bones and cut me to the heart.
Today I return the favor.
K-ZZZZAAAATT!!

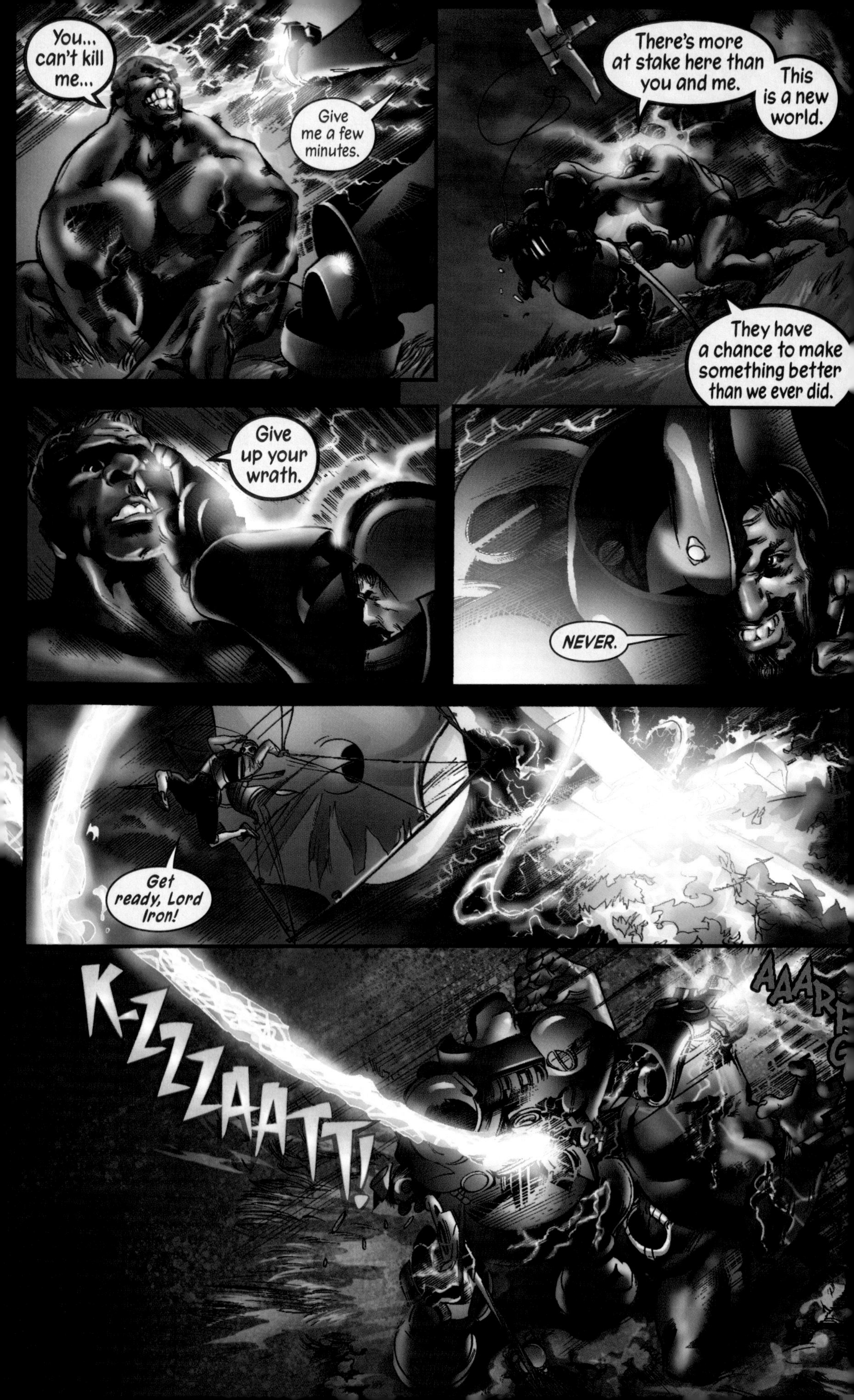
You... can't kill me...
Give me a few minutes.
There's more at stake here than you and me.
This is a new world.
They have a chance to make something better than we ever did.
Give up your wrath.
NEVER.
Get ready, Lord Iron!
K-ZZZAATT!
AAARG

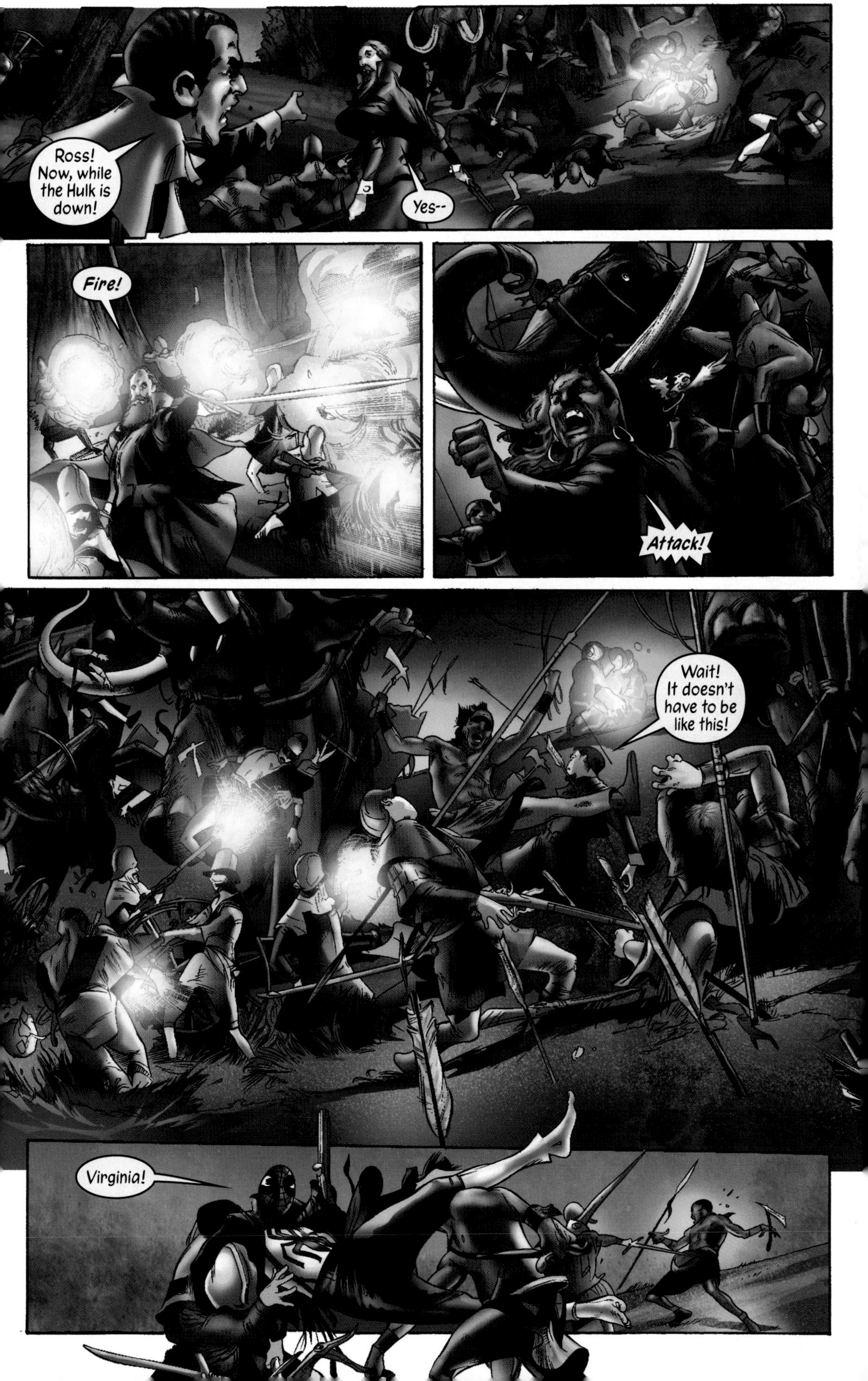
Ross! Now, while the Hulk is down!
Yes--
Fire!
Attack!
Wait! It doesn't have to be like this!
Virginia!

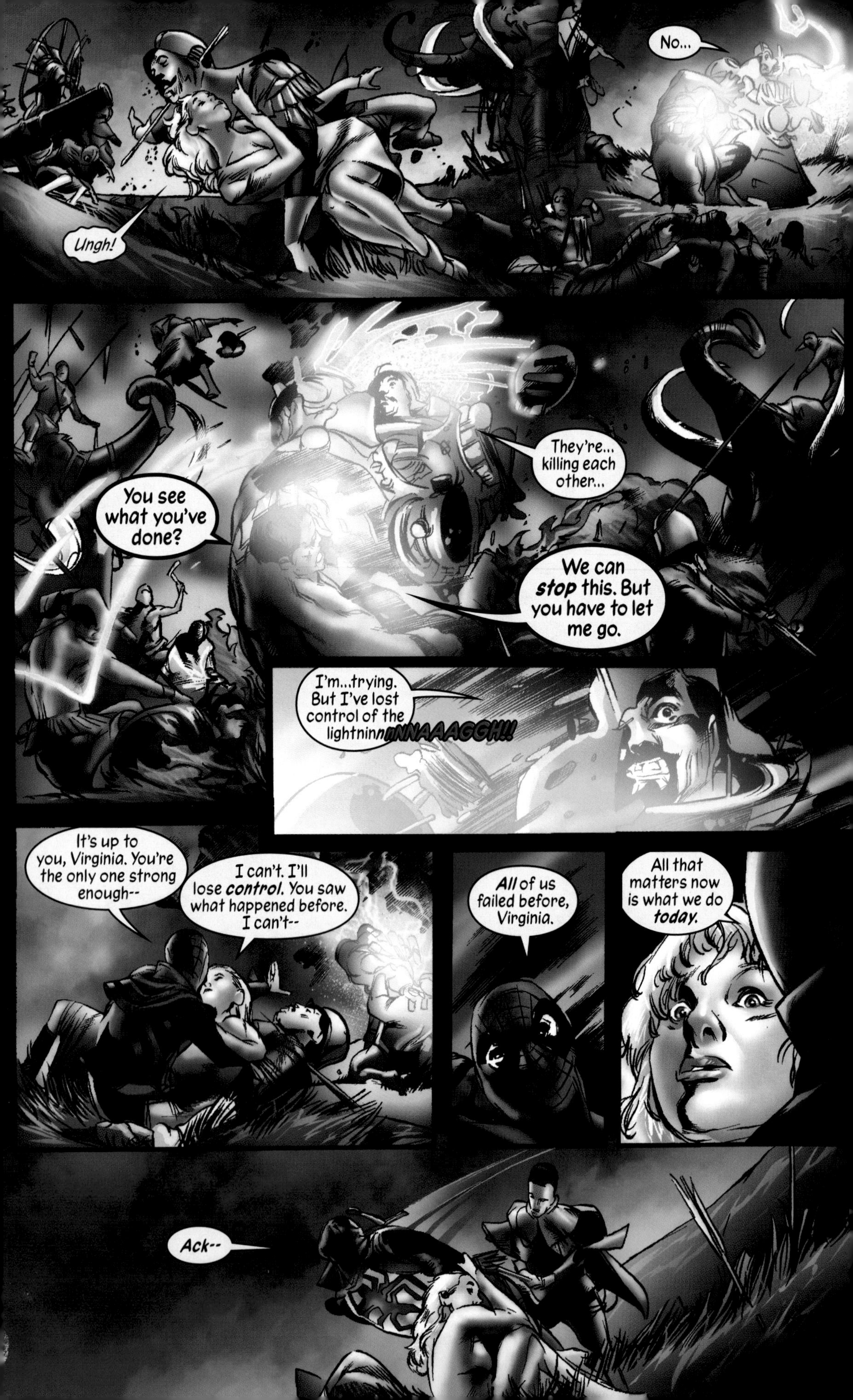
Ungh!
No...
They're... killing each other...
You see what you've done?
We can *stop* this. But you have to let me go.
I'm...trying. But I've lost control of the lightninnNNAAAAGGH!!
It's up to you, Virginia. You're the only one strong enough--
I can't. I'll lose *control*. You saw what happened before. I can't--
All of us failed before, Virginia.
All that matters now is what we do *today*.
Ack--

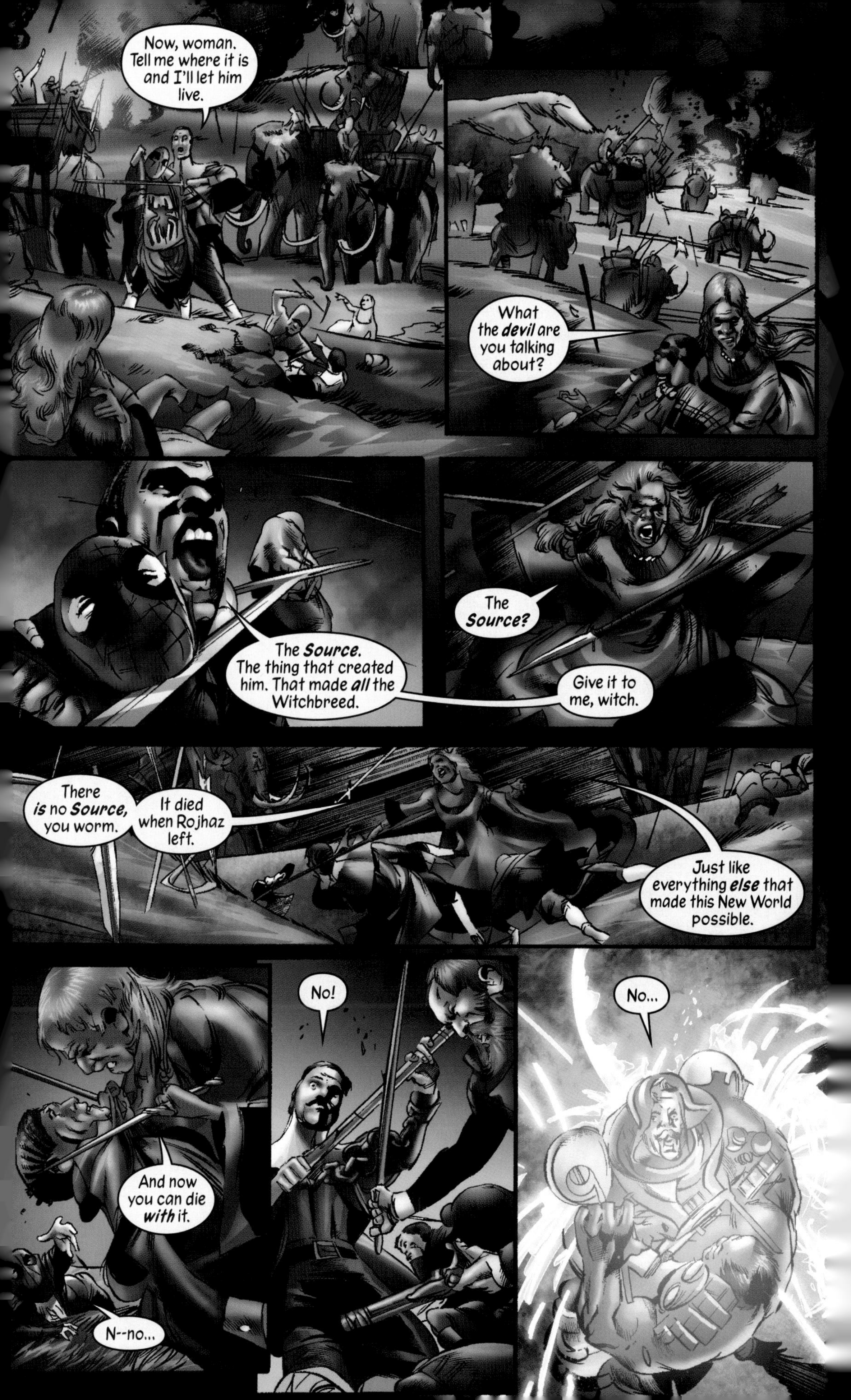
Now, woman. Tell me where it is and I'll let him live.
What the devil are you talking about?
The Source. The thing that created him. That made all the Witchbreed.
The Source?
Give it to me, witch.
There is no Source, you worm.
It died when Rojhaz left.
Just like everything else that made this New World possible.
And now you can die with it.
N--no...
No!
No...

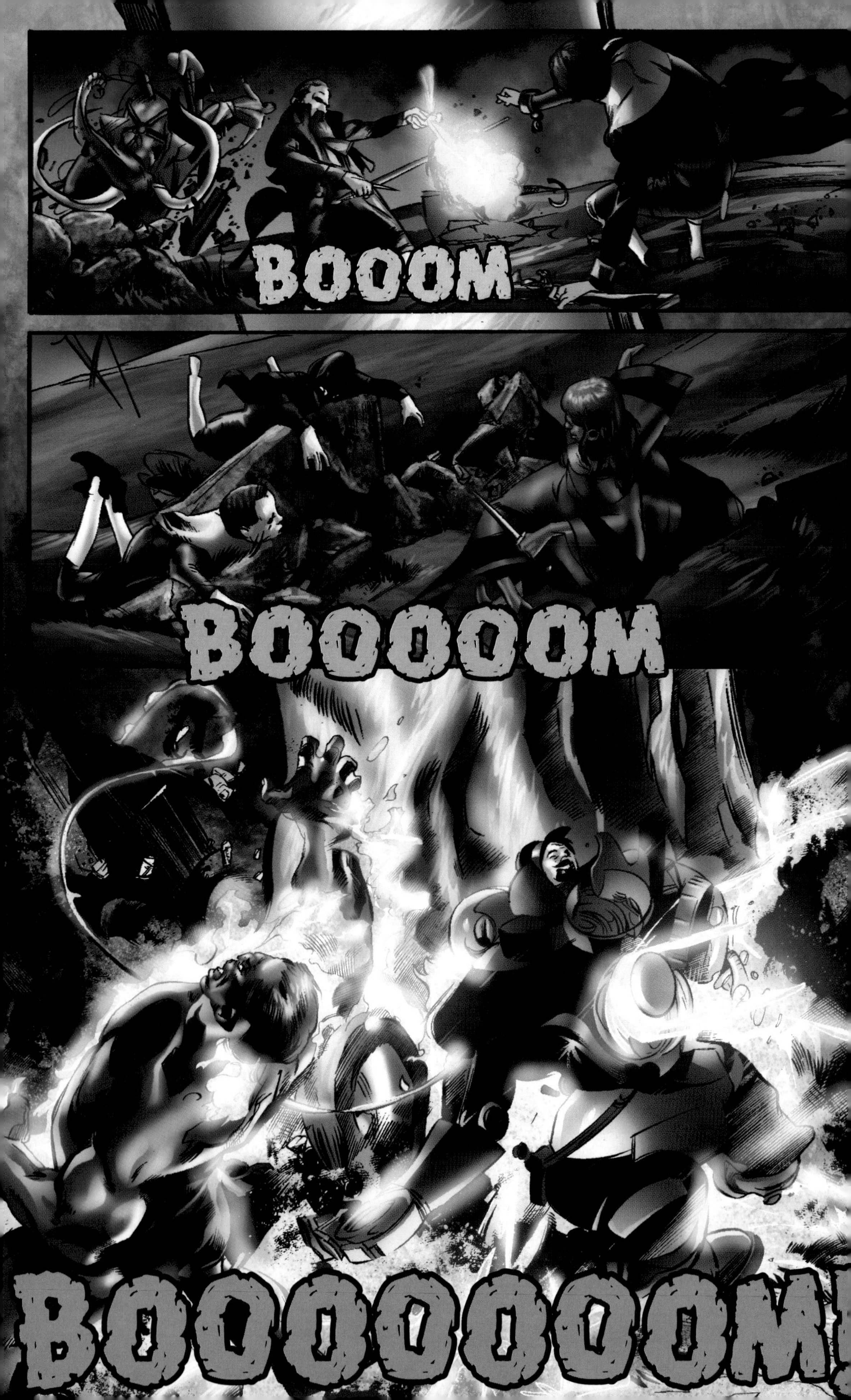
BOOOM
BOOOOOM
BOOOOOOOM!

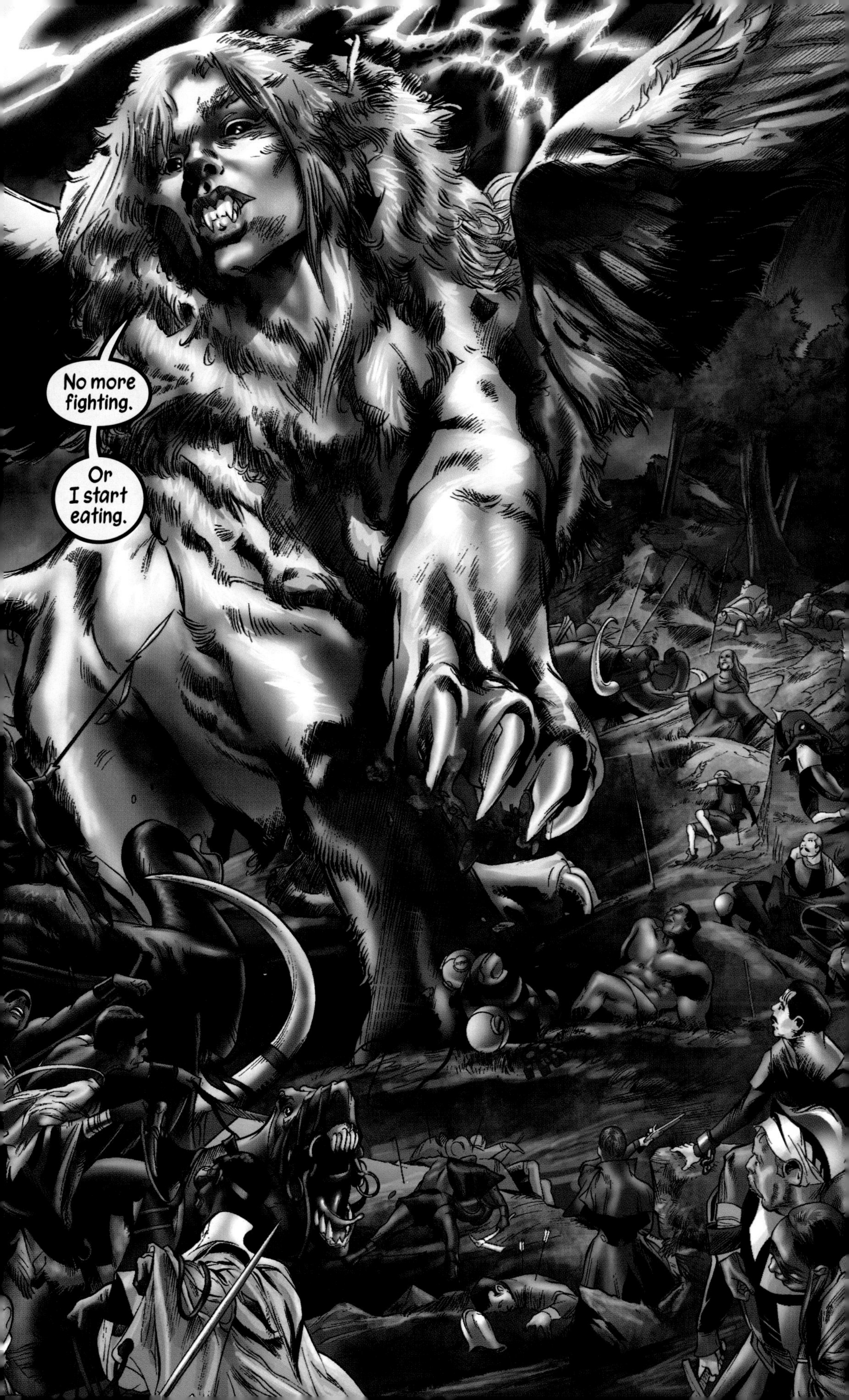
No more fighting.
Or I start eating.

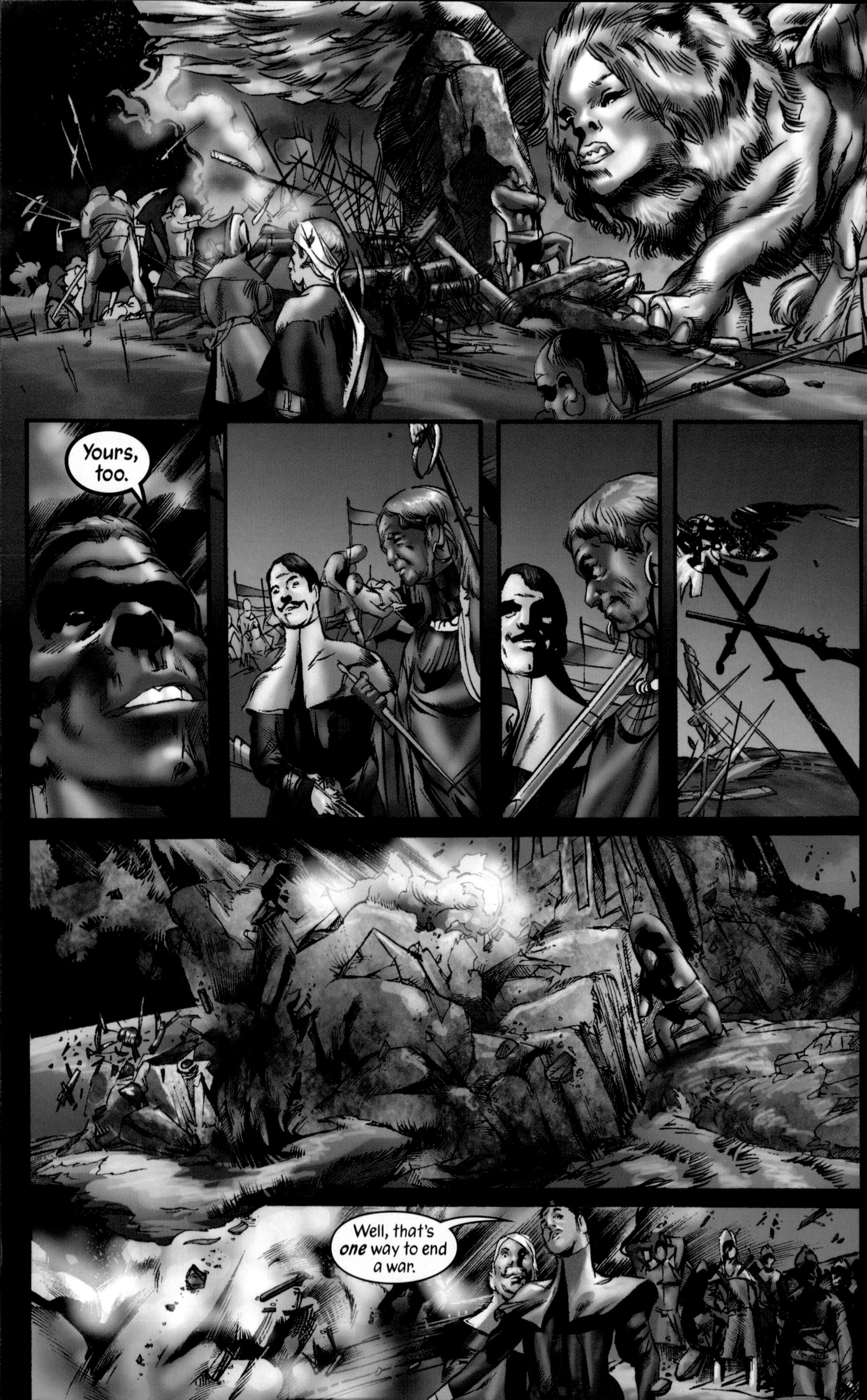
Yours, too.
Well, that's *one* way to end a war.

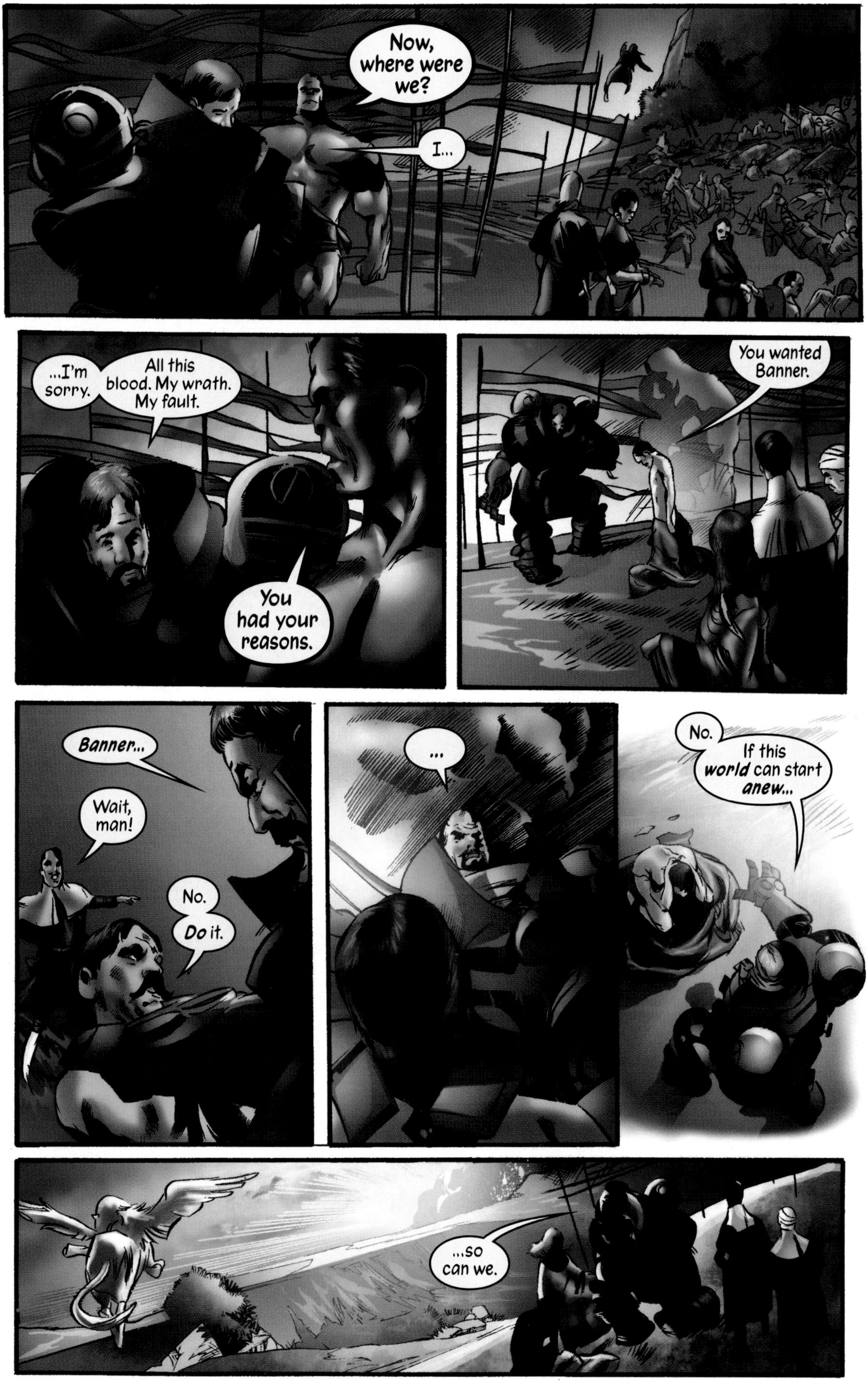
Now, where were we?
I...
...I'm sorry.
All this blood. My wrath. My fault.
You had your reasons.
You wanted Banner.
Banner...
Wait, man!
No.
Do it.
...
No.
If this world can start anew...
...so can we.

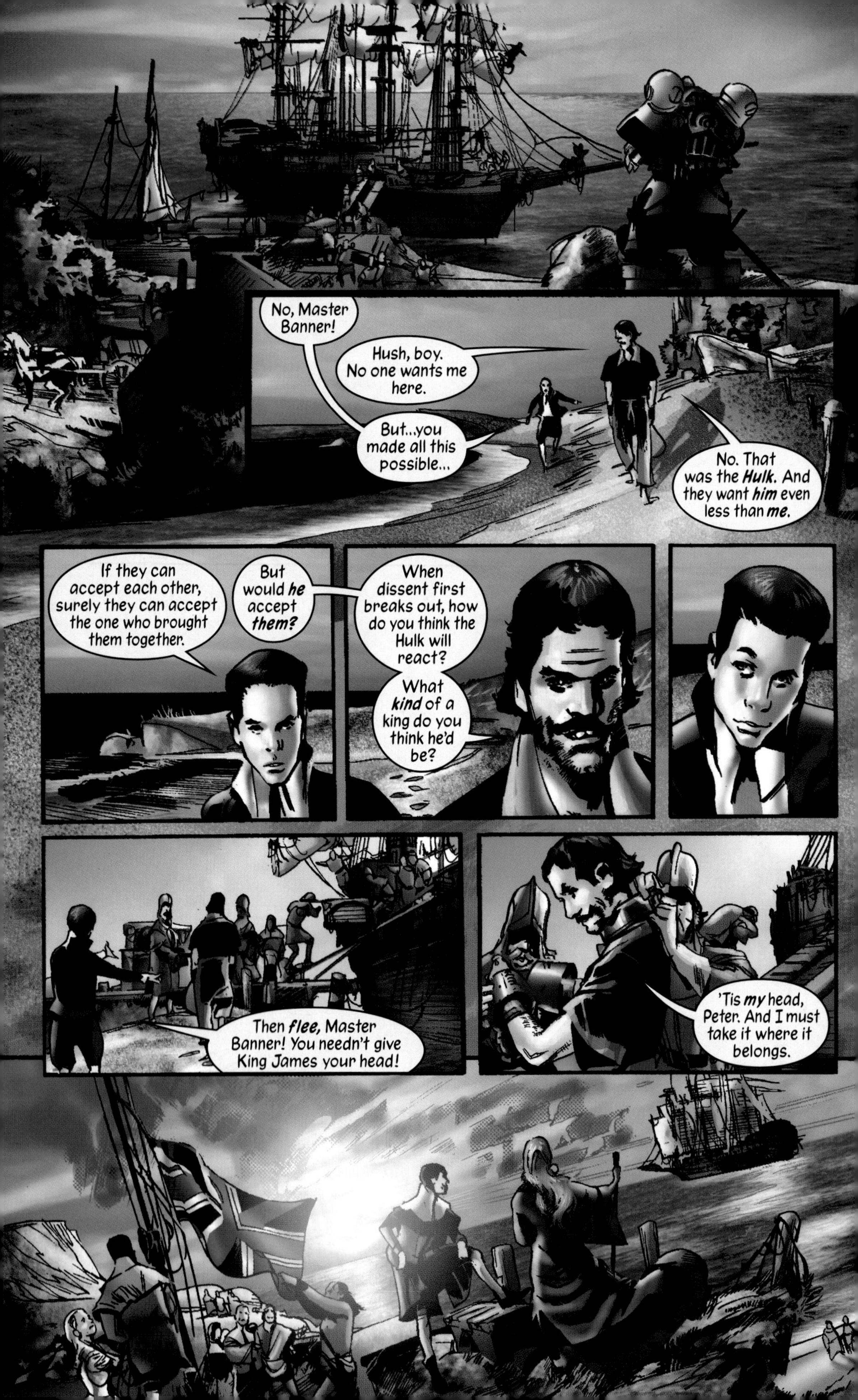
No, Master Banner!
Hush, boy. No one wants me here.
But...you made all this possible...
No. That was the Hulk. And they want him even less than me.
If they can accept each other, surely they can accept the one who brought them together.
But would he accept them?
When dissent first breaks out, how do you think the Hulk will react?
What kind of a king do you think he'd be?
Then flee, Master Banner! You needn't give King James your head!
'Tis my head, Peter. And I must take it where it belongs.

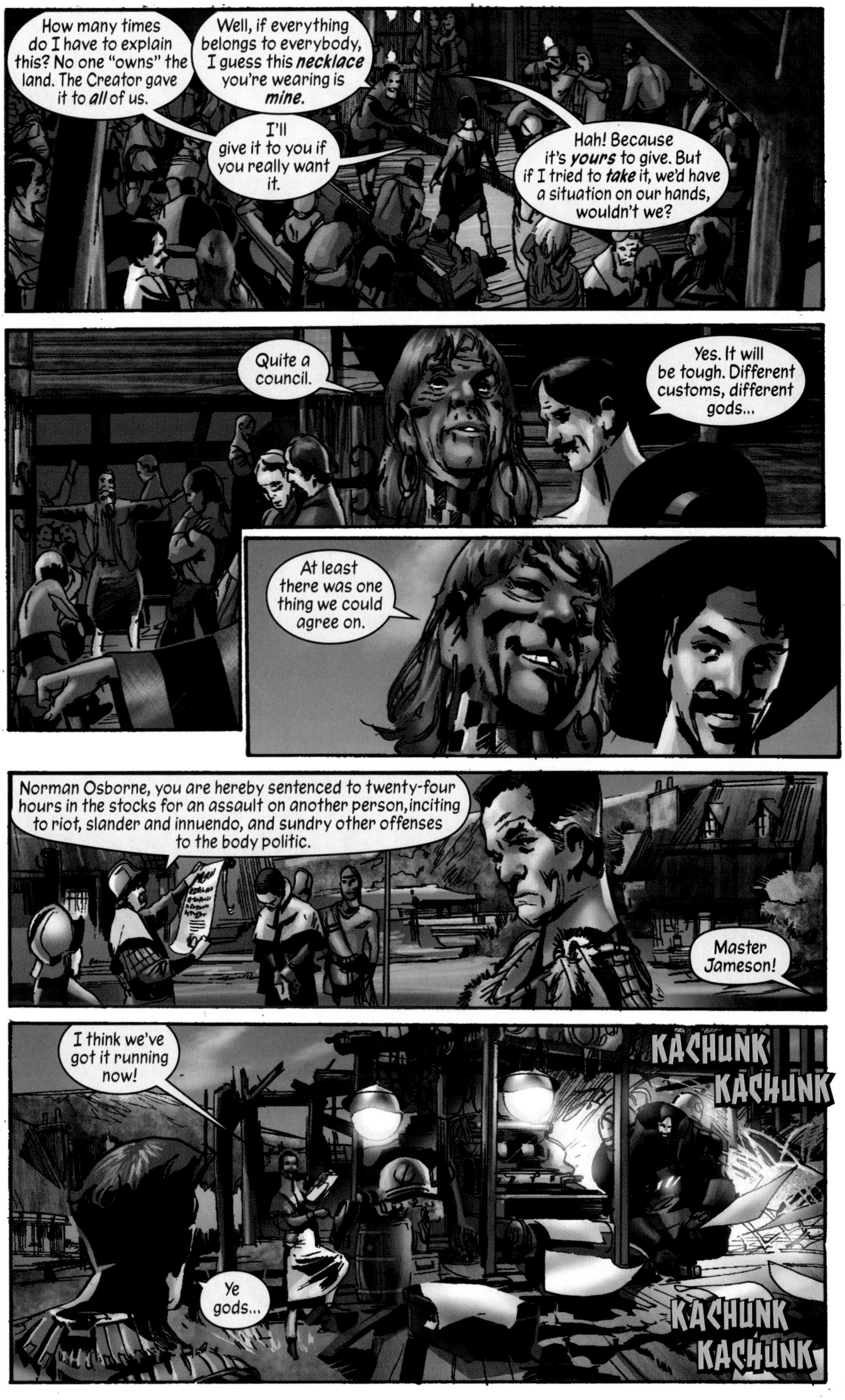
How many times do I have to explain this? No one "owns" the land. The Creator gave it to *all* of us.
Well, if everything belongs to everybody, I guess this ***necklace*** you're wearing is ***mine.***
I'll give it to you if you really want it.
Hah! Because it's ***yours*** to give. But if I tried to ***take*** it, we'd have a situation on our hands, wouldn't we?
Quite a council.
Yes. It will be tough. Different customs, different gods...
At least there was one thing we could agree on.
Norman Osborne, you are hereby sentenced to twenty-four hours in the stocks for an assault on another person, inciting to riot, slander and innuendo, and sundry other offenses to the body politic.
Master Jameson!
I think we've got it running now!
KACHUNK
KACHUNK
Ye gods...
KACHUNK
KACHUNK

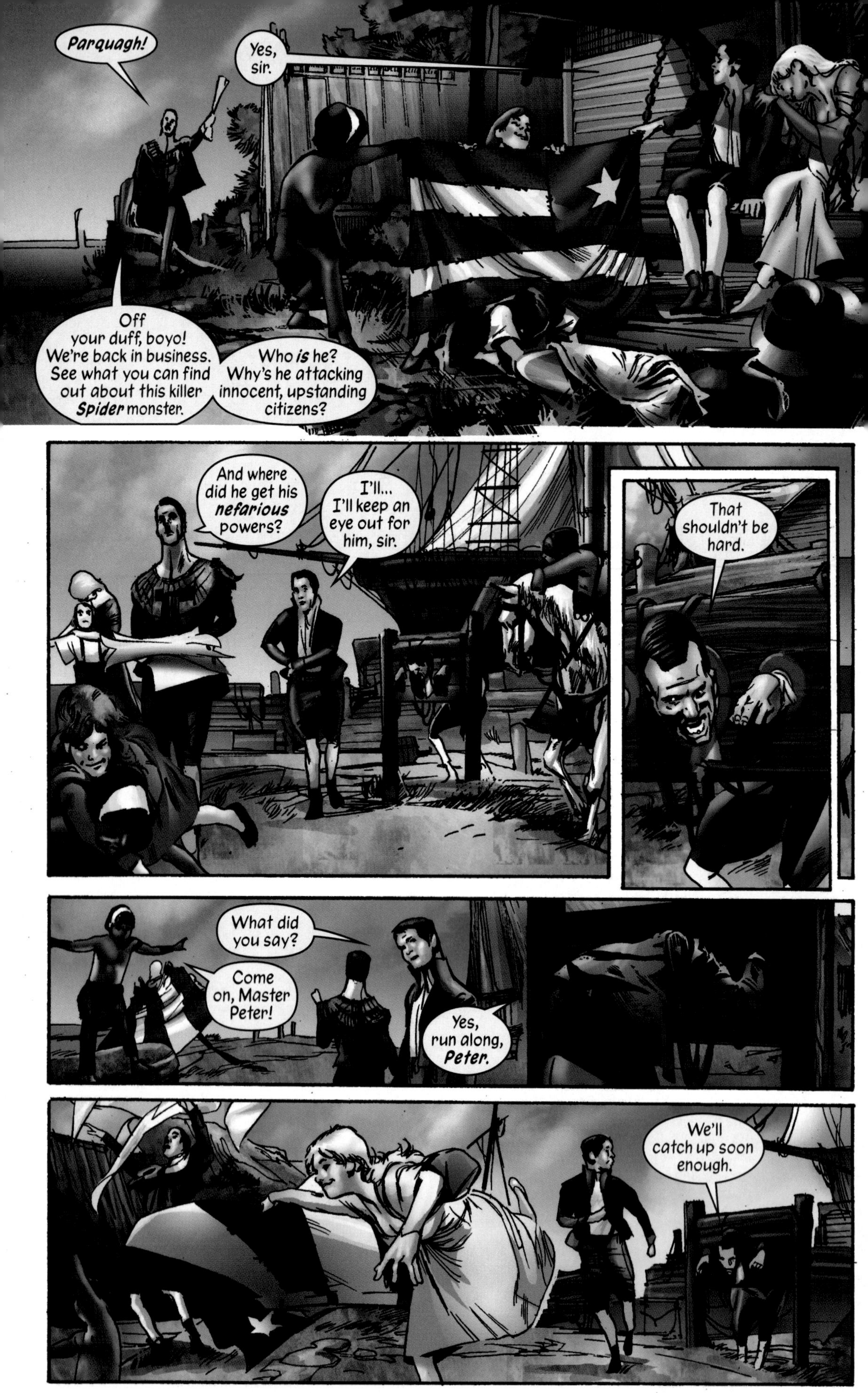
Parquagh!
Yes, sir.
Off your duff, boyo! We're back in business. See what you can find out about this killer *Spider* monster.
Who *is* he? Why's he attacking innocent, upstanding citizens?
And where did he get his *nefarious* powers?
I'll... I'll keep an eye out for him, sir.
That shouldn't be hard.
What did you say?
Come on, Master Peter!
Yes, run along, *Peter*.
We'll catch up soon enough.

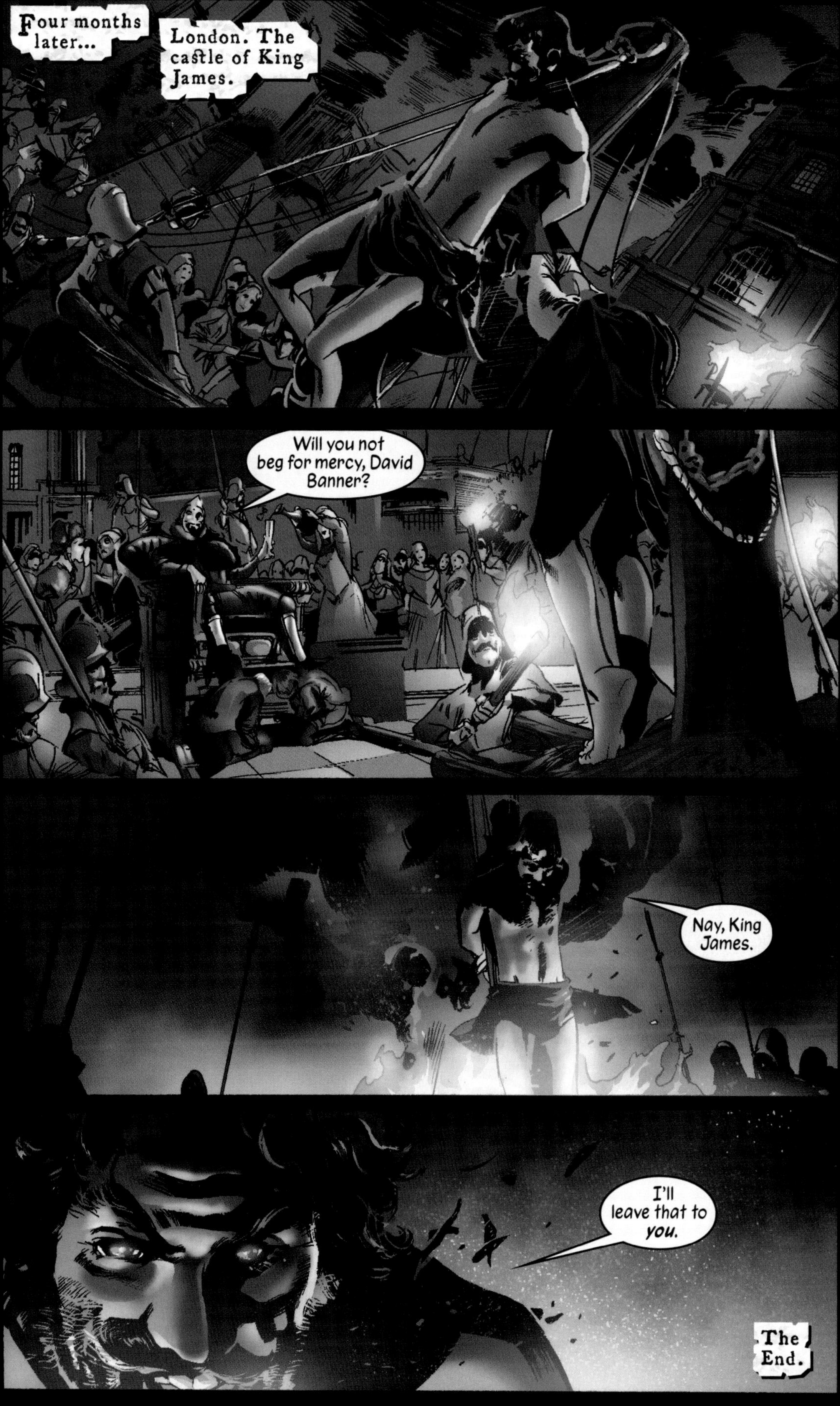
Four months later...
London. The castle of King James.
Will you not beg for mercy, David Banner?
Nay, King James.
I'll leave that to *you.*
The End.

LORD IRON AND SPIDER-MAN DESIGNS BY GREG TOCCHINI

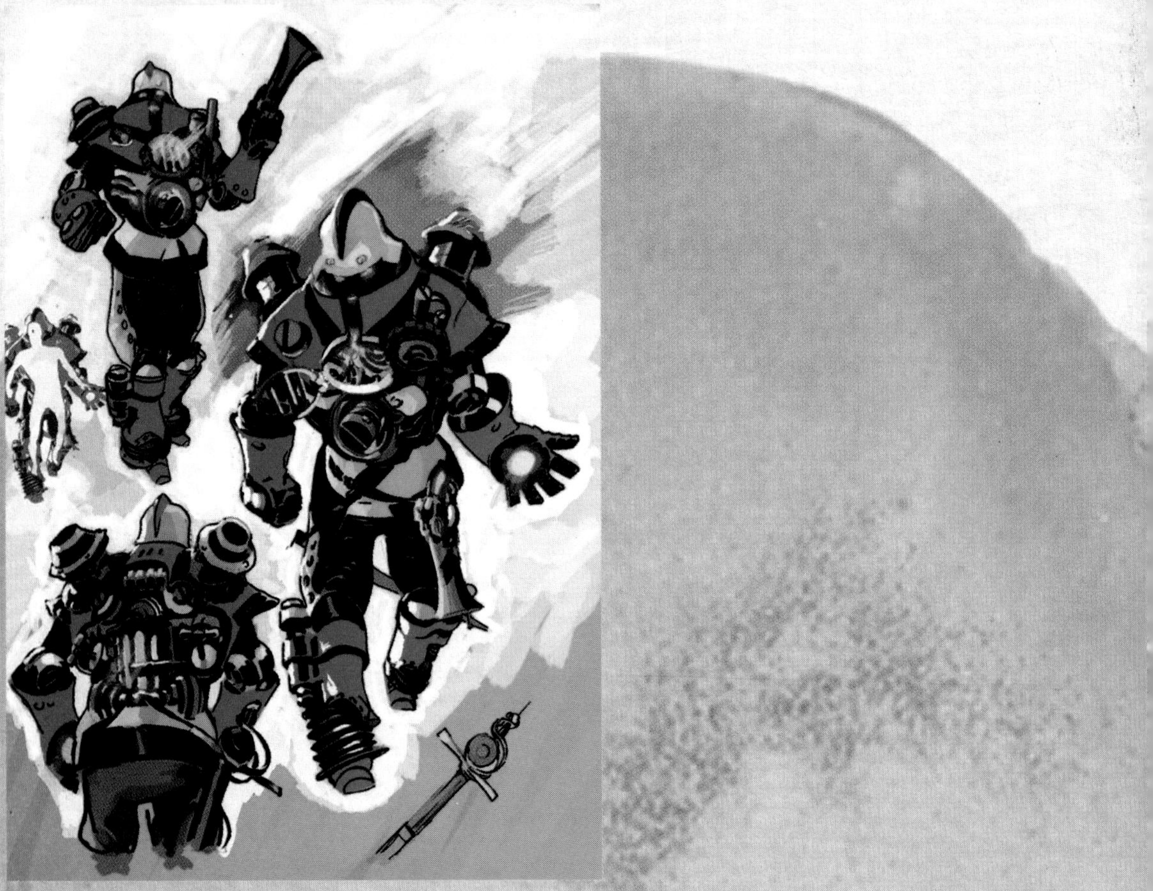

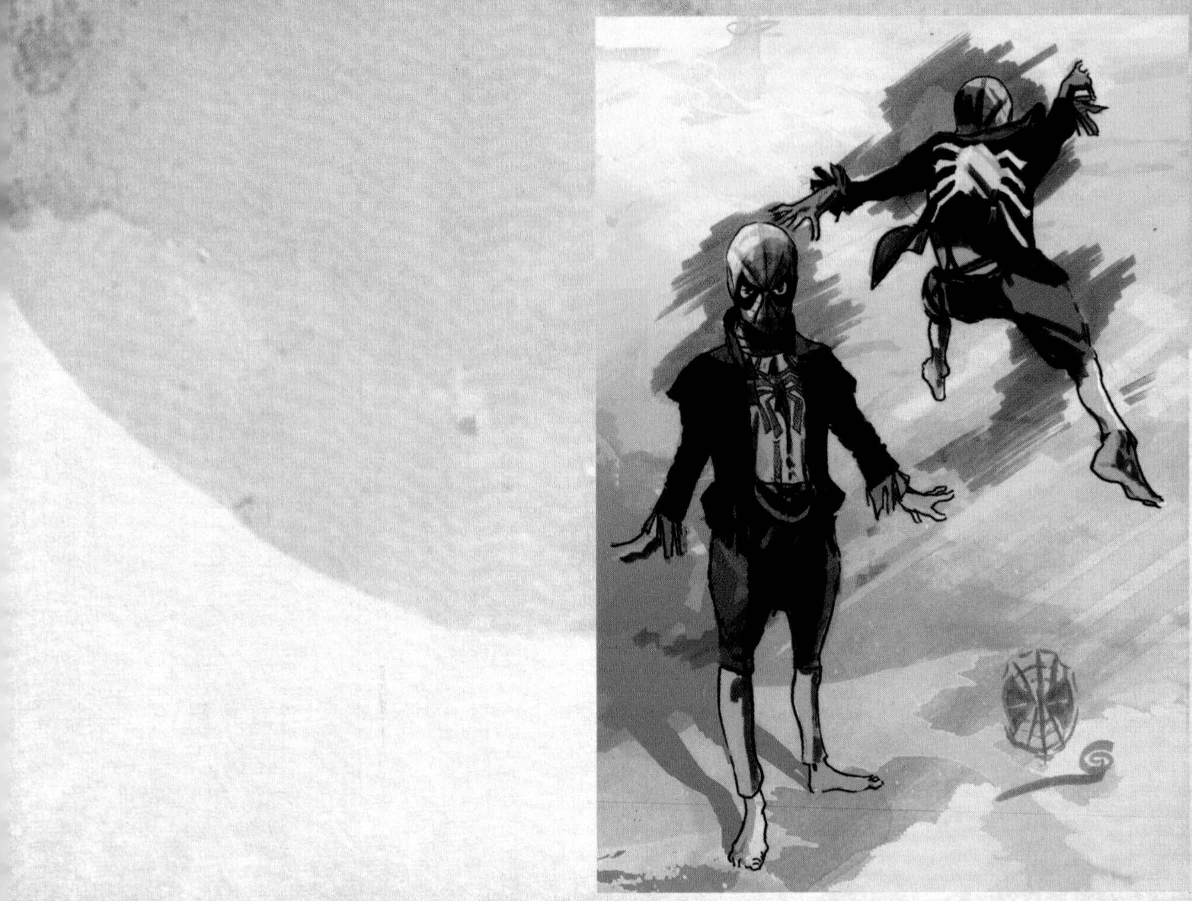